NEW STUDIES IN ARCHAEOLOGY

Culture contact and culture change:
Early Iron Age central Europe and the Mediterranean world

NEW STUDIES IN ARCHAEOLOGY

Other titles in the series include

Graham Connah, *Three Thousand Years in Africa*
Richard A. Gould, *Living Archaeology*
Ian Hodder and Clive Orton, *Spatial Analysis in Archaeology*
Kenneth Hudson, *World Industrial Archaeology*
Keith Muckelroy, *Maritime Archaeology*

Culture contact and culture change:

Early Iron Age central Europe and the Mediterranean world

PETER S. WELLS

Assistant Professor of Anthropology, Harvard University

Ella Machaman
London
1982

CAMBRIDGE UNIVERSITY PRESS

CAMBRIDGE

LONDON NEW YORK NEW ROCHELLE

MELBOURNE SYDNEY

Published by the Press Syndicate of the University of Cambridge
The Pitt Building, Trumpington Street, Cambridge CB2 1RP
32 East 57th Street, New York NY 10022, USA
296 Beaconsfield Parade, Middle Park, Melbourne 3206, Australia

First published 1980

Printed in Great Britain at the University Press, Cambridge

British Library Cataloguing in Publication Data
Wells, Peter S
Culture contact and culture change. – (New studies in archaeology).
1. Iron age – Central Europe 2. Etruscans
3. Civilization, Greek 4. Culture diffusion
5. Central Europe – Antiquities
I. Title II. Series
301.29′36 GN780.22.C46 80-40212
ISBN 0 521 22808 5

CONTENTS

LIST OF ILLUSTRATIONS

SOURCES OF ILLUSTRATIONS

Institut für Vor- und Frühgeschichte, Universität Tübingen:
figs. 3.3, 3.4, 3.5, 3.6

Württembergisches Landesmuseum, Stuttgart:
figs. 3.7, 3.8, 3.9, 5.11

R. Joffroy, Musée des Antiquités Nationales, St Germain-en-Laye:
fig. 3.11

Rheinisches Landesmuseum, Trier:
fig. 5.2

Rheinisches Landesmuseum, Bonn:
figs. 5.3, 5.4

Museum für Vor- und Frühgeschichte, Staatliche Museen, Berlin:
fig. 5.5

O.-H. Frey:
fig. 5.7 (from *Die Entstehung der Situlenkunst* (1969), p. 85 fig. 49, Verlag Walter de Gruyter, Berlin)

Historisches Museum der Pfalz, Speyer:
figs. 5.8, 5.9, 5.10

PREFACE

This book presents a case study in the analysis of contact between prehistoric societies and of the cultural changes associated with that contact. Its purpose is twofold. It offers a new perspective on the profound cultural changes which occurred during the Early Iron Age in central Europe and which were associated with the rapid growth of long-distance trade systems. The principal theoretical aim of the study is the development and explication of a general methodology for examining contact situations using archaeological data.

The study represents a new approach to a large body of archaeological material. Since the latter part of the nineteenth century, when objects manufactured in Greek and Etruscan workshops were identified in burial contexts in west-central Europe, much has been written on the subject of trade between Mediterranean societies and central Europe. Most of the literature has concerned itself with the chronology of the trade, the probable places of origin of imported objects, and routes by which they were brought to central Europe. Throughout this century such imports have continued to appear, and some of the most significant finds have been made in the past 30 years, such as at Vix, the Heuneburg, Grafenbühl, and most recently at Eberdingen-Hochdorf. Very little effort has been made, however, to understand the connections between the interactions which brought the imports to central Europe and the cultural changes which occurred in the regions in which the imports are most abundant.

Among anthropologically oriented archaeologists working in different parts of the world, concern with interaction between societies has been growing in recent years. The clearest manifestation of this trend is the productive work in the analysis of prehistoric trade systems (e.g. articles in Wilmsen 1972; Sabloff and Lamberg-Karlovsky 1975; Earle and Ericson 1977). The present study attempts to go a step beyond the analysis of trade and to examine the effects of the commercial interactions on the societies involved (see Renfrew 1969; 1972; Adams 1974).

The context under study provides a rich and varied data base. Working with this archaeological material I have formulated general models for mechanisms of exchange and processes of change based upon ethnographic and historical literature dealing with change in contact situations. I have not simply borrowed models from ethnographic contexts and applied them to archaeological problems. Since no two contact situations are ever identical, the processes documented in ethnographic and historical instances cannot be expected to be duplicated in prehistoric contexts. But there are certain regularities in the patterns by which cultural changes occur (Herskovits 1938; Kroeber 1948, 386–444; Barnett 1953; Rogers and Shoemaker 1971). Working with these regularities, I have attempted to develop general models for change processes in particular kinds of circumstances. I believe that such models can be usefully employed in studying cultural changes in prehistory.

By the very nature of this study – an attempt to explain patterns of interaction and change in a prehistoric situation – the models offered are tentative. My aim is not to be 'right' (to find the correct answers) if such a thing is ever possible about the distant past (see Gardiner 1952, 34–40; Carr 1961, 7–30). It is to present a coherent account of the mechanisms which were probably involved and an explanation of the changes observed, consistent with the archaeological evidence and with our current understanding of human behavior in traditional societies.

The central European Iron Age is divided into two periods: the Hallstatt (roughly 800–450 B.C.) and the La Tène (450 B.C.–Birth of Christ). The principal focus of this study is the Late Hallstatt Period, since during that time major culture changes occurred in association with contact with the Mediterranean world. The Early La Tène context is presented principally as a contrast with the earlier period, since during this later time the nature of the interactions was very different and no substantial cultural changes occurred.

Only a very small number of available excavated and published sites are brought into the discussion and are meant to serve as examples of the broader patterns. I have included photographs of all of the major categories of luxury imports discussed, as well as a few of local central European objects. A number of diagrammatic models are presented as visual aids in the understanding of the mechanisms and processes discussed.

The words 'chief' and 'headman' are used in a general way to designate the leading personages in Early Iron Age communities. Since no more appropriate terms exist, these are useful as long as they are understood to be employed without any specific cultural implications.

Information on ethnic groups during the period under consideration is sparse. Although I often speak of 'Celts' in central Europe, 'Greeks' at Massalia, and 'Etruscans' in Italy, the identification of ethnic groups is very difficult, and a great deal of ethnic mixing was probably going on.

This study was originally prepared and submitted as a doctoral dissertation to the Department of Anthropology of Harvard University in 1976. I wish to thank the Department of Anthropology for granting me an NDEA Title IV fellowship which helped to finance much of the research. I have made a number of changes in the text, including revising some of the data according to results of recent discoveries and analyses.

I have many people to thank for their help at various stages of the preparation of this study. Prof. C. C. Lamberg-Karlovsky of Harvard has provided me with much inspiration and enthusiasm about trade systems and culture change, and has helped to direct my studies of European prehistory since I was an undergraduate. Prof. Ruth Tringham, now of Berkeley, generously gave valuable advice and guidance throughout the preparation of my doctoral dissertation, and challenged me helpfully on many weak points in my developing arguments. Prof. David Gordon Mitten of Harvard has provided important guidance on the Greek and Etruscan materials and cultures, as well as constant encouragement throughout the preparation of this and other projects.

Dr Hugh Hencken has shared with me his vast knowledge of European archaeology and helped to arrange my year of graduate study at the University of Tübingen. During the academic year 1971–1972 and the three subsequent summers I worked at the Institut für Vor- und Frühgeschichte in Tübingen, where I benefited immensely from the generosity, kindness, and intellectual stimulation of Profs. Wolfgang Kimmig and Franz Fischer.

The background research for this study required considerable work in European museums as well as in libraries. Particularly during the summers of 1973 and 1974 I visited a large number of museums in West Germany, France, Switzerland, Italy, England, Luxembourg, and Belgium, and learned much through discussions with scholars in museums and universities in those countries.

For their kind advice, help, and generosity I wish to thank the following individuals: Prof. Robert McC. Adams (Chicago), Mr Richard Bartlett (Cambridge, Mass.), Dr Jörg Biel (Stuttgart), Prof. Larissa Bonfante (New York), Dr Jürgen Driehaus (Göttingen), Dr Alain Duval (St Germain-en-Laye), Dr Heinz-Josef Engels (Speyer), Prof. Otto-Herman Frey (Marburg), Dr Egon Gersbach (Tübingen), Dr Antonio Gilman (Northridge, California), Dr Alfred Haffner (Trier), Dr Hans-Eckart Joachim (Bonn), Prof. René Joffroy (St Germain-en-Laye), Dr Gustav Mahr (West Berlin), Dr Günter Mansfeld (Tübingen), Prof. Marcel Mariën (Brussels), Prof. Hallam L. Movius (Cambridge, Mass.), Ms Whitney Powell (Cambridge, Mass.), Prof. Colin Renfrew (Southampton, UK), Dr Ulrich Schaaff (Mainz), Dr Hilmar Schickler (Stuttgart), Dr Siegwalt Schiek (Tübingen), Dr Reinhard Schindler (Trier), Dr Peter Schröter (Munich), Dr Ian Stead (London, UK), Dr Hans-Peter Uerpmann (Tübingen), and Prof. Bernard Wailes (Philadelphia).

Finally, I wish to thank my wife Joan for her constant support and encouragement.

1

Culture contact and change:

delineation of a case study

1.1 *Contact and culture change*

Interaction with the outside world opens a community or a society to a theoretically unlimited range of available raw materials, finished goods, technical knowledge, and ideas. Furthermore, it brings about cultural changes in a society. Since all parts of a cultural system are interrelated, and change in any one necessitates changes in all others (Linton 1936, 347–366; Clarke 1968, 101–123), the introduction of a new element (such as bronze metallurgy in the ancient world or television in the modern) brings about changes in all aspects of a society's life (examples in Spicer 1952 and Walker 1972).

The results of interactions between communities and between societies account for many profound changes in all cultural contexts (see e.g. Linton 1936, 324–346; Redfield 1953; Braudel 1972; Adams 1977). In the discipline of archaeology investigators have recognized for a long time that certain raw materials and finished products are found in contexts removed from their areas of origin, suggesting some mechanisms of transmission, such as trade, between communities. The influences of foreign groups have also been seen in particular artistic styles and motifs, new technological practices, and new subsistence patterns. Such effects of interaction have been identified and described by archaeologists, but little attention has been paid to the systematic analysis of contact between societies and of the changes which occur as a result of contact (Adams 1974).

Systematic study of culture contact and its results began among American cultural anthropologists in the 1930s. Of particular influence was the *Memorandum for the Study of Acculturation* published by Redfield, Linton, and Herskovits in 1936. Both theoretical treatments of the subject (e.g. Herskovits 1938) and detailed studies of specific instances of contact and change followed (e.g. Keesing 1939; Linton 1940; Lewis 1942; Spicer 1952; Bohannan and Plog 1967; Walker 1972). On the basis of a large number of such case studies, anthropologists and sociologists have continued to develop the theoretical basis for the study of contact and change (Barnett 1953; Barnett *et al.* 1954; Spicer 1961; Foster 1962; Hagen 1962; Rogers and Shoemaker 1971). A number of archaeological studies have dealt with the subject (Willey *et al.* 1955; Hawkes and Hawkes 1973; C. M. Wells 1974; White 1975), some of them concerned particularly with the growth of trade systems and its effects on other aspects of cultural development (Flannery 1968*a*; Renfrew 1969; 1972; 1975; Rathje 1971; 1972; Adams 1974; 1975). But the possibilities of this line of inquiry for the understanding of processes of culture change in prehistoric contexts have not yet been fully realized.

This study will attempt to show the utility of concepts, developed by cultural anthropological studies of contact and change, in examination of archaeological contact situations. One context will be considered in some detail – that of interaction between west-central Europe and the Mediterranean world between about 600 and 400 B.C. Models for the mechanisms of contact and processes of change will be developed on the basis of data from ethnographic studies. These models will be employed to help to offer explanations for the patterns observed in the archaeological record.

The contact situation considered here is an instructive one for three reasons. First, archaeological evidence in west-central Europe is rich and of good documentary quality. Thousands of graves from the two centuries between 600 and 400 B.C. have been excavated and scientifically published, providing a broad data base. For over a century central European prehistorians have been refining the chronology of the period, hence the chronological controls are good – a requirement for any study of culture change. Settlements are not yet as well known as graves, but a few sites have been partially excavated and provide valuable information.

Secondly, the evidence for contact with the Greek and Etruscan societies to the south is abundant and clear. Greek pottery, bronze vessels and other crafts products, and Etruscan bronze vessels, are well represented at several settlements in many graves in west-central Europe. Many central-European products show the influence of Greek and Etruscan forms and techniques in their manufacture.

Thirdly, some textual information is available about aspects of Greek and Etruscan life that bear directly on the subject of interaction with other peoples. Greek literary sources tell much about trade and industry, interactions with non-Greek peoples, and establishment of colonies near central Europe for purposes of trade. More limited literary evidence regarding the Etruscans provides some important information concerning their interactions with central-European groups.

1.2 *Contact and change in the Early Iron Age*

During the period 600–400 B.C. a large number of objects manufactured in Greek and Etruscan workshops appear in archaeological contexts in west-central Europe. These imports are found to be associated with central-European materials of the Late Hallstatt and Early La Tène Periods on settlement sites and in graves. Most common of the objects from the Greek world are transport amphorae, Attic fine pottery, and bronze vessels; from the Etruscan sphere come bronze vessels.

In addition to the actual imports, other features in the archaeological record attest to contact between the Mediterranean world and west-central Europe. A wall of sun-dried clay bricks, patterned after Greek city walls, has been unearthed at the Heuneburg. At Hirschlanden, a stone statue has been found showing close familiarity with Mediterranean artistic traditions. Features of the local pottery point to Mediterranean models, and a variety of bronze vessels were manufactured after Etruscan prototypes.

At the same time that Greek and Etruscan objects appear in central Europe together with other evidence of contact, major culture changes are discernible in the archaeological record in west-central Europe. In the same areas in which the imports occur a series of richly outfitted burials make their appearance, containing Greek and Etruscan luxury objects as well as exceptional items of local manufacture. These 'princely graves' (*Fürstengräber*) are especially numerous in a part of central Europe consisting of southwest Germany, the Rhineland–Palatinate, the Saarland, eastern France, and northwest Switzerland. In these same regions there is evidence for the emergence of several centers of industrial activity, commerce, wealth, and political power. Most of the rich graves and the Mediterranean imports of the Late Hallstatt Period are associated with these centers. Like the rich graves, the centers are restricted chronologically to the period of contact with the Greek and Etruscan societies, and geographically to that part of central Europe where most of the imports have been found.

Investigators concerned with the Iron Age have commented upon the association of these changes in central Europe with the appearance of the imports. Yet the nature of the interrelation between these phenomena has not been systematically investigated (see, however, the important recent work of Kimmig 1969; Zürn 1970; Fischer 1973; Rowlands 1973; Frankenstein and Rowlands 1978; Pauli 1978). This study will investigate the nature of these interrelations. The changes in Early Iron Age west-central Europe will be examined in terms of the contact between that area and cultures of the Mediterranean world. Two main questions will be the focus of attention.

1. What was the nature of the contact between west-central Europe and the Greek and Etruscan worlds? (By what mechanisms did the

imports reach central Europe; why were central Europeans interacting with the Mediterranean societies; what segments of central European society were most directly affected by the interactions?)

2. What effects did contact and interaction with the Mediterranean cultures have upon culture changes in central Europe; how and why did the contact have these effects?

1.3 *Methods of approach and models*

For the Early Iron Age in central Europe there now exists an abundant literature on a wide variety of issues. Similarly for the Greek and Etruscan cultures with which central Europeans were interacting, much historical and archaeological evidence has been published and discussed. The first task of this study must be to select that evidence which is most directly relevant to the questions set forth above, with necessary background information to complete the picture. No attempt will be made here to deal with Early Iron Age central Europe in its entirety.

A single region within west-central Europe will be investigated in detail; the principal evidence for contact and change in that region will be examined. For the Late Hallstatt Period, Württemberg will be the focus of attention, because the evidence from that region is the most abundant. For the Early La Tène Period the greatest concentration of evidence for contact has been recovered in the Saarland, and this region will be the focus of attention for that period. In each instance reference will be made to patterns throughout central Europe and to important sites in other parts of that area.

On models in the sense used here see especially Carr 1961; Clarke 1968; 1972; Chorley and Haggett 1971; Sherratt 1972. All interpretation of information – historical and archaeological data or everyday occurrences such as traffic accidents – depends upon models. The interpreter's ideas about what happened and how it happened result from his view of how and why events take place. Models are the patterns we impose upon the real world, consciously or unconsciously, in order to make sense of various phenomena. Until recently, most archaeologists have been little concerned with the issue of models, and prehistory has often been written in the 'common sense' way (Carr 1961, 10). Here I shall try to be explicit about the sources and implications of the models employed.

A general systems model will be used to represent culture as a whole. Culture can be viewed as a system comprising a theoretically infinite number of subsystems interrelated in such a way that any change in one subsystem necessitates systemic readjustment of all other subsystems so that the equilibrium of the system is maintained. The utility of the systems model for the study of prehistoric culture has been demonstrated by many archaeologists (e.g. Clark 1957, 175 fig. 25; Clarke 1968; 1972; Flannery 1968*b*; Renfrew 1972; Hill 1977).

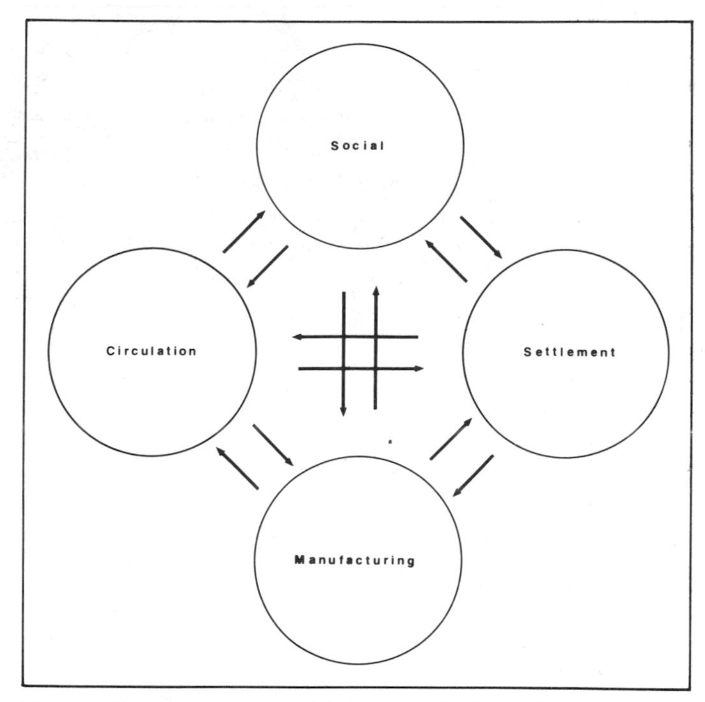

Fig. 1.1. Diagrammatic model showing the interrelatedness of the subsystems of a cultural system. A change in one subsystem will bring about changes in the others. For discussion of these four subsystems in the Early Iron Age see section 4.1.

Different models will be employed for consideration of the circulation of goods between central Europe and the Mediterranean world, and to define the social structure of Late Hallstatt and Early la Tène central Europe. In addition models will be used for study of the contact situations.

In developing models with which to work in this context, I have examined a wide range of cultural anthropological, sociological, and historical literature to study mechanisms of contact which might provide insight into the Iron Age case. In no instance do identical processes operate in two different contact situations, since all of the factors involved can never be precisely the same in any two cases. But patterns do recur in contact situations sharing certain features (Barnett 1953; Foster 1962, 28–43); hence models can often be formulated on the basis of ethnographic or historical data which can be productively applied to prehistoric contexts.

Since the point of departure of this study is the Greek and Etruscan objects in Iron Age central Europe, it is appropriate here to introduce several principles concerning the circulation of materials in traditional societies. Much work in the field of prehistory and early history has been

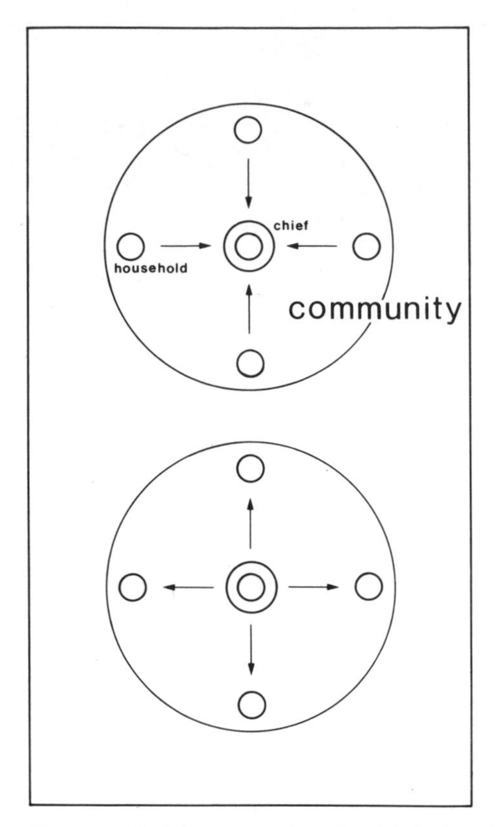

Fig. 1.2. Model representing the chief's function as economic coordinator of the community. *Top*: a portion of the produce of each household (food, manufactured goods) is given to the chief; time and energy are donated for chiefly and public labor projects. He consumes some of the goods, and redistributes others back to the individual households (*bottom*). The chief may trade some materials to outside groups; he may pass on some of the return goods to the households in his community. (For specific examples of these mechanisms see Bibliography for works by Firth and Sahlins.)

done with the assumption that economic systems in the past operated according to the same mechanisms as modern industrial economies. In 1944, Polanyi argued that, since the Industrial Revolution, the economic systems of Western nations have become divorced from other aspects of society, such as social organization (1944, chap. 4; see also Humphreys 1969; Laslett 1973). Before that change, he argues, production and circulation of goods were integrated in such a way that 'economic behavior' could not be separated from 'social behavior'.

Studies of economic processes (we are concerned primarily with the movement of goods) in non-Western societies have demonstrated that

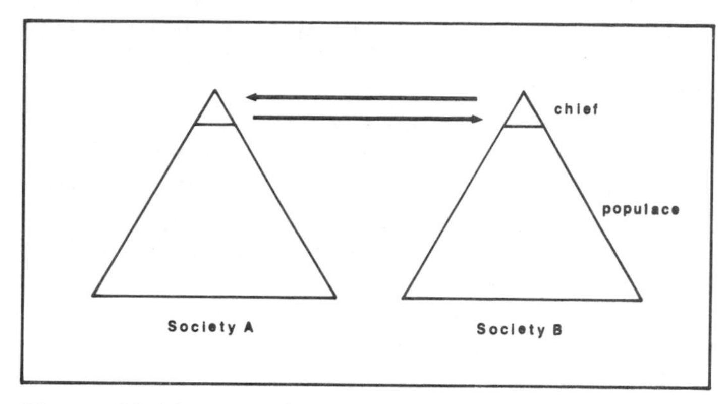

Fig. 1.3. Model representing an exchange system in luxury goods between the elite of two societies without the involvement of the respective populaces.

they cannot be understood when separated from the rest of a social system. Malinowski (1922, 156–194), Mauss (1967), Polanyi (1959), and Sahlins (1960*a*, *b*; 1963; 1965) have been particularly instrumental in showing the close connection between the circulation of goods and social behavior (see also Redfield 1947; Will 1954; Finley 1962; Wilmsen 1972; Duby 1974, 31–57; Renfrew 1975; Dalton 1977; Earle 1977). The patterns of circulation are determined by the social structure of a society, and the acts of giving, receiving, and exchanging all have their social as well as economic functions. Circulation of materials serves to maintain and to reaffirm social relationships, both within and between communities. (Some investigators argue that in traditional societies the passing of goods between individuals is often of secondary importance, while the social interaction behind that movement is more significant in the life of the society (Homans 1958; Sahlins 1965).)

In every cultural system the leader of the societal unit (headman, chief, king) plays a special role with respect to the circulation of materials. [In the text, I shall use the terms headman, chief, and king, with the understanding that these words designate positions in society which can be occupied by individuals of either sex.] As leader in political and social interactions, he is usually also coordinator of his community's economic activities. In most cases chiefs and kings act as economic centers, collecting, storing, and redistributing goods and services of their societies (Sahlins 1963; 1965; Firth 1965, 231–236; Finley 1965, 100; Duby 1974, 37, 42, 51–52). They also coordinate public activities involving group labor and the production of goods.

In his role as leader of the community and coordinator of its economic activities, the chief or king usually acts as its principal representative in interactions with foreigners. When relations are established with outside groups for purposes of trade, the chief or king generally controls the circumstances of the interactions – the place and time of meeting, the goods to be exchanged, and the rate of exchange. Often the rest of the society, aside from the chief's or king's agents, have little to do with the interactions with outsiders, and gain little or nothing as a result of the exchanges unless the chief redistributes some of the imported materials (examples in Arnold 1957; Hanks 1957; Ames 1962; Cipolla 1970). A flourishing intersocietal trade can exist between elite members of societies without the general populace taking any significant part in the interactions or their results (Malinowski 1922; Mauss 1967, 20; Bloch 1961, 65–69; Duby 1974, 48–57; for general discussion, see Bohannan and Dalton 1962, 13).

In any societal context, different goods circulate through different mechanisms depending upon the nature of the goods, the social subgroups involved in giving and receiving them, and the distances over which they are carried (for discussion of this principle in several different contexts see Bohannan and Dalton 1962, 3–5; Herlihy 1971; Renfrew 1972, 460–465; Struever and Houart 1972; Tourtellot and Sabloff 1972; Chang 1975). A variety of different mechanisms of circulation have been defined. Among those concerned with more-or-less voluntary circulation are barter (exchange of goods of equal value), gift-giving (Mauss 1967), administered trade (Arnold 1957), and market trade (Polanyi 1959, 177–178). Other mechanisms include payment of tribute, ransom, taxes, and tolls. Goods also circulate through violent means such as plunder in war or during raids (see Grierson 1959).

1.4 *Early Iron Age central Europe: the archaeological background*

Late Hallstatt Period

As it is generally understood among the prehistorians, the Early Iron Age material culture designated 'Hallstatt' covers the area of central Europe north and east of the Alps from Lyon and Paris in the west to Budapest in the east, and as far north as modern East Germany (fig. 1.5). On the basis of broad regional similarities in artifact assemblages, investigators speak of a western and an eastern Hallstatt culture-area, the dividing line running roughly north–south and passing close to the type-site of Hallstatt. (On development of the concept of the Hallstatt Iron Age, see Angeli 1970.)

This study is concerned with a part of the western Hallstatt area, that comprising Baden-Württemberg, northwest Switzerland, Burgundy, Alsace, Lorraine, the Saarland, and parts of the Rhineland–Palatinate. This region will be referred to as west-central Europe.

Relative chronology. The chronological scheme in use in west-central Europe is that developed by Reinecke (1911*a*) at the beginning of this

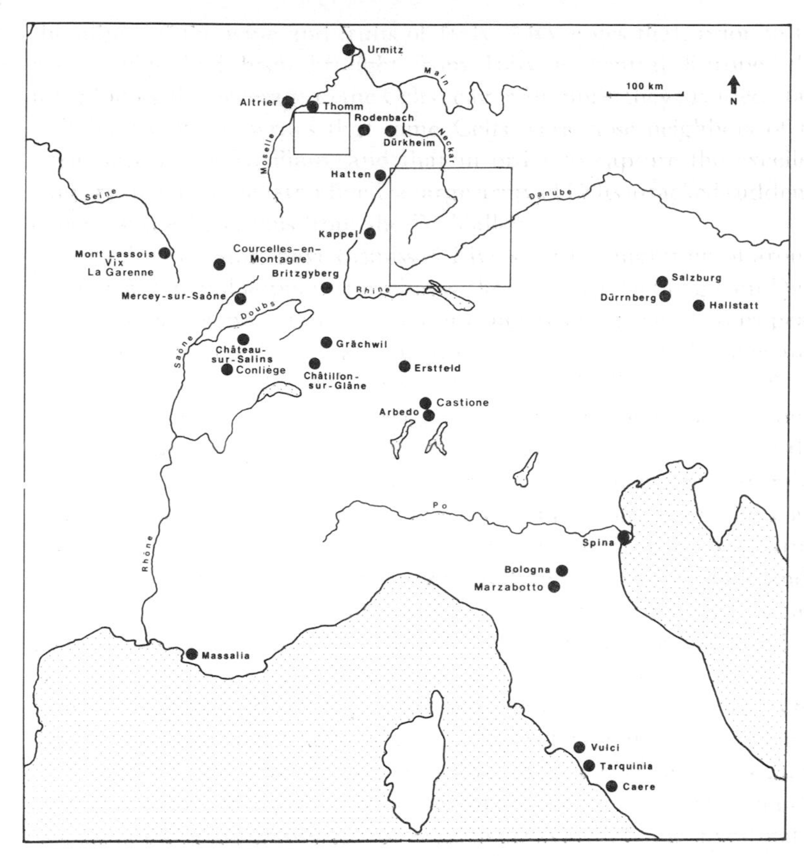

Fig. 1.4. Map showing location of important sites mentioned in text. For sites in the large box (Württemberg) see fig. 3.1, and for the small box (the Saarland) see fig. 5.1.

century and subsequently refined for southern Germany (Zürn 1942; 1952; Kossack 1959; Haffner 1969; Pauli 1972; 1978; Dämmer 1978) and for neighboring parts of France (Déchelette 1913*a*; Piroutet 1928; 1930*a*, *b*; Millotte 1963; Sangmeister 1969; Kilian-Dirlmeier 1970) and Switzerland (Drack 1949–1950; 1950; 1957). Reinecke divided the burial assemblages of the Hallstatt Period into four phases designated with capital letters. Hallstatt A and B are now treated as parts of the Urnfield tradition of the latest Bronze Age (Müller-Karpe 1959); phases C and D constitute the Early Iron Age. Hallstatt C is referred to as Early, Hallstatt D as Late Hallstatt.

The character of find-complexes of Late Hallstatt date is relatively uniform throughout west-central Europe, and the subdivisions D1 and D2 and perhaps D3 (Zürn 1952) appear to be valid throughout the area. Still there are difficulties involved in trying to establish contemporaneity between finds from different parts of the region. There is at present no

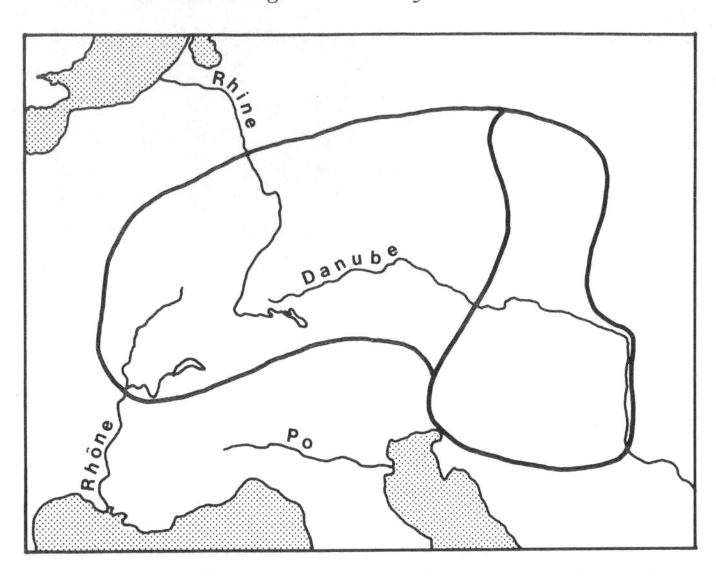

Fig. 1.5. Map indicating the region of Europe in which the classic Hallstatt material culture is found, divided into its western and eastern areas (adapted from Angeli 1970, 25 fig. 1).

technique of calculating the lapse of time between the introduction of a new type into one area and its introduction into another. Aside from the time it may have taken for specific fashions such as new fibula forms to spread from one end of west-central Europe to the other, it is possible that at the same time in neighboring valleys communities were using objects assigned by archaeologists to different phases in the relative chronology. These problems are inherent in the method of relative chronology and must be borne in mind.

Absolute chronology. The absolute dating of the periods in the relative sequence depends primarily on well-dated Greek and Etruscan objects associated with Hallstatt materials. The prehistoric archaeologist in this case is dependent upon the classical archaeologist and the art historian who provide the absolute dates for pottery, bronzes, and other materials in the Mediterranean world (Dehn and Frey 1962). It is not known how long it took for the Attic vases and bronze vessels to be brought from the workshops to central Europe and how long the objects were in central Europe before being deposited in the ground (Jacobsthal 1944, 143–152; Schefold 1950, 16; Dehn and Frey 1962, 202). In a few cases, such as the Grafenbühl grave (Zürn 1970), the patterns of association of dated objects from the Mediterranean world with characteristic Late Hallstatt types is so different from patterns in other contexts that investigators suggest the imports to have been some 50 or 100 years old when placed in the grave (Zürn 1970, 51). When such a great discrepancy between the dates of Mediterranean products and dates attributed through other

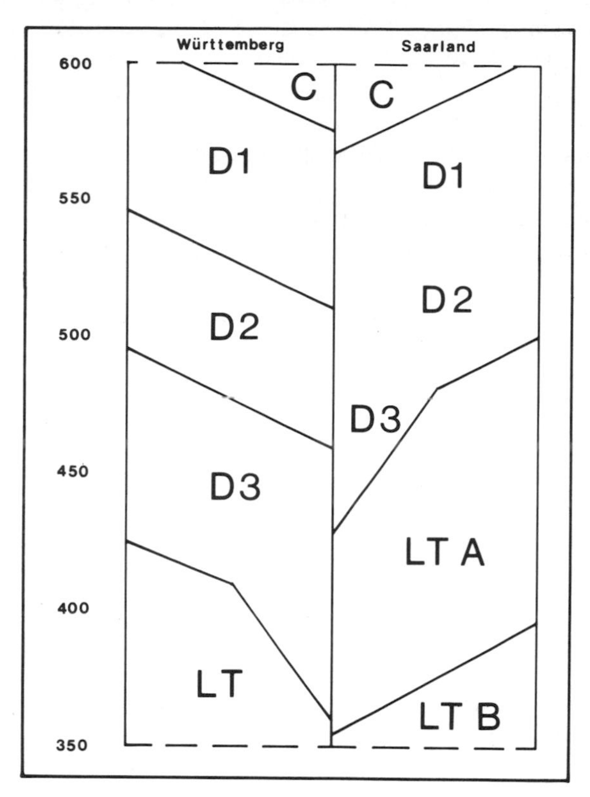

Fig. 1.6. Chart showing absolute dates B.C. for the phases of the relative chronological sequences of the Late Hallstatt and Early La Tène Periods in Württemberg and the Saarland. The oblique lines separating the phases are meant to indicate the coexistence of materials ascribed to different periods. (Based in part on Haffner 1976, 86 fig. 16; 99; Dämmer 1978, 67 fig. 11; Pauli 1978, 421 table 22; 425 table 23.)

associations to the local types does not exist, variations in the ages of the imports at the time of burial are extremely difficult to recognize.

For establishing absolute dates in central Europe, Attic painted pottery is the most useful kind of import because classical archaeologists are able to date most painted specimens within a decade or two. Bronze vessels from Greece, Magna Graecia, and Etruria yield some chronological information, but are less informative than Attic pottery, since they cannot be as precisely dated, even in their lands of manufacture. (On the dating of the phases of the relative sequence through use of Mediterranean imports, see Dehn and Frey 1962; Jucker 1966; 1973; Zürn 1970; on dendrochronology, see Hollstein 1973; 1976.)

The archaeological evidence. For the Late Hallstatt Period in west-central Europe, the number of known settlement sites is small compared to the number of cemeteries, and of the settlements only a few have been partly excavated (see Rieth 1938 on Swabia; Drack 1957 and 1974 on northwest Switzerland; Joffroy 1960*a*; 1976 and Millotte 1963; 1976*a*, *b* on eastern France; Haffner 1966*a*; 1976 on the Saarland; Engels 1967 and Joachim 1968 on the Rhineland–Palatinate). Of these, most have only been sampled by means of a few trenches and very limited surface excavation. No Late Hallstatt settlement has been completely excavated.

Thousands of graves of the period have been unearthed in west-central Europe, many well excavated and well published. Burial practices were relatively uniform throughout the area. The dominant form was inhumation under a tumulus, though some cremation graves are known from most regions. The tumulus sometimes consists of earth only, other times of earth and stones mixed; the prevalence of one kind of tumulus seems to depend largely on the nature of available soil (Engels 1967, 16). Stone pavings sometimes underlie the burials, and layers of stones often cover the graves. Remains of wooden coffins, boards on which the deceased were laid, and burial chambers, are often found.

In contrast to the common practice during the Early Hallstatt Period when only one grave was placed in each tumulus, during the Late Hallstatt the usual pattern was several graves per mound. In some areas the rule is three or four burials per tumulus (Engels 1967, 17); in others the number is higher. The Magdalenenberg tumulus at Villingen contained 127 graves (p. 34 below). Often the first grave in a tumulus was located at the center and base of the mound and was the most richly outfitted. Late Hallstatt tumuli usually occur in groups ranging from 4 to 10 mounds in some areas to upwards of 100 in others (Schaeffer 1930; Millottee 1963, 218; Engels 1967, 16; Zürn 1970). During the later phases of the Late Hallstatt Period (D2 and D3 of Zürn) large tumuli containing 15 or more burials became common in some parts of west-central Europe. These often occur alone rather than in groups and constituted cemeteries in themselves (Drack 1957, 10; Zürn 1970, 7–72), like the Villingen tumulus at an earlier date.

Grave goods of the Late Hallstatt Period differ from those of the Early Hallstatt Period. In Hallstatt C burials the dominant feature is pottery; metal objects are rare. In Hallstatt D, pottery is less abundant and metal objects are the principal burial goods (Rieth 1938, 96–97; Millotte 1963, 184–197; Haffner 1966*a*, 40; Engels 1967, 18). Bronze rings (neck, arm, and leg) are the most frequent objects. Fibulae are especially common in southwest Germany (Mansfeld 1973). Bronze belt plates are characteristic of Late Hallstatt graves in southwest Germany and occur often in Alsace and northern Switzerland as well (Maier 1958). Barrel-armbands are common in northern and western Switzerland (Rieth 1950). Bronze and iron daggers are most common in Germany but also appear in graves in Switzerland and eastern France (Rieth 1942, map 1; Drack 1972–1973). Arm rings made of lignite are common in several parts of west-central Europe (Rochna 1962). Other frequent items in the graves include bronze pendants and bronze and sometimes gold earrings.

Late Hallstatt burials range in richness from the spectacular *Fürstengräber*, containing wagons, ornate daggers, gold jewelry, and Greek and Etruscan bronze vessels, to graves containing a single object of bronze or no objects at all. No evidence has been identified to suggest other means of disposal of the dead besides burial (see discussion in Ucko 1969, 269).

Earliest La Tène Period (La Tène A)

In the Early La Tène context most of the imports from the Mediterranean world occur well to the north of the areas richest in imports during the Late Hallstatt Period. Württemberg and Burgundy are the regions yielding the most imports in Late Hallstatt times, while during the Early La Tène the greatest concentrations are in the Saarland and the Rhineland–Palatinate.

Relative chronology. As for the Hallstatt Period, for the La Tène the scheme developed by Reinecke (1902; 1911*b*) at the turn of the century, based on the earlier work of Tischler (1885), forms the basis for chronological systems in southern Germany. Schemes for eastern France (Déchelette 1914) and for northern and western Switzerland (Wiedmer-Stern 1908; Viollier 1916; Hodson 1968) have also been defind on the basis of Tischler's subdivisions.

The chronological relationships between Late Hallstatt and Early La Tène materials form a complex problem. Late Hallstatt and Early La Tène are viewed as chronological phases, but they overlap, as do all archaeological periods defined on the basis of change in artifact style. There is no evidence in the material for a gradual evolution of the Early La Tène style from Hallstatt elements (Reinecke 1902, 54 with n. 3; Jacobsthal 1944, 158), and objects which bear features characteristic of the two traditions are rare.

Throughout west-central Europe grave groups have been studied which contain objects belonging to both the Hallstatt and the La Tène traditions – for example a La Tène fibula in an otherwise pure Late Hallstatt assemblage (Piroutet 1930*a*; Millotte 1963, 234–235; Zürn 1970, 107–110). These stylistically mixed inventories demonstrate that Late Hallstatt and Early La Tène objects were circulating together for a time. The length of the period during which objects of both ornamental styles were being manufactured and used is unclear.

Two main schools of thought exist on the subject. One group adheres to the traditional model of the relative chronology and argues that the Early La Tène style was adopted quite rapidly all over west-central Europe, replacing the Late Hallstatt mode of ornamentation. In every local region, it is argued, stratigraphic evidence shows Early La Tène finds to be later than Late Hallstatt ones, and the few mixed inventories can be explained by referring to the introduction of Early La Tène objects from outside – from areas in which the Hallstatt–La Tène transition had already taken place (Haffner 1969; Schaaff 1971, 94; Lang 1974, 64).

Others view the Late Hallstatt and Early La Tène complexes more as material culture groupings than as chronological ones. They suggest that in some areas the Late Hallstatt material culture tradition survived longer than in others, so that the latest Hallstatt groups were contemporary with Early La Tène ones (Pauli 1972, 58–74; 1974, 685; 1978, 418–442; Kimmig 1975*a*, 198). Zürn (1952, 40–41) points out that type-fossils of Reinecke's La Tène A are rare in southwest Germany where the latest Hallstatt phase (D3) is well represented (see also Bittel 1934; Liebschwager 1972). Of the few typical La Tène A finds which do occur, some appear in contexts earlier than some of the latest Hallstatt ones (Pauli 1974, 685). From this evidence some investigators suggest that Hallstatt D3 and La Tène A were largely contemporary, and were only geographically mutually exclusive (fig. 1.4); Uenze (1964, 96–110), for example, suggests that the Vix burial (Hallstatt D3) may be contemporary with the Reinheim grave (La Tène A). There is evidence in some areas that the Late Hallstatt–Early La Tène distinction was not only chronological and geographical, but also social. Wahle (1940–1941, 24) suggests that in some cases elite members of society (those in the rich graves) already had jewelry and weapons ornamented in La Tène style while the rest of the populace was using material of the Hallstatt tradition (see also Engels 1967, 52–53; Pauli 1978, 420, 436).

Absolute chronology. Absolute dating of the Early La Tène Period is also accomplished through the Greek and Etruscan imports (Dehn and Frey 1962; Frey 1955; Bouloumié 1968; 1973; Schaaff 1969). All of the datable Mediterranean imports in Early La Tène associations belong to the fifth or very end of the sixth century B.C.

The archaeological evidence. For the Early La Tène Period information about settlements is even poorer than for the Late Hallstatt. Many sites have been located by the discovery of characteristic Early La Tène metal types and pottery, but none has yet been extensively excavated in the area under consideration here.

Burial practices were similar to those of Late Hallstatt. The dead were buried in tumuli; usually several in each mound. Stone circles around the graves, pavings beneath them, and stone packings covering them are common features (Haffner 1966*a*, 30; 1976; Engels 1967, 40; Joachim 1968, 94–97). Tumuli occur in small groups, as during the Late Hallstatt. None of the Early La Tène tumuli contains the large number of graves unearthed in such mounds as the Magdalenenberg at Villingen.

Among the plain graves, characteristic grave goods include bronze jewelry, iron weapons, and ceramic vessels. Women's graves contain neck, arm, and leg rings, and fibulae. The men's graves have fibulae and iron weapons – often a spear and sometimes a sword (Haffner 1966*a*, 34; Engels 1967, 41). The exceptionally rich graves are characterized by gold jewelry and bronze weapons ornamented in the Early La Tène style, Etruscan bronze vessels, and two-wheeled chariots or carts.

2

Imported objects in archaeological contexts:

the Greek and Etruscan objects in west-central Europe

The clearest evidence for contact and interactions between Early Iron Age inhabitants of central Europe and people of the Mediterranean world is the presence of objects of Greek and Etruscan manufacture in archaeological contexts in west-central Europe. The dating of the imports helps to define the chronology of those interactions. The character of the imports and the nature of the contexts in which they are found provide information about the interactions and their significance to central European societies.

For identification of the place of manufacture and for absolute dating of individual imports we must rely upon classical archaeologists who specialize in the study of the Greek and Etruscan products. The attribution and dating of specific imports is sometimes revised in the light of new information and new analyses (see e.g. Shefton 1979, 1–6). The attributions used here are those current in the literature. Revisions in them with advancing knowledge should cause no substantial changes in the thesis and argument of this study.

GREEK MATERIALS IN WEST-CENTRAL EUROPE 600–400 B.C.

Attic pottery: settlements

Mont Lassois (Joffroy 1960*a*, 120–121)
Heuneburg (Kimmig 1971, 40–41)
Château-sur-Salins (Dayet 1967, 98–99)
Britzgyberg (Schweitzer 1971; 1973)
Châtillon-sur-Glâne (Schwab 1975, 80–81; 1976, 3–4)
Ipf (one sherd: Schultze-Naumburg 1969)
Würzburg (two sherds: Mildenberger 1963)
Pretin (one sherd: *Gallia* **16**, 1958, 343 fig. 1)
Zurich-Uetliberg (one sherd: Reim 1968)
Urmitz-Weissenthurm (one sherd: Jacobsthal 1934, 17)

Attic pottery: graves

Vix (two kylikes: Joffroy 1954)
Kleinaspergle (two kylikes: Jacobsthal and Langsdorff 1929, 30–31)
Rodenbach (kantharos: Engels 1972)
Courcelles-en-Montagne (kantharos: Déchelette 1913*b*)

Greek ceramic amphorae: settlements

Mont Lassois (Joffroy 1960*a*, 123)
Heuneburg (Kimmig 1971, 41–43; 1975*a*, 200)
Château-sur-Salins (Dayet 1967, 99)
Montmorot (Benoit 1965, 186)
Mont Guérin (Benoit 1965, 186)
Britzgyberg (Stahl-Weber and Schweitzer 1972, 45)
Châtillon-sur-Glâne (Schwab 1975, 81; 1976, 4)

Greek ceramic amphorae: graves

Mantoche (Benoit 1965, 186)
Savoyeux (Benoit 1965, 186)
Mercey-sur-Saône (Perron 1882, pl. 3.1)

Bronze vessels and stands (all from graves)

Vix krater (Joffroy 1954)
La Garenne tripod and cauldron (Joffroy 1960*b*)
Grächwil hydria (Jucker 1966; 1973)
Grafenbühl tripod (Herrmann 1970)
Hochdorf cauldron (Biel 1978)
Kappel jug (Kimmig and Rest 1954)
Vilsingen jug (Schiek 1954)

Other Greek products (all from graves)

Vix silver phiale mesomphalos (Joffroy 1954; Strong 1966*a*, 56)
Vix gold diadem? (Joffroy 1954; on origin see Megaw 1966, 41)
Grafenbühl carved sphinxes (Herrmann 1970, 25–28)
Grafenbühl ivory lion's foot (Herrmann 1970, 27–28)
Grafenbühl ivory, amber, bone ornaments (Herrmann 1970, 28–30)
Römerhügel amber ornaments (Zürn 1970, 14 fig. 6 nos. 8, 9; 125)

ETRUSCAN MATERIALS IN WEST-CENTRAL EUROPE 600–400 B.C.

Schnabelkannen (for literature see Frey 1969, 116–117)

Armsheim
Vicinity of Armsheim
Berschweiler (Niederhosenbach)
Besseringen
Dürkheim
Vicinity of Haguenau
Hatten
Hermeskeil (Rascheid)
Hillesheim
Hoppstädten
Horhausen
Iffezheim
Kärlich 4
Marpingen
Mercey-sur-Saône
Oberwallmenach
Remmesweiler-Urexweiler
Rodenbach
Schwarzenbach I
Schwarzenbach II
Sessenheim
Siesbach
Soufflenheim
Theley
Thomm
Urmitz
Urmitz-Weissenthurm
Vix
Waldgallscheid (Dörth)
Weiskirchen I
Weiskirchen II
Vicinity of Wiesbaden
Worms-Herrnsheim
Zerf

Stamnoi (see Jacobsthal 1944, 135–137 on all but Altrier)
- Altrier (Thill 1972)
- Basse-Yutz (2)
- Courcelles-en-Montagne
- Dürkheim
- Kleinaspergle
- Weiskirchen II

Stamnos-situla
- Schwetzingen (Jacobsthal 1944, 140)

Basins (see Schaaff 1969, 195–196, 198–199 on all but Vix)
- Armsheim (2)
- Fellbach
- Hermeskeil (Rascheid) (2)
- Reinheim (2)
- Rodenbach (2)
- Thomm
- Vix (2) (Joffroy 1954)
- Waldgallscheid (Dörth)
- Zerf (2)

Trefoil-mouth jug
- Hatten (Frey 1957)

Boss-rimmed bowls (Frey 1963, 22-3)
- Giessübel-Talhau (6 total)
- Römerhügel
- Portalban

Other bronze vessels
- Conliège amphora (Lerat 1958)
- Dürkheim tripod (Neugebauer 1943, 222)
- Ferschweiler kyathos (Steiner 1930)
- Schwarzenbach amphora (Neugebauer 1943, 235)
- Vix bowl (Joffroy 1954)
- Kastenwald ribbed bowl and pyxis (Jehl and Bonnet 1968)

Other Etruscan material
- Ceramic mold for Silenus head, Heuneburg (Kimmig and von Vacano 1973)
- Weiskirchen gold leaf band? (Jacobsthal 1944, 140; see Megaw 1975, 24)
- Jegenstorf gold ball? (Jucker 1966, 122; see also Kimmig and Rest 1954, 202; Torbrügge 1968, 99; Lang 1974, 47)
- Ins gold ball? (Jucker and Jucker 1955, 146; Lang 1974, 47)

OTHER MEDITERRANEAN LUXURY GOODS IN WEST-CENTRAL EUROPE

- Silk textile, Hohmichele Grave 6 (Hundt 1969)
- Silk textile, Altrier (Megaw 1975, 19–20)
- Ivory plaque, Grafenbühl (Herrmann 1970, 30–31)
- Coral. Coral occurs as inlay on metal objects of the Late Hallstatt and Early La Tène Periods, as beads, as spheres constructed of carved pieces, and as natural branches (see Reinach 1899; Paret 1935; 1938; 1951; Millotte 1963, 241–242, 304; Kimmig 1971, 57–59; Champion 1976).

Greek and Etruscan products in west-central Europe

Greek. Attic pottery is the best-represented and most accurately datable category of Greek material in central Europe. According to the ceramic chronology almost all of the black-figure pottery at central-European sites (all in Late Hallstatt contexts) dates to the final third of the sixth century B.C.; all of the red-figure ware (which occurs in Early La Tène contexts) dates to the fifth century B.C. The greatest quantities of Attic pottery have been found at settlement sites of the Late Hallstatt Period – Mont Lassois (24 identifiable vessels and fragments of others: Joffroy 1960*a*, 120–121), the Heuneburg (over 50 sherds: Kimmig 1975*a*, 200), Château-sur-Salins (11 identifiable vessels: Dayet 1967, 98–99), Châtillon-sur-Glâne (4 or 5 vessels: Schwab 1975, 80–81), and the Britzgyberg (4 identifiable vessels: Stahl-Weber and Schweitzer 1972, 44–45). At Château-sur-Salins both black- and red-figure pottery are present.

Concentrations of different kinds of Greek materials occur at several Late Hallstatt sites. At Mont Lassois are Attic pottery, other Greek fine ceramics, and amphorae. Just below the Mont Lassois settlement in the Vix grave were found two Attic kylikes, the bronze krater, silver phiale, and gold diadem; at nearby La Garenne a tripod and cauldron were recovered. Attic pottery and transport amphorae occur together at the Heuneburg. Not far to the west at Vilsingen a Greek trefoil-mouth bronze jug was found in a moderately rich grave. Associated with the settlement at Hohenasperg the rich graves of Grafenbühl and Kleinaspergle both contain Greek materials. At Châtillon-sur-Glâne are Attic black-figure pottery and a fragment of a Massaliote amphora. In addition to Attic pottery, other ceramics attributed to Greek manufacture have been recovered at the same Late Hallstatt settlements yielding Attic wares (Joffroy 1960*a*, 121–122; Benoit 1965, 163; Kimmig 1971, 44–46). Further study is needed of the origins of these materials.

Attic pottery is much less frequent in Early La Tène contexts, and its distribution does not indicate concentrations at particular sites. Four Early La Tène graves, each in a different part of west-central Europe, contain one red-figure vessel each; the Kleinaspergle grave contained two Attic cups. The settlement finds at Château-sur-Sâlins and Urmitz-Weissenthurm are not associated with any of these burials.

Etruscan. Etruscan materials in west-central Europe are almost exclusively bronze vessels, in contrast to Greek products which are predominantly fine pottery. About 73 Etruscan bronze vessels have been found in west-central Europe, compared to seven Greek bronzes (see lists above). Associated with Late Hallstatt materials are the Hatten jug, the Conliège amphora, boss-rimmed bowls from three sites, two basins and a bowl from Vix, and the *Schnabelkannen* from Vix, Hatten, and Mercey-sur-Saône.

Associated with Early La Tène materials are the rest of the *Schnabelkannen*, all of the basins except those from Vix, the stamnoi, the Dürkheim tripod, the Ferschweiler kyathos, and the Schwarzenbach amphora. All of the Etruscan bronze vessels were recovered in graves except the boss-rimmed bowl from Portalban, Switzerland, which was found in a settlement deposit.

The Weiskirchen gold leaf band and the gold balls from Ins and Jegenstorf are grave finds. From the settlement at the Heuneburg comes the ceramic mold for a Silenus head. (In a tumulus that contained a Late Hallstatt grave at Corminboeuf in Switzerland was found a bronze leg from a human figurine (Drack 1964, 14–18) which may be Etruscan (Schwab 1976, 24). Dehn (1965, 129) calls into question the association of the leg fragment with the Late Hallstatt grave.)

Other evidence for central European–Mediterranean contact

Much of the literature on the Mediterranean luxury imports in Late Hallstatt and Early La Tène central Europe implies that the contact was a new phenomenon and that these objects constitute the only evidence for contact during the period 600–400 B.C. Neither is the case.

By the Late Stone Age inner Alpine regions were inhabited (see Drack 1969). From the Early Bronze Age the similarity of metal objects north and south of the Alps suggests regular contact (Erb 1969; Drack 1971). During Urnfield and Hallstatt times many complex metal forms occur on both sides of the Alps (Müller-Karpe 1959; Primas 1977). When Etruscan bronze vessels appear in central European graves they represent only a change in the kinds of materials carried across the mountains, not the beginning of contact.

For the Hallstatt and Early La Tène Periods, Pauli (1971) has documented the presence of large numbers of fibulae, knives, and pendants of Italic origin, north of the Alps, particularly in Switzerland, eastern France, and southwest Germany. His maps and discussion show that small bronze objects were being carried across the Alps regularly during the Hallstatt Period. Mansfeld (1973) demonstrates the *circum*-Alpine distribution of several types of Late Hallstatt fibulae (also Frey 1971*a*, 358 fig. 1).

The hoard of bronze objects found at Arbedo at the confluence of the Misox into the Ticino, near Bellinzona, is of special importance for the Early La Tène Period. Among the 1000+ items were several fragments of Etruscan bronzes, including the handle of a stamnos and part of a boss-rimmed bowl, and three fibulae and four end-fragments of arm rings of types common in central Europe (Crivelli 1946, pl. 11; Primas 1972, pl. 15 and fig. 1). The Etruscan materials indicate a date for the hoard of *c.* 450 B.C. It is significant that both Etruscan and central European objects were present in this hoard recovered at the southern end of the Alpine valleys at a time when Etruscan bronze vessels were appearing in graves in west-central Europe.

At Erstfeld, just north of the St Gotthard Pass through the Alps, was found a cache of four gold neck rings and three gold arm rings ornamented in the same style as those in the rich graves in the middle Rhineland. They were probably made in the same workshops as those found in the Rhineland, and perhaps even by the same craftsmen (Megaw 1970, 80–81; Wyss 1975). Their location of discovery suggests that they were related to the movement of persons between central Europe and northern Italy.

Many other examples of evidence for interaction across the Alps could be cited. These few suffice to indicate that contact existed long before 600 B.C., and that during the Late Hallstatt and Early La Tène Periods other archaeological materials, in addition to the luxury imports, attest to regular contact across the mountains (see also Primas 1974; Wyss 1974, 130).

3
The nature of the contact:
end of the Early Iron Age

3.1 *Patterns in the archaeological evidence*

A single region, Württemberg, will be examined in detail. As throughout west-central Europe, most of the known finds from the Late Hallstatt Period in Württemberg come from graves. Burial mounds often survive with little erosion and are recognizable today. Numerous museums in Württemberg contain large collections of objects recovered from Hallstatt graves during the last century; often there is no accompanying information concerning grave groups. A few cemeteries excavated during the last century such as Tannheim and Zainingen were carefully investigated and are of scientific value today. During the past half-century a number of tumuli and some complete tumulus cemeteries of Hallstatt date have been excavated in Württemberg. Several of these will form the basis for discussion here.

Among settlements of the Late Hallstatt Period only the Heuneburg has been intensively studied, using modern excavation techniques; about one-fifth of the settlement has been excavated (Dämmer 1978, 5.6 fig. 1). Research at the Goldberg was thorough, but many of the finds and excavation records were lost during the last war. Other sites have been sampled and have yielded finds of Late Hallstatt date, but little information has been obtained regarding the character of these sites. At some known Hallstatt Period settlements, such as the Hohenasperg (Zürn 1969) and the Hohennagold (Fischer 1967, 82), medieval building has badly disturbed, and prevented study of, the Iron Age remains.

Settlements

Heuneburg. The Heuneburg is situated on a spur of land extending eastward from the Swabian Alb overlooking the Danube south of Riedlingen (for an aerial view see Kimmig 1968, foldout between pp. 24 and 25). Its surface area is about 3.2 ha. Around the Heuneburg are many tumuli of Hallstatt date, including 11 exceptionally large ones (fig. 3.2). In 1876–1877 Paulus excavated three of the Giessübel-Talhau

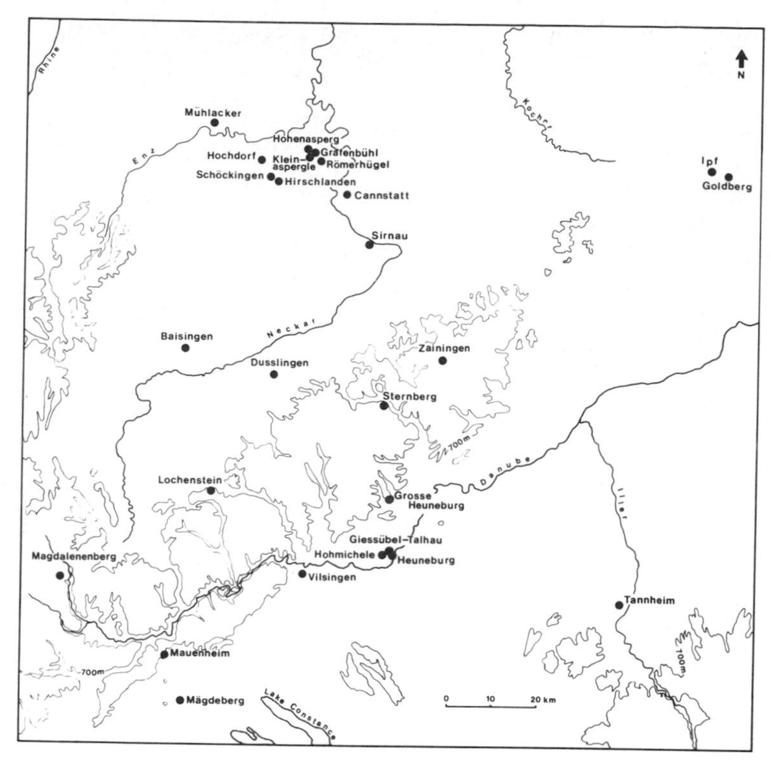

Fig. 3.1. Map of Württemberg showing sites discussed. The highlands running southwest–northeast are the Swabian Alb, or Jura.

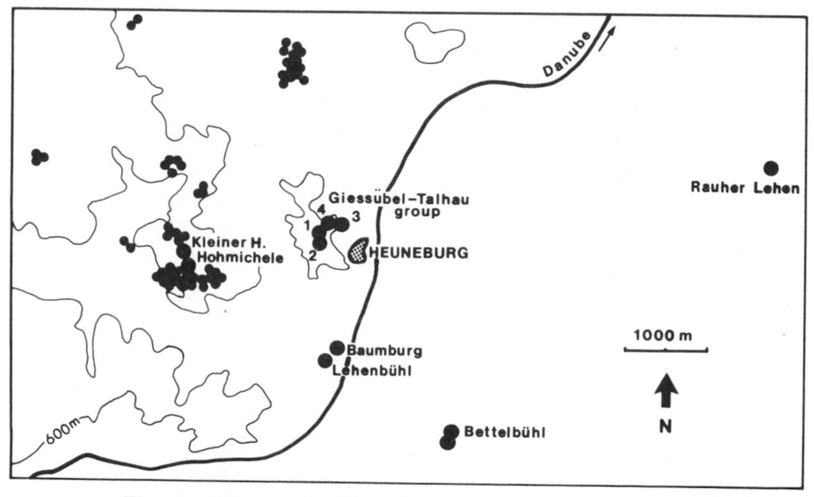

Fig. 3.2. Plan of the Heuneburg and its vicinity, showing the 11 exceptionally large tumuli and numerous smaller ones. Kleiner H. = Kleiner Hohmichele (adapted from Kimmig 1968).

Fig. 3.3. Section of the wall of sun-dried clay bricks at the Heuneburg, standing on a foundation of roughly hewn stone blocks. The dark and light sections of the ranging rod are each 0.5 m long.

mounds, finding grave goods of much richer character than those recovered from most mounds of the region. Among the finds were four gold neck rings, 15 bronze vessels, and two four-wheeled wagons. In the 1930s, Riek excavated the Hohmichele, the largest mound associated with the Heuneburg, and found two richly equipped graves as well as 11 others.

In 1950 the first test excavations were carried out on the Heuneburg settlement, and work has continued since. Several periods of occupation are represented in the one-fifth of the surface area so far excavated (Kimmig 1968, 1975*a*, *b*; Gersbach 1976). The Late Hallstatt occupation, dating from Hallstatt D1 to Hallstatt D3 (Kimmig 1975*a*, 196; Spindler 1975*a*; Dämmer 1978, 67 fig. 11), is of concern here. In the southeast corner of the site, which has been completely excavated, six main phases of building activity during Late Hallstatt times have been identified (Dehn 1957; Gersbach 1971; 1976). The amount of building and re-building, together with the dense concentration of pottery, animal bones, and other cultural materials, indicate an intensive occupation of the site. Gersbach's plans (1971, foldouts 1–6) show the size and character of the structures.

During the Late Hallstatt occupation the settlement was surrounded by defensive wall structures; like the settlement, the walls were rebuilt

Fig. 3.4. Sherds of Attic pottery recovered in the settlement deposits at the Heuneburg.

several times. Most of the phases of the wall are characterized by earth, stone, and timber construction, a technique of building typical of Iron Age central Europe (Dehn 1974). But in phase IVa a wall built of sun-dried clay bricks resting on a foundation of roughly hewn stone blocks lines the settlement's perimeter (fig. 3.3; Kimmig 1968, plan 2; most recently Gersbach 1978). This brick wall is the only one of its kind known in central Europe, but the type is well represented in the Mediterranean world (Kimmig 1968, 47–57; Griffo and von Matt 1968, 183–184).

Many of the finds from the Heuneburg attest to contact with Mediterranean peoples. Over 50 sherds of Attic pottery have been recovered from the settlement, most dating to the end of the sixth century B.C. (fig. 3.4; Kimmig 1971, 40–41; 1975*a*, 200). The sherds represent a variety of different vessel forms including drinking bowls and large mixing vessels (Kimmig 1971, 41). Fragments of at least 15 transport amphorae from the Greek world have also been found (fig. 3.5 and Kimmig 1975*a*, 200); they are of types manufactured in Greek southern France and recovered at numerous sites in the Rhône valley and eastern France (Benoit 1965, 186; Kimmig 1971, 41–43).

Several kinds of locally made pottery provide further evidence of contact with the Mediterranean world. Kimmig (1971, 24–40) suggests that decorative motifs on polychrome pottery at the Heuneburg are

Fig. 3.5. Restored ceramic amphora and fragments of others from the Heuneburg.

imitations of ornamentation on pottery in use in Greek southern France. A dark gray, hard-fired pottery with sharp profile is among the earliest known pottery in central Europe made on a fast-turning wheel (Dehn 1962–1963; Lang 1974; 1976). Some of the vessel forms produced in this pottery copy those of bronze vessels of Etruscan manufacture found in rich graves in central Europe (Lang 1976, 46, 51).

Coral objects at the Heuneburg also point to interaction with the Mediterranean world. The substance occurs most frequently as inlay in Late Hallstatt fibulae (Kimmig 1971, pl. 6 nos. 1, 2). Recovery of a partly worked coral branch (Kimmig 1971, pl. 8 no. 5) suggests that coral was brought to the site in its natural state, then worked into different forms. The settlement deposits have also yielded a clay mold of Etruscan origin intended for casting a Silenus head at the lower attachment of the handle

Fig. 3.6. Casting made from the ceramic Silenus mold found at the Heuneburg. Height 4.6 cm.

on a bronze jug (fig. 3.6). The object has been dated at *c.* 480–460 B.C. (Kimmig and von Vacano 1973, 85).

During excavation of Giessübel-Talhau Tumulus IV, Schiek discovered remains of another settlement beneath that mound. Traces of this settlement, dating to Hallstatt D1, extend across the entire area covered by the four Giessübel-Talhau tumuli; its limits have not yet been found. Questions concerning its relation to the Heuneburg settlement, 500 m away and also occupied during Hallstatt D1, remain unanswered (Schiek 1959; Gersbach 1969; Spindler 1975*a*).

The location of the 11 exceptionally large tumuli around and within sight of the Heuneburg, and their contemporaneity with the settlement remains, indicate that they and the Heuneburg are parts of a single complex. The graves contain important evidence for contact with the

Mediterranean world, and are among the most richly outfitted burials of the period in central Europe (see below).

The Heuneburg is unique in southern Germany both because it is the most thoroughly investigated major Hallstatt settlement and because it has yielded more evidence of material wealth and of contact with the Mediterranean world than any other. A brief review of some other partly excavated settlements of Hallstatt date in Württemberg will call attention to the contrasts between them and the Heuneburg.

Goldberg. The Goldberg is a flat-topped limestone block rising from the plain on the western edge of the Nördlinger Ries; its surface measures about 250 by 150 m (Schröter 1975, 100 fig. 3). Excavations there were conducted between 1911 and 1920 by Bersu. He was primarily concerned here with distinguishing different phases of occupation and the settlement structures associated with each. About three-quarters of the surface area were excavated; numerous structures were identified and great quantities of finds recovered.

Bersu never published more than a series of articles dealing with specific phases at the site (references in Schröter 1975, 113 note 1). Most of the finds were destroyed during the Second World War, and for those which survive, find locations and associations are often unclear. Metal objects from the Hallstatt settlement suggest that the site was occupied throughout the Late Hallstatt Period (Schröter 1975, fig. 14). About the character of the settlement little is known. Schröter's recent studies have brought into question the accuracy of Bersu's plan of the Hallstatt settlement (Childe 1950, 224 fig. 178). Some of the structures (houses?) on the plan are probably of later date, and Schröter (1975, 111) doubts that all of the features shown are contemporary (see also Kimmig 1969, 98–99).

Topographical features at the Goldberg and the Heuneburg are similar (flat plateau surfaces bounded by steep slopes) and the sizes of the surface areas are comparable. Significant is the absence at the Goldberg of imported luxury items which are well represented at the Heuneburg, such as Attic pottery, transport amphorae, large pieces of coral, and anything comparable to the clay mold. Had such materials been recovered, Bersu would surely have cited them in his articles. In his researches on the surviving finds, notes, and plans Schröter has not encountered any evidence of such finds (personal communication).

No exceptionally large tumuli are known in the vicinity of the Goldberg comparable to the 11 around the Heuneburg, nor have richly outfitted graves been found near the site. The available evidence thus suggests that the Goldberg was of essentially different character from the Heuneburg.

Compared to the Heuneburg and the Goldberg, no other Late Hallstatt settlement in Württemberg has been more than sampled.

Lochenstein. Lochenstein is also a flat-topped block of limestone with steep sides rising above the surrounding land; its surface area is about 2.5 ha. Lochenstein is situated on the northern edge of the Swabian Alb at the head of a natural pass connecting the Neckar and Danube valleys. During two months in 1923 the site was tested by means of narrow trenches; in two places slightly broader areas were opened. Thus the materials recovered from the site lack the context of an excavated settlement structure. From the Late Hallstatt phase of occupation were recovered quantities of pottery, bronze jewelry, and other objects. Several houses were excavated, dated by the Late Hallstatt pottery in them, one of which has been published (Bersu and Goessler 1924, figs. 1–2). On the basis of the settlement area excavated little can be said about the structure of the site.

No imported materials from the Mediterranean world have come to light among the finds, yet since so little has been excavated, it would be premature to suggest that such items are not present. As at the Goldberg, no large tumuli have been located, nor especially rich graves found, in the vicinity.

Grosse Heuneburg bei Upflamör. This site is situated in the southern part of the Swabian Alb about 15 km north of the Heuneburg. Its surface area is surrounded by artificial walls which date at least in part to the Late Hallstatt Period (Bersu 1922, 51). Bersu dug a series of test pits and recovered small quantities of sherds of Late Hallstatt pottery, but found no culture layer (*ibid.*). On the northern and western edges of the site remains of structures were found and designated 'dwellings' by Bersu (*ibid.* 56).

Mägdeberg. This site is on a steep hill rising from a side valley of the Aach River in Mühlhausen, north of Singen. In the process of gravel quarrying in 1934–1935 on the north slope of the hill, a thick culture layer was found, containing Hallstatt and Early La Tène pottery. Excavation in 1935 produced quantities of pottery and animal bones, as well as the ground plans of two small structures, one of Hallstatt and the other of La Tène date (Garscha and Rest 1938). No imports from the Mediterranean world were found, and the one Hallstatt house plan provides little information about settlement character.

Hohenasperg. Like the Heuneburg and the Goldberg the Hohenasperg is a flat-topped hill rising from surrounding flat land. It is located in the middle of the Neckar Basin north of Stuttgart. On top of the hill is a medieval fortress, the building of which disturbed the entire surface of the hilltop. A few sherds of pottery found are of Late Hallstatt character (Fischer 1967, 81), but possibilities for future research at the site are very limited.

The graves around the hill provide important evidence about the site (Zürn 1970, pl. *B*). Like the Heuneburg, the Hohenasperg is surrounded by a number of large tumuli which contain graves of exceptional richness. In the immediate vicinity are Grafenbühl, Römerhügel, and Kleinaspergle; at a somewhat greater distance from the hilltop site are the two at Bad Cannstatt, one at Esslingen-Sirnau, and the recently excavated burial at Eberdingen-Hochdorf (Zürn 1970, pl. *B* and p. 123 fig. 78; Biel 1978; 1979). As at the Heuneburg the proximity of the great tumuli to the settlement and the contemporaneity of settlement and graves indicate that all are part of a single complex. Like those associated with the Heuneburg, the large tumuli around the Hohenasperg contain graves outfitted with rich goods including luxury products from the Mediterranean world, gold, and a variety of local fine crafts products.

Ipf. The Ipf is a steep hill with a flat top located just west of the Nördlinger Ries near the town of Bopfingen. A system of massive walls surrounding the summit dates largely to Hallstatt times. Excavations in 1907 and 1908 recovered materials ranging from Neolithic through Early La Tène; Middle and Late Hallstatt occupation was especially well represented (Dehn 1950, 15–16). Among the finds a single sherd of Greek pottery has been identified (Schultze-Naumburg 1969). Since only a very small portion of the settlement was excavated, this site offers possibilities for future study of Mediterranean imports in central Europe.

Hallstatt Period settlements have been ascertained at many other locations, and a few others have been partly excavated (e.g. Ströbel 1961; Joachim and Biel 1977); none yet discovered has yielded Mediterranean imports or signs of exceptional wealth such as are evident at the Heuneburg and the Hohenasperg. *In toto*, the quality of the evidence regarding settlements of the Late Hallstatt Period is poor. Only at the Heuneburg are good data available, and four-fifths of that settlement remain to be excavated. None of the other sites mentioned provides such useful information regarding settlement structure, size, or organization, nor such a comprehensive sample of finds.

All of the sites reviewed above are situated on hilltops. Hilltop settlements are easier for the archaeologist to find than others; lowland sites tend to be covered quickly by sediments. In addition, hills with level summits of appropriate size for habitation and with convenient water supply are limited in number. To what extent hilltops were preferred as settlement locations is unclear; they were certainly not avoided. The sections in the volumes of *Fundberichte aus Schwaben* (now *Fundberichte aus Baden-Württemberg*) which report finds made in the course of building and farming operations show that numerous Hallstatt settlements are discovered each year in lowland areas of Württemberg. Most go unexcavated (an important exception is reported by Joachim and Biel 1977); hence the hilltop settlements of this period are much better known.

Cemeteries

Heuneburg group

Giessübel-Talhau. Four large tumuli form the group known as Giessübel-Talhau, situated just northwest of the Heuneburg settlement area (fig. 3.2). Mounds I–III were excavated by Paulus in the years 1876–1877. In the 1950s Schiek re-excavated Mound I and found in it an undisturbed burial (personal communication), thus bringing into question the thoroughness of Paulus' investigation of all three tumuli. In a wooden chamber in Tumulus I Paulus found the remains of three skeletons accompanied by four spearheads, a dagger, and amber and gold ornaments. Outside of the burial chamber were an additional five graves containing between them four gold neck rings (similar to fig. 3.7), two gold arm rings, three bronze vessels, bronze belt plates, iron daggers, spearheads, and the remains of a wagon (Schiek 1956). In Tumulus II Paulus found one grave, in a wooden chamber in the center of the mound. This grave contained only fragments of bronze and iron. A number of objects were recovered in the fill of the mound, suggesting that other graves had been missed by the excavator. These finds include four bronze boss-rimmed bowls of Etruscan manufacture (p. 52 below) and two bronze basins. In Tumulus III Paulus found only a central chamber grave which contained an iron dagger and an iron spearhead. Among the objects recovered in the mound fill were an iron dagger, two spearheads, a ribbed bucket of bronze, and a bronze basin. Found by Paulus in his excavations of the three tumuli, but not now attributable to any one tumulus, were at least five more bronze basins and two gold earrings.

Paulus did not investigate the fourth mound of the group. In his excavation of it in 1954, Schiek found in the center a wooden burial chamber which had been robbed (Schiek 1959, 127–128). Scattered on the floor of the chamber were remains of a wagon and parts of harness fittings, a bronze belt plate, and other fragments. Twenty-five other inhumation burials were found by Schiek in the tumulus. Among the grave goods in them were iron spearheads, two bronze Etruscan boss-rimmed bowls, a bronze basin with cross-attachments, bronze leg and arm rings, fibulae, a silver earring with gold covering, and a wooden bowl.

Of special significance from the Giessübel-Talhau tumuli is the abundance of objects otherwise rare in west-central Europe: gold neck rings (4 in Mound I), wagons (in Mound I, secondary burial 1; and in Mound IV, central burial), daggers (5 total), and bronze vessels (15 total, 6 of them Etruscan). Schiek's excavation of Mound IV and re-study of I provide important information about the group. He found that the central grave of IV had been robbed shortly after burial. It is now apparent that most of the exceptionally large tumuli in Württemberg were looted in antiquity: grave robbery has been demonstrated at the Hohmichele and at Grafenbühl as well as at Giessübel-Tahlau IV (Zürn 1970, 128). It is likely that mounds I, II, and III at Giessübel-Talhau had also been robbed (Sperber 1979, 35). In the central chamber of I Paulus found fibulae and bronze fragments scattered about on the floor; similarly scattered materials were found on the floors of chambers in Mound IV at Giessübel-Talhau and at Grafenbühl (Zürn 1970, 11 fig. 4). Robbery of Tumuli I–III might also make understandable the relative poverty of the central burials compared to the subsequent graves. In Hohmichele and Giessübel-Talhau IV, the central (looted) grave was poorer in grave goods than some secondary burials in the mounds. Tumuli I, II, and III contained more graves than Paulus recognized, as Schiek's discovery of an untouched grave in I demonstrates.

Hohmichele. The Hohmichele is surrounded by some 30 smaller mounds also of Hallstatt date (Goessler and Veeck 1927, 64–66). In his excavations in 1937–1939 Riek investigated the central chamber and found 12 secondary burials. Much of the tumulus was left unexcavated (Riek 1962, 7 fig. 2), and other graves may remain in the mound. The central chamber tomb had been robbed shortly after burial (*ibid.* 1962, 42). Among the materials left in the chamber were thin sheet gold bands apparently once woven into textile, around 500 glass beads, the remains of a wagon, and fragments of silk (Hundt 1969). Grave 6, with two skeletons in it, also contained exceptional objects including the remains of a wagon and bronze harness fittings, three bronze vessels, a leather quivver containing 51 iron-tipped arrows, a perforated piece of iron ore, a coral ring, four amber rings, four boar tusks mounted in bronze fittings, two animal incisors mounted in bronze fittings, a string of 351 amber beads, and one of 2360 glass beads.

Little is known about the other six large tumuli around the Heuneburg. The Kleiner Hohmichele was largely destroyed in 1884 for its soil. In 1893 a quick excavation of the remains of the mound brought to light finds of bronze, iron, wood, and pottery, but all have disappeared (Kimmig 1968, 100). In 1897 a shaft was sunk into the center of the Lehenbühl. The excavator found remains of a wooden burial chamber and a few grave goods. On the basis of the small number of unexceptional objects, Kimmig (1968, 107) suggests that this grave may have been robbed. The Rauher Lehen was dug into in 1934 by amateurs who found among other items several bronze vessels and glass and amber jewelry; the objects are preserved, but without information about associations (Paret 1933–1935; Kimmig 1968, 112–114). 'Rich finds' have been mentioned from the Bettelbühl, but no materials survive. The mound next to the Bettelbühl remains to be excavated (Kimmig 1968, 111–112). The Baumburg seems to be untouched (*ibid.* 107–110). In the case of five of these six tumuli, some graves probably survive; only the Kleiner Hohmichele appears to have been severely damaged.

Three other well-excavated cemeteries in southern Württemberg will be considered here.

Tannheim. Tannheim is located in the valley of the Iller River at the eastern edge of the hills of upper Swabia. The cemetery was excavated by Geyr von Schweppenburg in the 1890s, and the results published in 1910 by the excavator and Goessler. Excavation procedure and publication were of high quality, and the results are valuable today. Twenty-five graves were excavated; seven were found to have been disturbed by ploughing or later burials.

The cemetery has been dated to Hallstatt C on the basis of the presence of three Hallstatt swords. Yet many features suggest a Hallstatt D date. All graves are inhumation rather than cremation; four contain lignite arm rings (see p. 39 below); a Late Hallstatt dagger is present in one burial. Finally, the general abundance of metal grave goods – jewelry, weapons, and bronze vessels – is a feature of Hallstatt D but not of Hallstatt C.

Five graves at Tannheim contained wagons. Bronze vessels (none of them imported from the Mediterranean world) were found in two graves, five in Tumulus II and two in XIV. A sword was present in three graves, a dagger in one. No gold jewelry, glass beads, or materials from the Mediterranean world were found at Tannheim. Only amber beads (a total of 44 in 4 burials) represent imports from outside central Europe. Though many of the Tannheim graves were more richly equipped than most Early Iron Age graves in terms of wagons, bronze vessels, and weapons, none compares with the rich graves of the Hohmichele and Giessübel-Talhau tumuli at the Heuneburg.

Mauenheim. Mauenheim is situated north of the town of Engen in the Hegau in Baden, just west of southern Württemberg. After several tumuli in a group of some 20 were leveled mechanically, rescue excavations were conducted on some of the partly surviving mounds in 1957 and 1958 by the Freiburg office of the Staatliches Amt für Ur- und Frühgeschichte and by the Institut für Ur- und Frühgeschichte of Freiburg University. Aufdermauer published a report (1963) on the results of the excavations of the first 12 tumuli investigated. A total of 28 graves were found, 14 of them cremation and 14 inhumation. The former Aufdermauer dates to the Early Hallstatt phase (Hallstatt C), the latter to Hallstatt D (1963, 41). Of the 14 inhumation burials, 2 were badly damaged by the mechanical digging operations preceding the archaeological work, hence our sample here consists of 12 undisturbed inhumation burials of the Late Hallstatt Period. Of these 12, 1 contained weapons (a dagger and 2 spearheads) and another fragments of amber. No wagon or gold object was found in these 12 graves.

Magdalenenberg at Villingen. Villingen is located at the eastern edge of the Black Forest on the Brigach, one of the two streams that join at Donaueschingen to form the Danube. The site is on the natural route of passage between the upper Danube and Neckar valleys. First excavation at the great Magdalenenberg tumulus was carried out in the 1890s, when a trench was dug to study the central burial. A wooden chamber was found, together with scattered burial remains, and evidence of robbery shortly after burial (Spindler 1971). In 1970 Spindler began to excavate the entire mound with the intention of re-studying the central burial and locating any subsequent graves.

Around the central chamber 126 graves were found (Spindler 1971; 1972; 1973; 1975*b*; 1976; 1977). Seven contained cremation burials; four contained only a cremation, three were double graves containing a cremation and an inhumation. The other graves contained inhumations, eight double and the rest single. All of the Magdalenenberg graves date to Hallstatt D1 (Spindler 1975*b*, 223). Only the central chamber grave, which was robbed in antiquity, contained a wagon. Twelve graves contained weapons, a total of five daggers, eleven spearheads (four pairs and three singly), and a group of seven arrowheads in one grave. The only gold present was a wire spiral. Other relatively uncommon materials include jet and lignite bracelets and beads, nine glass beads distributed among six graves, amber beads and pendants, and in one grave seven coral beads.

Hohenasperg group. As at the Heuneburg, around the Hohenasperg are a number of exceptionally large tumuli (Zürn 1970, pl. *B*). Three have been excavated and have yielded graves of great richness: Römerhügel, Grafenbühl, and Kleinaspergle. Other finds recovered in the area probably came from rich graves whose mounds have been destroyed through farming activity or erosion (Zürn 1969, 5). (A series of large burial mounds containing rich graves has been found at somewhat greater distances from the Hohenasperg; it includes Eberdingen-Hochdorf (Biel 1978; 1979), Schöckingen (Paret 1951), Bad Cannstatt 1 and 2 (Paret 1935; 1935–1938), and Esslingen-Sirnau (Paret 1938). The relation of these slightly removed graves to the Hohenasperg settlement must be clarified through future archaeological research.)

Römerhügel. In 1877 the city of Ludwigsburg excavated part of this tumulus during construction of a reservoir; two rich burials were found. Enlargement of the reservoir in 1926 resulted in the discovery of 15 plain graves. Among the objects found in the first rich grave were a gold neck ring (fig. 3.7) and another gold ring, perhaps an arm ring; four bronze vessels including an Etruscan boss-rimmed bowl, a ribbed bucket, and two basins; the remains of a wagon; and an iron dagger with iron and bronze sheath with amber inlay (Schiek 1926, 47–51). The glass

Fig. 3.7. Neck ring of sheet gold from the first rich grave in the Römerhügel tumulus. Diameter 23 cm.

bottle once attributed to the grave (Paret 1921, 180) is now thought not to belong to the burial (Dehn 1951). Among the objects in the second rich grave were fragments of sheet gold, a bronze dagger handle, and carved amber ornaments (Schiek 1956, 47–51).

Grafenbühl. This tumulus was excavated in 1964–1965 by Zürn. In addition to the central chamber grave, 33 other burials were found, some of which had been disturbed (Zürn 1970, 39–50). Zürn (1970, 9) believes that other graves probably had existed in the tumulus but were destroyed during building operations.

The central chamber grave had been robbed shortly after the burial (*ibid.* 1970, 9–16). The objects that the robbers left behind constitute one of the richest grave inventories of prehistoric Europe. Among them were two bronze tripod feet of Greek manufacture; a bronze kettle and fragments of another bronze vessel; two carved sphinxes, one of ivory and the other of bone and amber (fig. 3.8), of Greek southern Italian origin; an ivory plaque from the East Mediterranean; an ivory lion's foot of Greek origin; numerous carved pieces of amber and bone from Mediterranean workshops; the remains of a wagon; and small gold ornaments including threads (Zürn 1970, 13–24; Herrmann 1970). Study of the skeletal remains indicates that the individual was male and around thirty years of age (Zürn 1970, 13).

Kleinaspergle. A tunnel was dug into the mound of Kleinaspergle in 1879. In the center was found a wooden burial chamber which had been robbed. A second chamber grave was discovered, this one containing a rich assemblage comprising a variety of gold ornaments including two end-pieces of drinking horns, four bronze vessels including

Fig. 3.8. Sphinx of bone with amber face and two gilded bronze rivets, from Grafenbühl. Height 4.8 cm, length 5.2 cm.

an Etruscan stamnos, and two Attic kylikes (Zürn 1969, 5). The local objects from this second grave (see Jacobsthal 1944 for illustrations) are all ornamented in the Early La Tène style rather than that of the Late Hallstatt; the grave will be considered in the discussion of Early La Tène below.

Zainingen. Zainingen is located in the Swabian Alb near its northern edge about 15 km southeast of Kirchheim. The cemetery was excavated at the end of the last century and beginning of this one; from the surviving notes and grave groups Zürn (1957*a*) has published the results. In the cemetery of 36 tumuli, 36 graves are recorded. Chronologically the cemetery extends from Hallstatt B2 to Hallstatt D1; most of the graves are cremations of Hallstatt C type, and contain much pottery but few or no metal objects. Zainingen is brought into the present discussion for comparison with the Hallstatt D cemeteries with which this study is directly concerned.

Hirschlanden. The tumulus at Hirschlanden was excavated by Zürn in 1963–1964 and found to contain a small cemetery of 16 graves (Zürn 1970). On top of the mound had stood a life-size sculpted stone statue of a man, the only such statue known from Early Iron Age central Europe and exhibiting a familiarity with Mediterranean artistic traditions (fig. 3.9).

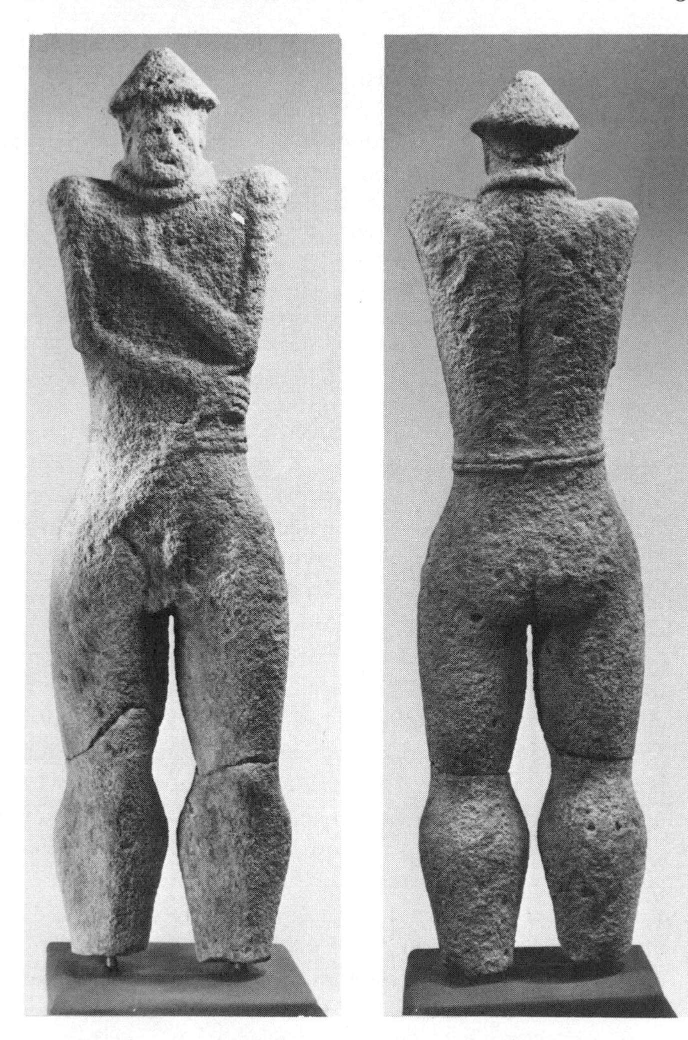

Fig. 3.9. Sandstone stele from Hirschlanden. Height 1.5 m. The modeling of the legs shows familiarity with Mediterranean artistic traditions. The neck ring, belt, and dagger are objects typical of Late Hallstatt Württemberg.

The 16 graves were all inhumations and date from Hallstatt D1 and D2. The grave goods are similar to those from the 33 secondary burials at Grafenbühl, and consist primarily of bronze jewelry with occasional beads of amber, glass, and lignite. Only two weapons were present in the 16 burials – both spearheads. Amber is the only material aside from copper and tin which had to come from outside the immediate area.

Mühlacker. Mühlacker is located on the river Enz about 20 km west of the Hohenasperg. The cemetery consists of 12 tumuli containing a total of 46 graves. Zürn directed excavations here during 1964–1967. All 46 graves contained inhumations; objects in them date the cemetery to Hallstatt D1 and D2. The grave inventories at Mühlacker are comparable to those of the Grafenbühl secondary graves and of Hirschlanden. Only one weapon was present: a spearhead. No bronze vessels or wagons were found. Three graves contained small amounts of gold: a pair of earrings in two burials and 23 small wire rings in another. Four amber beads were recovered in one grave. The only objects from the Mediterranean world were eleven coral beads in one grave and one in another.

Circulation of materials

As indicated in the foregoing discussion, at many Late Hallstatt sites in Württemberg materials occur which were not available locally. The most important group for this study comprises the luxury products from the Mediterranean world – Greek pottery, Greek and Etruscan bronze vessels, and items such as carved ivory and amber ornaments. In this section a different series of materials which were also circulating in Late Hallstatt Württemberg will be considered.

In most parts of west-central Europe, all of the basic necessities for maintaining life and some degree of comfort were available to Hallstatt communities in their immediate environments. The subsistence base was broad; by the Hallstatt Period a wide range of domesticated plants were cultivated and domesticated animals are well represented. Grains grown include rye, oats, einkorn, emmer, and spelt wheat, barley, and millet. Among legumes, the field pea, lentil, vetch, and bean are documented; flax and hemp were also present. Fruits represented include apple, pear, plum, sweet cherry, and wild grape (Jankuhn 1969, 71–75). Cattle, pigs, sheep, goats, horses, and dogs were being kept (*ibid.* 75–81).

A variety of important raw materials were locally available to most communities in central Europe. Clay (for ceramics and wall plaster), wood (for buildings, vehicles, tools, weapons), iron, and a variety of plant and animal products (linen, wool, horn, antler, bone) were readily available (Kossack 1959, 69). Beyond these basic substances communities needed to go outside their own territories to procure desired materials.

Patterns of distribution of substances not available in every locality provide evidence about the systems through which those materials circulated. Based on their source areas, the materials under consideration can be divided into three general groups.

Source in Württemberg: iron, lignite, jet, gold (?)
Source in central Europe, but not Württemberg: copper, tin (?), salt
Source outside central Europe: amber, coral

Two subjects are of concern here: the distribution of these materials at the settlement and cemetery sites under consideration, and their areas of origin.

Iron. Iron occurs in abundance throughout much of central Europe and in the Iron Age needed only to be collected or excavated at the surface (Frei 1965–66; Pleiner 1976). In Württemberg it occurs as granular ore in various locations in the Swabian Alb (Seibold 1959, 44; Eichler 1961, fig. 1). The ore is found associated with limestone outcroppings and is relatively abundant (as far as Iron Age needs were concerned). In Late Hallstatt graves iron occurs in the form of weapons (spearheads, daggers, arrowheads), jewelry (fibulae, belt hooks, rings), and fittings for wagons and harnesses. A table showing numbers of iron objects of four main categories at two cemeteries gives an impression of the quantities present.

	Spear-heads	Knives	Fibulae	Belt Hooks
Magdalenenberg (126 graves)	11	9	11	8
Mühlacker (46 graves)	1	1	2	3

Bronze objects are more numerous than iron ones in Late Hallstatt contexts; the most abundant items, such as rings of various kinds, are almost always of bronze. Most fibulae are bronze as are most belt hooks. Only spearheads and knives are consistently of iron in this period.

Since evidence for extracting and forging of iron is rare in Hallstatt Europe (Rieth 1942; Pleiner 1962; Haffner 1971), little can be said about the organization of iron metallurgy. As the ore is abundant throughout the Alb, it is possible that many communities smelted the ore and made iron objects. Study of large numbers of iron objects may provide information about workshop distribution.

Lignite and jet. Lignite and jet are forms of coal, and appear in Late Hallstatt graves as jewelry, particularly as bracelets and beads. Rochna (1962, 70) has shown that the lignite in southwest German Late Hallstatt contexts came from shale deposits in the Swabian Alb, not from lignite deposits in northern Germany. The same appears to be true for the jet (*ibid.*, 69).

Both materials appear in the archaeological record of southwest Germany during Hallstatt D. Lignite bracelets are most often associated with finds of phase D1, though a small number occur in Hallstatt C2 and D2 contexts. Jet objects are almost completely restricted to D2 (Rochna 1962, 54, 67, 69).

Rochna's (1962, 45 fig. 1, 47 fig. 2) distribution maps of finds of lignite and jet show concentrations of both materials in the Heuneburg area, in the upper Rhine valley, and around the northeast end of Lake Neuchâtel in Switzerland. Outside of these areas is a rapid fall-off in finds. Kossack (1959, 70) comments on the rarity of these substances in southern Bavaria and indicates that the few finds which do occur are probably objects manufactured in southwest Germany. Recent studies of lignite and jet in Late Hallstatt graves at Dürrnberg in Upper Austria have shown them to have been imported from southwest Germany (Rochna and Mädler 1974).

Lignite and jet are represented at Tannheim, Mauenheim, Magdalenenberg, and at the Heuneburg in southern Württemberg, and jet is present in several graves at Mühlacker and Hirschlanden in the north. Examination of the graves in which lignite and jet items occur shows a pattern of some significance. Both substances appear in graves above average in wealth but not exceptionally rich. None of the chamber graves of the Heuneburg or Hohenasperg tumuli yielded any objects of lignite or jet among the abundant luxury items present. For all except Hohmichele 6, it might be argued that such materials may have been removed by the robbers, but among the goods left in such graves as Grafenbühl and Hohmichele 1 some trace (such as a bead) might be expected (after all, many fragments of gold were left behind in these graves). Lignite and jet jewelry seems to be associated with the richer graves in hinterland areas, but not with the very rich burials at the major centers. Lignite was recovered at the Heuneburg in the settlement deposits (both on the main settlement and in that beneath the Giessübel-Talhau tumuli), where the finds include scrap fragments suggestive of manufacture at the site (Kimmig 1975*b*, 56).

Lignite and jet at the sites examined

Tannheim Grave 5	Lignite bracelet
Grave 15	Lignite bracelet
Grave 19	2 lignite bracelets
Grave 23	2 lignite bracelets
Mauenheim	
Tumulus H, Grave 1	Lignite barrel bracelet; pin head
Magdalenenberg	
Grave 10	2 jet barrel bracelets
Grave 13	2 jet barrel bracelets
Grave 16	Jet ring
Grave 30	Jet bead
Grave 56	2 lignite bracelets
Grave 65	2 jet bracelets
Grave 68	2 jet bracelets
Grave 72	2 jet barrel bracelets
Grave 78	2 jet barrel bracelets
Grave 96	2 jet wide bracelets
Grave 120	2 jet wide bracelets
Heuneburg tumuli:	
Hohmichele	None
Giessübel-Talhau group	None
Rauher Lehen	Fragments of lignite bracelets
Zainingen, Tumulus 3	Jet ring
Hirschlanden, Grave 7	305 jet beads
Grave 11	37+ jet beads
Grave 13	7 jet beads

Mühlacker	
Tumulus I, Grave 2	Jet bead
Tumulus IV, Grave 1	250 jet beads
Tumulus IV, Grave 2	357 jet beads
Tumulus IV, Grave 6	16 jet beads
Tumulus IX, Grave 4	13 jet beads
Tumulus IX, Grave 5	35 jet beads
Hohenasperg tumuli:	
Grafenbühl	None
Römerhügel	None

Copper. Most of the objects found in Late Hallstatt graves are made of bronze; the metal was used for the manufacture of jewelry (rings, fibulae, belt plates, buttons of various kinds, pins), vessels, tools, weapons, and wagon and harness fittings. Great quantities of copper were required for the production of the bronze in Late Hallstatt Württemberg, and since it does not occur in the region copper or its alloy had to be imported.

Archaeological evidence documents the mining of copper in the eastern Alps from the Early Bronze Age onwards (Jankuhn 1969, 82–83). Rich evidence of prehistoric copper mining has been found in the Salzburg region and in the Tirol (Neuninger *et al.* 1969; Pittioni 1976*a*, *b*). The copper in southwest Germany was probably coming from such Austrian Alpine sources; archaeological evidence indicates active trade between Germany and this part of Austria (see e.g. Rochna and Mädler 1974; Pauli 1978).

Tin. The quantities of tin required to manufacture bronze are smaller than those of copper, and tin is considerably less available in nature than the other metal (Charles 1975, 19–20). Within central Europe the Erzgebirge of East Germany has been cited as having been a possible source for tin during this period (Hencken 1974; Piggott 1977, 141; see Jankuhn 1969, 94). Other parts of Europe which may be involved are Cornwall, Brittany, and Iberia (Muhly 1973, 248–261).

Gold. During the Early Iron Age, gold was probably obtained in Württemberg, principally from rivers bearing Alpine mineral sediments (Hartmann 1978, 601), though other source areas in Europe have been considered as well (Schüle 1965; Jankuhn 1969, 87; Hartmann 1970, 49). Most gold objects from Late Hallstatt Württemberg were probably made locally; techniques of manufacture and styles of ornament correspond closely to those employed in the production of bronze objects in the same area (see Megaw 1970).

At several sites considered here no gold objects have been found, viz. Tannheim, Zainingen, and Hirschlanden. A single small gold wire spiral occurs at Magdalenenberg. At Mühlacker three graves contain small gold objects: two have in them a pair of earrings, the third 23 small rings.

Some of the graves around the Heuneburg and the Hohenasperg

contained large gold objects and often numerous small gold ornaments: the five secondary burials in Giessübel-Talhau I contained between them four gold neck rings and two gold arm rings. In Hohmichele 1 (robbed) were thin gold bands once woven into textile. The Grafenbühl grave (robbed) still contained a variety of small gold ornaments. Römerhügel 1 had in it a neck ring and arm ring similar to those in the Giessübel-Talhau secondary graves; Grave 2 in the same tumulus contained small objects of sheet gold.

The pattern apparent is one of extraordinary richness in gold at the Heuneburg and Hohenasperg and relative poverty in the metal elsewhere. Had the central burials in the Giessübel-Talhau tumuli, Hohmichele, and Grafenbühl not been looted, the quantity of gold at these sites would surely be considerably greater. Outside of west-central Europe gold objects are rare at this time (Kimmig 1975*b*, 41 fig. 18*b*). Kossack's (1959, 70) comprehensive study of southern Bavaria records only three gold objects from the Hallstatt Period, at least two of which were almost certainly manufactured in Württemberg.

Gold at the sites examined

Tannheim	None
Mauenheim	None
Magdalenenberg	
Grave 42	Small wire spiral
Heuneburg tumuli:	
Hohmichele	
Grave 1	Sheet bands (woven into textile)
Grave 11	2 earrings
Giessübel-Talhau group	
Tumulus I, Chamber Grave 1	Small bosses (on textile)
Tumulus I, Grave 1	Neck ring
Tumulus I, Grave 2	Neck ring, bracelet
Tumulus I, Grave 3	Neck ring
Tumulus I, Grave 4	Bracelet
Tumulus I, Grave 5	Neck ring
From Tumuli I–III	2 earrings
Rauher Lehen	None
Heuneburg settlement	Gold straining spoon
Zainingen	None
Hirschlanden	None
Mühlacker	
Tumulus IV, Grave 1	2 earrings
Tumulus IV, Grave 2	2 earrings
Tumulus X, Grave 1	23 wire rings
Hohenasperg tumuli	
Grafenbühl Central Grave	Sheet ornament on fibulae; sheet mount; covering on rivets; threads; sheet covering on iron belt piece
Römerhügel	
1	Neck ring, bracelet
2	Sheet fragments; rivets

Salt. At Hallstatt and at the Dürrnberg at Hallein in Upper Austria there is good evidence for trade in salt over substantial distances during the Early Iron Age (Kromer 1959; 1964; Maier 1974; Pauli 1978). Objects from west-central Europe in both cemeteries suggest that salt was being traded from the Hallstatt and Dürrnberg mines to Württemberg (Kromer 1963, 25; Jankuhn 1969, 85; Pauli 1978). In west-central Europe evidence for salt production during the Hallstatt Period has been found at sites in eastern France (Nenquin 1961, 30–31. 34–35, 38–39). Recent work at Seille in Lorraine suggests a high level of salt production through evaporation of brine during the Late Hallstatt Period (Bertaux 1977).

Amber. Amber is represented at all of the sites considered here. Most of the finds consist of one or two small beads or rings. Exceptional numbers of amber beads occur in Tannheim Grave 19 (27 beads) and in Hohmichele Grave 6 (351 beads). Amber heads for bronze pins are numerous at the Heuneburg settlement and occur in some graves. The carved amber face of the bone sphinx from Grafenbühl (fig. 3.8) and the carved plaquettes from Grafenbühl and Römerhügel 2 are products of Mediterranean workshops (Herrmann 1970).

Spectrographic studies of the amber from the Heuneburg and other sites in Württemberg suggest that the substance is Baltic amber (Kimmig 1971, 56–57; see also Beck *et al.* 1975). Kimmig (1971) and Kossack (1959, 116) suggest the East Hallstatt area as a possible immediate source for southwest German amber, a suggestion supported by the work of Malinowski (1971) and Bohnsack (1976). Since peoples in the Italian peninsula were importing large quantities of amber from the Baltic region during this period (Strong 1966*b*, 7–8, 24, 27–28), much of the amber in west-central Europe probably came by way of Italy, as the Grafenbühl sphinx and the carved plaquettes almost certainly did.

Amber at the sites examined

Tannheim	
Grave 10*b*	4 beads
Grave 16	7 beads
Grave 19	27 beads
Grave 20	6 beads
Mauenheim	
Tumulus E, Grave 1	Fragments (bead?)
Magdalenenberg	
Grave 5	2 beads
Grave 16	Ring
Grave 56	2 pendants, 10 amber pinheads
Grave 68	2 beads
Grave 97	191 beads
Grave 99	7 beads
Heuneburg tumuli:	
Hohmichele	
Grave 1	2 beads

Grave 6	4 rings, 351 beads
Grave 12	Bead
Giessübel-Talhau group	
Tumulus I, Chamber Grave 1	3 plaquettes, hemisphere, club-shaped fragment
Tumulus I, Chamber Grave 3	2 plaquettes
Tumulus I, Grave 4	4 pinheads
Rauher Lehen	8 rings, 3 rings with drop-shaped appendage
Heuneburg settlement	Heads of bronze pins
Zainingen	
Tumulus III	Ring
Hirschlanden	
Grave 5	2 pendants
Grave 11	Ring, 6+ beads
Mühlacker	
Tumulus X, Grave 1	4 rings, inlay in bronze ring, inlay in bracelet
Hohenasperg tumuli:	
Grafenbühl	
Central Grave	Carved face on sphinx, carved plaquettes, bead, fragments
Grave 3	4 beads
Grave 5	2 beads
Grave 14	Bead
Grave 15	Beads
Römerhügel	
Grave 1	Inlay in dagger hilt
Grave 2	2 plaquettes from earrings, plaquettes identical to those in Grafenbühl

Coral. Like amber, the coral found in Württemberg was brought from some distance. It is found in southwest Germany principally in the form of beads and inlay in bronze fibulae (Champion 1976, 30 fig. 1). But unlike amber, which occurs in earlier contexts in central Europe, coral first appears in the area in the Late Hallstatt Period (Reinach 1899; Kimmig 1971, 58).

In addition to numerous fibulae with coral inlay (Mansfeld 1973), a coral branch with signs of working (perforation and file marks) was recovered in the settlement deposits of the Heuneburg (Kimmig 1971, pl. 8 no. 5). This object indicates that coral branches were imported to central Europe and there worked into desired forms. Other coral branches in Late Hallstatt contexts in west-central Europe have been found at the settlement of Mont Lassois in eastern France (Joffroy 1960*a*, pls. 17, 18) and in several graves (see p. 18, above). Coral branches have also been recovered at a number of coastal settlements in Provence and eastern Spain dating to this same time (Jacobsthal 1944, 133; Kimmig 1971, 58). Benoit (1965, 195–196) reports a coral-fishing device found south of Marseille and suggests that it may have been used in collecting coral for trade to central Europe.

Coral at the sites examined

Tannheim	None
Mauenheim	None
Magdalenenberg	
Grave 122	7 beads
Heuneburg tumuli:	
Hohmichele, Grave 6	Ring
Giessübel-Talhau group	None
Rauher Lehen	None
Heuneburg settlement	Worked branch, fibula inlay
Zainingen	None
Hirschlanden, Grave 11	Inlay in 2 fibulae
Mühlacker	
Tumulus IV, Grave 1	11 beads
Tumulus IV, Grave 5	Inlay in fibula
Tumulus IV, Grave 6	Bead
Tumulus X, Grave 1	Inlay in 2 fibulae, in bracelet, in small ring, and in link belt
Hohenasperg tumuli:	
Grafenbühl	
Grave 3	Inlay in fibula
Grave 12	Inlay in fibula
Grave 24	Inlay in fibula
Grave 25	Inlay in 2 fibulae
Römerhügel	
Grave 1	None
Grave 2	None

Glass. In contrast to the substances considered above, glass is a finished product rather than a raw material. Since glass was manufactured and traded widely in Late Hallstatt central Europe, distribution of glass products is of direct interest to this study. Glass beads were probably being produced in central Europe from Urnfield times on (Neuninger and Pittioni 1959; Haevernick 1978). Nearly all of the glass objects at the sites examined here are beads, and they most often occur singly or in pairs. Exceptional are the quantities in the two Hohmichele graves (508 and 2360 respectively) and the 75 from Rauher Lehen. If the colored glass beads were manufactured in central Europe, and it is probable that at least some varieties were (Haevernick 1975), it is unlikely that they were produced in small dispersed workshops because glass production is a difficult process (Haevernick 1960, 1–38). The rarity of glass finds at the sites considered here also argues against any widespread local industries. Those that were made locally in west-central Europe were probably manufactured at a few large workshops at the major centers.

Glass at the sites examined

Tannheim	None
Mauenheim	None
Magdalenenberg	
Grave 5	Bead

Grave 10	Bead
Grave 16	Bead
Grave 68	4 beads
Grave 79	Bead
Grave 99	Bead
Heuneburg tumuli:	
Hohmichele	
Grave 1	508 beads, pendant
Grave 6	2360 beads, glass slag bead
Giessübel-Talhau group, Tumulus I, Grave 2	Bead
Rauher Lehen	75+ beads
Heuneburg settlement	Small ring and unpublished finds
Zainingen	None
Hirschlanden, Grave 7	235 beads
Mühlacker	None
Hohenasperg tumuli:	
Grafenbühl	
Grave 5	2 beads
Grave 14	Bead
Grave 15	Bead
Römerhügel	
Grave 1	None
Grave 2	None

Many of the materials considered here appear in quantity for the first time during the Late Hallstatt Period. Coral has not been found in contexts earlier than Hallstatt D (Kimmig 1971, 58). Amber is rare during the Bronze Age and Urnfield Period (Kimmig 1940; Müller-Karpe 1959), but relatively abundant during the Late Hallstatt. At no time before the Late Hallstatt is gold as plentiful in southwest Germany. Glass is present in only very small quantities before Hallstatt D (Haevernick 1978). Lignite and jet jewelry first appear at the very end of Hallstatt C and are most abundant during Hallstatt D. Iron is also much more plentiful during the Late Hallstatt Period than during the Early (Rieth 1942). Coral, amber, gold, glass, lignite, and jet are all much more abundant on archaeological sites in Württemberg, and in west-central Europe generally, than in surrounding parts of central Europe (compare Kossack 1959 for southern Bavaria, Joachim 1968 for the middle Rhineland, Polenz 1973 for the Rhine–Main area).

New patterns in the evidence

Among the changes in the patterns of the evidence from the Early to the Late Hallstatt Period, four are most important to this study.

1. Luxury products from the Mediterranean world appear in burial and settlement contexts. Before Late Hallstatt times, many objects were transported across the Alps (see pp. 20–21 above), but only with the beginning of this period do such materials as bronze vessels, fine pottery, transport amphorae, and other luxury items arrive in quantity.

2. Circulation of materials in central Europe intensifies. A number of luxury substances are well represented at cemetery and settlement sites during the Late Hallstatt Period which were absent or very rare during earlier times. The most apparent are amber, coral, glass, gold, jet, and lignite.

3. Differentiation in grave wealth increases. During the Late Hallstatt Period the difference in grave equipment between the richest and the poorest burials is far greater than during the Early Hallstatt and Urnfield Periods. In Württemberg a series of richly outfitted graves is characterized by the presence of four kinds of rare luxury goods: four-wheeled wagons (Schiek 1954), ornamental daggers of bronze and iron, gold jewelry, and luxury products from the Mediterranean world. At the other end of the scale are numerous burials containing no grave goods or only a single object.

4. A few settlement complexes emerged as centers in Late Hallstatt Europe. Evidence from the Heuneburg indicates the following special features not shared by most settlements: dense concentration of population; active commerce within central Europe and beyond, including the Mediterranean world; concentrations of material wealth; active and varied industrial systems. The Hohenasperg in north Württemberg and Mont Lassois in the Côte-d'Or were centers of a character similar to that of the Heuneburg. Château-sur-Salins in Franche-Comté, the Britzgyberg in Alsace, and Châtillon-sur-Glâne in Switzerland may have shared these features as well; further research at the last three will clarify their character. [The term 'center' is used here in a general way to designate a site which acted as a collecting, producing, and distributing unit in a cultural landscape (Haggett 1965, 121). No attempt is made to quantify the role played by the Late Hallstatt centers in production and trade because the data base does not at present permit such quantification.]

3.2 *A model for the social structure*

Much has been written on the subject of reconstructing social structure from burial evidence (e.g. Otto 1955; Ucko 1969; Rathje 1970; Brown 1971 (various articles); Renfrew 1972; 1974; Pauli 1972; 1978; Randsborg 1973; 1974; Kossack 1974; Shennan 1975; Dušek 1977; Moberg 1977; Frankenstein and Rowlands 1978). Without dealing here in detail with the various issues concerning interpretation of burial patterns in terms of social patterns, I wish to present a simple model of the relation between burial wealth and social structure. A few examples drawn primarily from early European textual sources will help to define working hypotheses.

In many documented instances a rich burial assemblage is associated with an individual of high social status. The grave of the Frankish King Childeric is a good example because from historical evidence we know something about his position in his society. The grave contained a variety of precious goods including a set of weapons (axe, spear, long and short swords – the swords and their scabbards decorated with gold and garnet), a gold seal ring, a gold fibula, a gold bracelet, many bee-shaped gold studs, and over 300 Roman coins (Böhner 1970, 84–88). Herodotus' description of the extraordinary goods placed in the graves of Scythian kings (IV 69–72) is similarly instructive. Ucko (1969, 267) cites further examples from ethnographic contexts.

In other cases individuals of high status are not buried with goods which archaeologists would perceive as exceptional (see *ibid.*). Of Germanic groups Tacitus writes 'in their funerals there is no pomp; they simply observe the custom of burning the bodies of illustrious men with certain kinds of wood... Monuments with their lofty splendor they reject as oppressive to the dead' (*Germania* **27**). Thus the absence of exceptionally rich graves does not necessarily mean that a society did not recognize status differences.

Are there cases of rich graves associated with persons who are not of high social status? If they exist, they are extremely rare; in his study Ucko does not cite any such instances (see also Trigger 1974, 100). Ucko (1969, 268–269) discusses the association of elaborate grave monuments with persons of differing status, but that is another matter since the monuments are community projects and not individual graves.

Here, I shall work with two hypotheses:

1. Exceptionally rich graves are those of individuals of high status in the society.

2. In contexts in which both rich and poor graves occur, the poor graves are those of individuals not of high status.

Hagen (1962, 59) distinguishes two kinds of persons in traditional societies – the 'simple folk' (peasants, artisans, craftsmen) and the 'elite' (warriors, priests, chiefs, kings). In archaeological contexts in which plain and rich graves can be easily separated, we can hypothesize that the plain graves are those of the common people, the richer ones those of the elite. These distinctions are apparent in the graves of Hallstatt west-central Europe.

In the Early Hallstatt Period, many cemeteries have one or two graves containing a long sword of bronze or iron (Rieth 1942; Kossack 1959, 125; 1972, 90) and sometimes several exceptionally fine ceramic vessels (Neuffer 1974, 2–5 with fig. 1). The majority of graves contain smaller numbers of vessels. The known cemeteries of the Early Hallstatt Period in central Europe probably represent settlement units on the scale of individual farmsteads or hamlets, generally with fewer than 40 inhabitants (Rieth 1938; Kossack 1959, 86; 1972, 92). The individuals buried with swords might be characterized as the heads of extended family groups or headmen of hamlet communities. Only the presence of the sword and sometimes the quantity and ornamental quality of the pottery distinguish these graves from the rest; very few gold ornaments, wagons, and bronze vessels are present to suggest a substantial social distance between them and the others.

The pattern changes in the Late Hallstatt Period, with the appearance of the rich graves. The earlier rich graves (Hallstatt D1, dating roughly to 600–550 B.C., such as Hohmichele Grave 6 and Vilsingen) are less richly outfitted that the later ones (Grafenbühl, and Vix in eastern France), but still much more sumptuously equipped than the majority of graves of the period. In addition to ornate daggers and four-wheeled burial wagons these graves contain bronze vessels (some imported from the Mediterranean world, others made locally) and gold jewelry. They are very different from the sword graves of the Early Hallstatt Period, and their burial equipment sets them well apart from the great majority of graves.

At the same time other changes in the patterns of the archaeological evidence suggest important changes in social and political structure; archaeologists often associate these changes with the rise of chiefdoms (Renfrew 1972, 364–365; 1974). Centers of industrial and commercial activity such as the Heuneburg assumed major roles in economic activity. Craft specialization is evident in several new industries, including those producing gold jewelry, bronze vessels, fibulae, and pottery. The centers performed important redistributive functions in producing finished goods for smaller communities in their regions (see Kimmig 1975*a*, *b*). Public labor projects, such as the construction of the fortifications around the Heuneburg settlement and the building of exceptionally large tumuli around the centers, are evident. Warfare assumed a greater significance as evidenced by the increase in the number of weapons in the graves and the new emphasis on the fortification of many sites. A wide range of new luxury goods became available for consumption by the elite including both locally made products, many of rare materials, and exotic imports. The towns such as the Heuneburg were occupied by much larger populations than any known Early Hallstatt settlements in the area, and there is evidence that population grew substantially in west-central Europe as a whole (Jankuhn 1969, 61–64). As community size grew, a more complex social and political organization was required to control and regulate the workings of the cultural system, and more positions in the social and political hierarchies developed (see Shennan 1975, 283; Gall and Saxe 1977).

Among the Late Hallstatt rich graves in Württemberg, different degrees of wealth can be recognized. Grafenbühl stands out particularly (as does Vix in France) by virtue of its extraordinary wealth in exotic luxury objects imported from the Mediterranean world. Other contemporary graves contain such exceptional goods as gold neck rings and four-wheeled wagons, but not the great wealth of Grafenbühl. Zürn (1970, 125–126) has defined two categories of rich graves and has tentatively suggested the recognition of a third. Frankenstein and

Rowlands (1978, 84–85) identify a four-tiered hierarchy of chiefs on the basis of the burial evidence and analogy with ethnographic contexts: paramount chiefs, vassal chiefs, sub-chiefs, and village chiefs.

Several aspects of the role of the chief in traditional societies are of particular interest to this study. The chief plays a special role in the circulation of goods (see pp. 6–7 above). He acts as the center of the economic system and collects and redistributes materials (and services) in his community (see Sahlins 1965; Firth 1965, 187–236; Odner 1972, 643–644). The chief also acts as the liaison between the community and outsiders. When representatives of a foreign group enter a territory for non-hostile purposes, they are usually brought into contact first with the local chief (e.g. Hanks 1957; Cipolla 1970). The chief decides whether or not friendly relations are to be established and sets down regulations governing interactions (Arnold 1957; Rogers and Shoemaker 1971, 340–342). Sometimes he regards the benefits of interaction with outsiders as his exclusive prerogative and establishes regulations preventing interaction between his people and the foreigners. By keeping the advantages derived through interaction to himself and his followers, he can often enhance his status and position (Barnett 1953, 305; Rogers and Shoemaker 1971, 340–342). The chief is often allowed by his people to retain certain privileges such as the accumulation of wealth and display of material riches (Dalton 1977, 197); often he is expected to live a lavish and flamboyant life (Hocart 1936, 197–209; 214–215; Duby 1974, 52).

3.3 *The evidence for contact*

Three kinds of archaeological evidence in Württemberg attest to contact with the Mediterranean world: imports, imitation of objects and elements by central European craftsmen, and application of technical knowledge gained from Mediterranean peoples.

Imports

The distribution of the imports, the contexts in which they occur, and their character all provide useful information.

Distribution. Fig. 3.10 shows the location of luxury imports of Greek and Etruscan origin in Late Hallstatt Württemberg; the concentrations around the Heuneburg and the Hohenasperg are apparent. In the settlement deposits of the Heuneburg have been found transport amphorae, Attic fine pottery, and the clay mold from Etruria. In Hohmichele Grave 6 were fragments of silk. Giessübel-Talhau Tumulus II yielded four Etruscan boss-rimmed bowls, and Tumulus IV, Grave 2 of the same group contained two more of the same. (Had Hohmichele Grave 1, Giessübel-Talhau Tumulus IV, Grave 1, and probably the three other

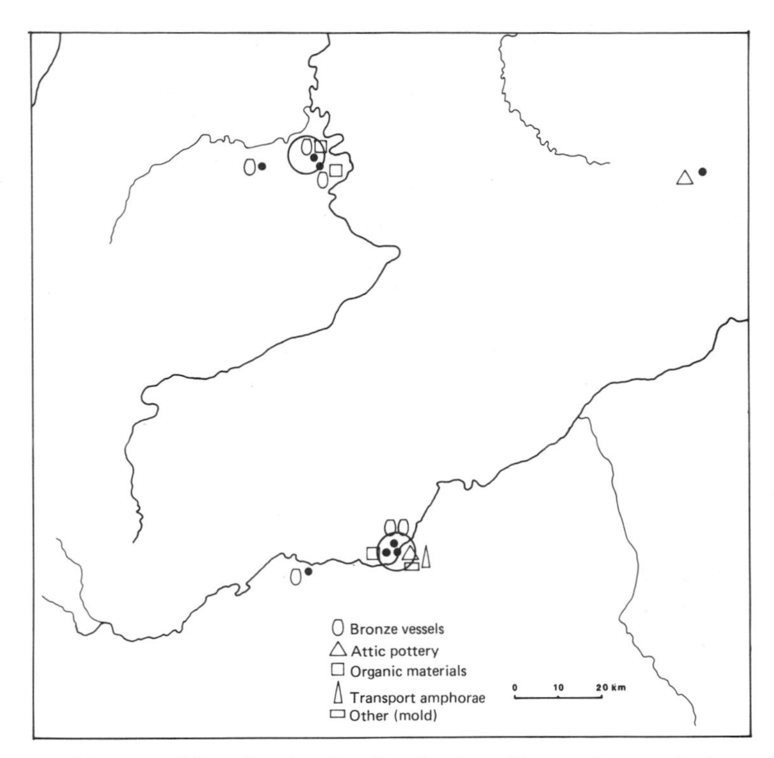

Fig. 3.10. Map showing the distribution of luxury imports in Late Hallstatt Württemberg (compare fig. 3.1). The map indicates the presence of each category in each grave, but not the quantity.

Giessübel-Talhau central graves, not been robbed shortly after burial; by comparison, additional southern imports would probably have been recovered in them.) At Vilsingen, about 18 km up the Danube from the Heuneburg, a Greek trefoil-mouth bronze jug was found in a grave dating to Hallstatt D1 (Schiek 1954).

In north Württemberg a similar concentration of imports occurs around the Hohenasperg.

No such luxury imports have been found at the other cemeteries considered here – Tannheim, Magdalenenberg, Mauenheim, Hirschlanden, Mühlacker, or Zainingen.

Context. All of the Mediterranean imports occur in settlement deposits and in graves; none has been found in other contexts such as hoards. Except for the Ipf, at which a single Greek sherd was identified, the Heuneburg is the only settlement site in Württemberg which has so far yielded imported luxury items. In many respects Mont Lassois on the upper Seine is comparable to the Heuneburg (Joffroy 1960*a*). Transport amphorae, Attic fine pottery, and other ceramics from the Mediterranean world, have been found at both sites, and around both settlements there are richly outfitted graves.

The best-respresented kind of Mediterranean import in the settlement deposits is pottery; in graves it is bronze vessels. Greek and Etruscan products occur in only a tiny fraction of known Late Hallstatt graves in Württemberg. All of the graves containing Mediterranean imports are also distinguished from the majority of graves by the presence of exceptional materials of local manufacture such as large pieces of gold jewelry, bronze vessels, and four-wheeled wagons. All of the graves in Württemberg containing Mediterranean imports, with the exception of Vilsingen, are closely associated with the settlements at the Heuneburg and the Hohenasperg.

Character of the imports

Bronze vessels

BOSS-RIMMED BOWLS. With seven specimens from three (or more) graves, these bowls are the best-represented group of imported bronzes in Württemberg (Hencken 1958, 265–267). They were probably made in Etruria, where the greatest number have been found (Frey 1963, 22; Dehn 1965, 133; Lang 1974, pl. 32). In the Mediterranean world they occur in burials dating from around 700 B.C. to the second half of the sixth century B.C. (Hencken 1958, 265–266; Lang 1974, 46). In central Europe the form occurs consistently in Hallstatt D contexts; besides the Württemberg bowls, specimens have been recovered in a Late Hallstatt grave at Pürgen in Bavaria, at the lakeshore settlement at Portalban on Lake Neuchâtel (Hencken 1958, 267), and at Chaveria in the French Jura (Kimmig 1974, 87 n. 33).

No specific information is available regarding the use of these bowls in Etruria. All of the Italian finds are from graves except one bowl in a 'votive deposit' at Broglio, between Arezzo and Chiusi (Hencken 1958, 266).

TREFOIL-MOUTH 'RHODIAN' JUGS. One such jug was found in the grave at Vilsingen and another in Baden at Kappel on the Rhine, also in a rich Late Hallstatt burial (Kimmig and Rest 1954). Different scholars have argued that these vessels are Greek or Etruscan in origin (Jacobsthal 1929; Villard 1956; Frey 1963); the most recent study (Shefton 1979) suggests that they are Greek. In Italy, where the majority of these jugs have been found, they occur in burials of the late seventh and early sixth centuries B.C. (Villard 1956, 49–50; Frey 1963, 19–20; Shefton 1979, 16–17). Paintings on Attic pottery show jugs of similar form (probably often clay versions) being used in pouring libations and in serving wine.

TRIPODS. The Grafenbühl tripod is the only one found in Württemberg, but another was recovered in a grave at La Garenne near Mont Lassois. (An Etruscan tripod thought to have been found at Auxerre in Burgundy will not be treated here, since its location of discovery is uncertain: Rolley 1962; 1964.) Of the Grafenbühl tripod only the two cast bronze feet with remains of iron connecting rods survive; the rest of the object and any cauldron which may have been associated with it were probably removed when the grave was looted shortly after burial. The specimen is a rod-tripod (Riis 1939) and according to Herrmann's reconstruction belongs to Riis' 'Fittings Group' (Herrmann 1970, 32–33 with fig. 9). That found at La Garenne, complete with a protome cauldron (Joffroy 1960*b*), belongs to the same group.

Eight other rod-tripods of the Fittings Group are known (Riis 1939, 18–22; Liepmann 1968). The Grafenbühl, La Garenne, and Kourion tripods are attributed to Greek manufacture, the other seven to Etruscan (Riis 1939, 21–22; Liepmann 1968, 53 n. 25; Herrmann 1970, 34). Herrmann (1970, 34) suggests a Peloponnesian origin for the Grafenbühl tripod on the basis of the style of the cast bronze feet, and he dates it to sometime before the middle of the sixth century B.C.

In the Greek world, remains of rod-tripods and of protome cauldrons (such as that in La Garenne) are found principally in sanctuary deposits (Riis 1939; Jantzen 1955, 9; Herrmann 1966, 4–5). In Etruscan contexts they and their imitations occur in graves (Riis 1939, 18–22; Janzten 1955, 42). The contexts in which they are found in the Greek world, and literary references to tripods in Greek literature, suggest that tripods had a significance beyond that of everyday household utility. (Rod-tripods have been found in graves elsewhere on the borders of the Greek world, for example in the rich graves at Trebenischte in Macedonia: Filow 1927.)

VIX KRATER. Though not found in Württemberg the Vix krater will be mentioned as it is of special importance to this study. The krater (fig. 3.11) is a vessel of hammered and cast bronze standing 1.64 m high and weighing 208 kg, with Gorgon figures ornamenting the two volute handles and a frieze of separately cast and applied hoplites and horse-drawn chariots on the neck (Joffroy 1954). On the basis of comparisons of the cast figural ornament with those on other Greek bronze vessels the Vix krater is dated to around 530–520 B.C. (Vallet and Villard 1955; Jucker 1966, 107–112). Although its place of origin is not certain, most scholars favor a Greek workshop in southern Italy as the place of manufacture (Charbonneaux 1953; 1959, 45, 88; Homann-Wedeking 1958; Vallet 1958, 228–234).

Closest parallels are a series of three complete bronze volute kraters (Trebenischte Grave 1: Filow 1927, 39–47, pls. 7–8; Trebenischte Grave 8: Vulić 1934; 'Campania' in the Antikensammlung, Munich: Sieveking

Fig. 3.11. Vix krater.

1908), and handles of four others (two from a krater purchased in Italy, one in the Louvre and one in the Musée de Nîmes: Héron de Villefosse 1887), 'Italy' in the British Museum (Walters 1899, 85 no. 583), 'Cilicia' in the de Clerq Collection, Louvre (Joffroy 1954, 26), and Mostanosch (Martonosha), southern Russia, from a tumulus grave (Hoving 1975, no. 46). These volute kraters with cast Gorgon figures on the handles have all been found in areas involved in interactions with the Greek world during the latter half of the sixth century B.C. (see Boardman 1973). Unique among the known bronze kraters is the size of the Vix specimen. Another exceptionally large volute krater is also represented in a non-Greek context – painted on the wall of the Tomb of the Lionesses at Tarquinia in Tuscany (Ducati 1937, pl. 2).

Herodotus mentions metal kraters as gifts presented to potentates and as dedications to gods. Gyges sent six gold kraters to Delphi as offerings (I 14) and Croesus sent a gold krater and a silver one there (I 51). Herodotus describes one huge bronze vessel 'graven outside round the rim with figures, and large enough to hold twenty-seven hundred gallons,' commissioned by the Lacedaemonians as a gift for Croesus (I 70). These passages suggest that metal kraters played a special role in the Greek world as gifts presented for political reasons to powerful individuals or, in the case of Delphi, to their gods.

GRÄCHWIL HYDRIA. Among the roughly 300 known bronze hydriai (von Bothmer 1965, 599), the specimen from Grächwil in Switzerland (Jucker 1973) and the two from Treia, Province Macerata, Italy (Jucker 1966), constitute a special group of ornate hydriai. Jucker suggests a south Italian origin for the group and Tarentum as the most likely center for their manufacture (*ibid.*, 76–107; see also Charbonneaux 1959, 87); he dates the Grächwil hydria to 580–570 B.C. (1966, 119).

These three are distinct from other bronze hydriai in that the vertical handle is replaced by a delicate, cast, figural ornament. Such ornamental handles are probably non-functional, being too delicate to support the weight of a full hydria and providing no convenient grip. They may have been manufactured as decorative objects, perhaps as household trophies, prizes, offerings, or as grave goods (Jucker 1966, 15–16). Use of bronze hydriai as burial urns, as in the Grächwil grave (Jahn 1852, 82), is well documented in the Greek world (Diehl 1964, 146–168). What relation there might be between Greek use of hydriai as urns and the same function at Grächwil is unclear; since the great majority of Late Hallstatt burials in west-central Europe are inhumations, the Grächwil find is of particular interest for its burial rite.

Attic pottery. Attic pottery has been found in two Late Hallstatt associations in Württemberg – at the Heuneburg and at the Ipf. Over 50 sherds have been recovered on the Heuneburg (see fig. 3.4) representing a variety of different vessel forms (Kimmig 1971, 40–41; 1975*a*, 200); from the Ipf comes a single unpainted sherd (Schultze-Naumburg 1969). Attic pottery has been recovered from several other Late Hallstatt sites in west-central Europe (Reim 1968, 277 fig. 1; Kimmig 1975*b*, 47 fig. 20*b*). It was manufactured in Attica, in and around the city of Athens. Most of the finds in Late Hallstatt contexts date between 540 and 500 B.C. (see literature cited on p. 16 above).

During the sixth century B.C. and particularly in the years 550–500 B.C., Attic pottery was transported widely throughout the Mediterranean world and bordering inland regions. It was popular among a wide variety of peoples in the ancient world and was a good trade item for any merchants traveling in Mediterranean waters. Bailey's map (1940, 67 fig. 4) showing the distribution of Attic black-figure pottery dating to the years 560–520 B.C. indicates some of the areas in which the pottery has been found (see Boardman's (1973, xxii) more recent map showing distributions of all Greek objects in the ancient Mediterranean area; also

Kimmig 1974, 63 fig. 8). Of sites north of the Alps only the Heuneburg, Mont Lassois, and Château-sur-Salins have yielded substantial quantities; the Britzgyberg and Châtillon-sur-Glâne may yield more as excavation work continues. Unlike some of the bronzes discussed above, Attic pottery was manufactured in large quantities for both local use and export (Cook 1959; 1972).

Transport amphorae. Greek amphorae found in central Europe were almost certainly brought from the Mediterranean world for their contents. They are unpainted and otherwise undecorated and are of coarse fabric. In Württemberg, only at the Heuneburg have such amphorae been found to date; at least 15 vessels can be reconstructed from the sherds recovered there (Kimmig 1975*a*, 200). Similar amphorae have been recovered at several other sites in west-central Europe (see distribution maps in Kimmig 1971, 42 fig. 8; 1975*b*, 46 fig. 20). The amphorae at the Heuneburg and the other sites were probably made in the Marseille area of southern France (Benoit 1965, 167; Kimmig 1971, 41–42). Large numbers of the same kind have been recovered along the coast of southern France from Nice to the Spanish border as well as in sunken ships off the coast; finds are especially abundant in the lower Rhône valley.

In the Greek world such amphorae were used to store and carry various liquids and solid foods, particularly wine, oil, and grain (Kimmig 1971, 42–43). Ceramic amphorae are well suited to sea transport since they are easy to make, pack well, and can be reused indefinitely. Land transport was more difficult because the weight of the container is great relative to that of the substance in it. The association on several sites (Heuneburg, Mont Lassois, Château-sur-Salins, Britzgyberg, Châtillon-sur-Glâne) of Attic wine serving and drinking vessels (see Kossack 1964) together with transport amphorae makes the carrying of wine in these amphorae into central Europe very likely (Kimmig 1971, 43).

Silk fragments, Hohmichele Grave 6. The silk from Hohmichele Grave 6 is the only documented example from Hallstatt central Europe (Hundt 1969). Its origin is unknown; it probably came from the Near East or further eastward, via Greek southern France with the other imports.

Sphinxes, Grafenbühl. One is of bone with a face of amber (fig. 3.8); the other of ivory and lacking the face (Zürn 1970, pl. 66, 2). Such carving in amber, ivory, and bone was highly developed in the Greek world during the seventh and sixth centuries B.C.; Herrmann (1970, 25) suggests an origin in the Greek city of Tarentum in southern Italy around 600 B.C. The original use of these unique ornaments is unclear; remains of a dark substance on the back suggests that they were attached to another object.

Ivory lion's foot, Grafenbühl. This object was once part of a piece of furniture and originated somewhere in the Greek world. Its features suggest a date around the end of the seventh century B.C. (Herrmann 1970, 27).

Ivory plaque, Grafenbühl. This enigmatic object probably came from the eastern Mediterranean – from northern Syria or southeastern Anatolia (Herrmann 1970, 30–31).

Carved plaquettes of bone, ivory, and amber, Grafenbühl. A variety of different forms including palmettes, rhomboids, and rectangles of these substances occur in this grave and came from the Mediterranean world. Herrmann (1970, 28–30) suggests that they originally ornamented one or more pieces of furniture in the grave.

Carved plaquettes of amber, Römerhügel Grave 2. In the second rich grave at Römerhügel were found carved amber plaquettes identical to those at Grafenbühl (Schiek 1956, 51; Zürn 1970, 14 fig. 6; pl. 3 nos. 12–24).

Silenus head mold, Heuneburg (fig. 3.6). This object is not a luxury product in its own right but was intended to be used in the production of luxury objects, namely bronze vessels. The fabric of the clay mold indicates that it was made in Etruria; the style of the Silenus head is Etruscan, and von Vacano suggests a date of 480–460 B.C. (Kimmig and von Vacano 1973, 85). The mold is the only find in central Europe representing the tools of production of Etruscan bronzes. No finished bronzes have been found in central Europe with Silenus heads resembling the mold; nor have close parallels been cited among bronze vessels from Italy.

Domestic chicken. Recovery of bones of domestic chickens at the Heuneburg suggest the introduction from the Mediterranean world of this bird during the Late Hallstatt Period (Jankuhn 1969, 76; Kimmig 1975*b*, 50).

Imitation of Mediterranean elements

At least two different kinds of bronze vessels in Württemberg and elsewhere in west-central Europe in Late Hallstatt contexts are probably local imitations of Etruscan vessels. One is a variation of the boss-rimmed bowls discussed above (p. 52). Local versions of these bowls have been found in Württemberg in Hohmichele Grave 6 and in the settlement deposits at the Heuneburg (Dehn 1965; 1971).

The second local bronze vessel form based on Etruscan prototypes is the hemispherical kettle with iron ring-handles (Hawkes and Smith 1957,

191–198; Pauli 1974, 684). Most of the known finds occur in southwest Germany, particularly in Württemberg (Hawkes and Smith 1957, 194 fig. 12). At the Heuneburg these kettles have been found in Hohmichele Grave 6, in Giessübel-Talhau Tumuli I–IV (a total of 12 in the 4 mounds), and in the Rauher Lehen tumulus (Paret 1933–1935). Other finds in Württemberg include those in the Vilsingen grave and in Cannstatt Grave 1 (two kettles) and Grave 2.

All of the grave groups in which these kettles have been recovered date to Hallstatt D. Among the probable Etruscan prototypes are vessels in the Regolini-Galassi tomb at Cerveteri (Pareti 1947, pl. 38 no. 304), in the Tomba dei flabelli di bronzo at Populonia (*Monumenti antichi* **34**, 1932, pl. 9 no. 2), and in Grave 1 of Cemetery C at Narce (*Monumenti antichi* **4**, 1893, 428–429 no. 9; pls. 4, 5 figs. 4–4*a*). These three Tuscan finds are dated to the second half of the seventh century B.C. (Lang 1974, 47).

The painted pottery from the Heuneburg possesses a variety of decorative features which can be traced to Greek traditions present in southern France and to parts of the Italian peninsula (Kimmig 1971, 25–40; 1975*b*, 49, 56; Lang 1974; 1976; Dämmer 1978, 42–55). As Dämmer points out, the origins and development of many of the features in question can only be documented in detail when additional pottery assemblages from sites between central Europe and the Mediterranean area become available for study. Other varieties of pottery at the Heuneburg also show influences of artistic traditions of the Mediterranean lands, for example the ceramic imitations of bronze trefoil-mouth jugs and *Schnabelkannen* (Lang 1976, 46, 51).

The gold straining-spoon from the Heuneburg settlement may also be an imitation of an Etruscan bronze implement (Kimmig 1975*a*, 200, 202 fig. 13).

Technical knowledge from the Mediterranean world

Potter's wheel. Pottery made on the fast wheel appears in central Europe for the first time during the Late Hallstatt Period; at the Heuneburg its earliest occurrence is at the end of Hallstatt D1 (Lange 1974, 37, 59). Wheel-made pottery occurs at other Late Hallstatt sites at about the same time (Dehn 1962–1963; Lang 1974, 3–25). The nature of the introduction and dissemination of this new technique is still unclear. Familiarity with the fast-turning wheel was probably transmitted directly from craftsman to craftsman (see Pauli 1978, 445). Central European potters may have learned the technique directly from Greek potters (or from others who had learned the Greek techniques) either in southern France or from Mediterranean potters working in central Europe (Dämmer 1978, 55).

At the start of the Late Hallstatt Period, there appear also objects of metal and wood which were probably made with the use of a lathe, suggesting introduction of this device at this same time (Pauli 1978, 402).

Heuneburg brick wall. The wall of sun-dried clay bricks belonging to Heuneburg phase IVa is the only defensive wall of clay bricks known in west-central Europe (Dehn 1957; 1974), and has its parallels at cities in the Mediterranean world (Kimmig 1968, 47–57; Griffo and von Matt 1968, 183–184). It may have been a novelty and a sign of connections with the outside world, erected as a showpiece by a local chief, rather than a strictly military structure (Dehn 1974, 130).

Someone brought not only information about the existence of clay brick walls, but also the technical knowledge of how to build such a wall, from the Mediterranean world to central Europe. Construction involved first the laying of a foundation of cut stone blocks (Kimmig 1968, figs. 18, 23), then the digging and preparation of the clay, manufacture of the bricks, drying, and building. The knowledge of how to build such a wall was probably not brought by a central European visitor to the Mediterranean world, nor by Greek merchants trading in Württemberg. It was built by someone specifically trained in construction of brick walls. The architect may have been a Greek or someone else in southern France who had learned the techniques from Greeks, or perhaps a central European who studied the methods in southern France.

Hirschlanden stele. The nearly life-size statue of a warrior cut from north Württemberg sandstone (see fig. 3.9) was found at the base of the Hirschlanden tumulus (Zürn 1970, 55 fig. 23; 67–68 fig. 35; pl. *A*). Breaks at the ankles and the position of the stele at the time of discovery indicate that it had stood on top of the mound as a burial monument.

The statue is the earliest life-size human figure of stone sculpted in the round known from central Europe and the only one from a Hallstatt context. Modeling of the legs, with representation of musculature, points to prototypes in the Mediterranean world. Potential prototypes for the stele have been suggested in east-central Italy (see Cianfarani 1969, pls. 86–93 nos. 180–182), but the familiarity with Mediterranean stone carving may have come from the stone sculpting tradition developing in southern France at this time (see van Dorp and van Royen 1977).

3.4 *Greek commerce with non-Greeks*

Most of the Mediterranean luxury products in Hallstatt west-central Europe probably arrived via the Greek colony of Massalia (Marseille) and thence up the Rhône valley into the heart of the continent. Earlier in this century many investigators argued in favor of routes across the Alps from Italy along which the imports were carried northward (see summary of the arguments in Lang 1974, 49–52). Most scholars now agree that the Greek objects were transported up the Rhône valley rather than across the Alps (Carcopino 1957; Kimmig 1958; Blanc 1958; Gallet de Santerre 1962, 392; Pauli 1974, 684; Shefton 1979, 21). Amphorae of the same form and composition as those in Late Hallstatt contexts are abundant in the vicinity of Marseille (Benoit 1955) as well as along the Rhône valley northward (see p. 56 above). Attic pottery is well represented at Marseille (Villard 1960) and at other sites in the lower and middle Rhône valley; distribution of this pottery north of Marseille suggests that the fragments found at Late Hallstatt sites were brought up the Rhône route (Villard 1960, 133; Reim 1968, 275 fig. 1; Stahl-Weber and Schweitzer 1972, 45; Kimmig 1975*b*, 47 fig. 20*b*).

For the Etruscan bronze vessels in Late Hallstatt graves routes across the Alps to central Europe are often suggested. But these are likely to have been brought up the Rhône valley together with the Greek materials (Benoit 1956*a*, 19–20; Hatt 1959, 23–26; Megaw 1966, 40). The Etruscan bronze vessels found in Late Hallstatt contexts include the Conliège amphora (Lerat 1958), *Schnabelkannen* from Vix, Mercey-sur-Saône, and Hatten, the Hatten trefoil-mouth jug, and the pyxis and bowl from Kastenwald (Jehl and Bonnet 1968). In the first three instances the Etruscan objects were found either in direct association with Greek ceramics or in localities at which Greek pottery has also been recovered. Evidence is abundant for an active commerce between Massalia and Etruria during the sixth century B.C. (see below), hence the presence of Etruscan bronzes in Greek southern France is not unexpected.

Thus the problem of imports in Hallstatt contexts and their relation to interactions between central Europeans and the late archaic Mediterranean world can be reduced to the relationship between Hallstatt Europe and the Greek city of Massalia. A few imports may, of course, have arrived across the Alps, but the archaeological evidence cited here suggests that most were transported up the Rhône valley. (Distribution of small objects such as bronze pendants north and south of the Alps (Frey 1957, 244–245; Pauli 1971) tells us nothing about the route used for transport of the luxury objects. The mechanisms by which the luxury products were exchanged to central Europeans and those involved in the circulation of the small metal trinkets were probably very different: see pp. 20–21.)

Pre-600 B.C. Greek activity in southern France

No evidence has been found at Marseille of Greek presence before the foundation of Massalia about 600 B.C. (Villard 1960, 76). But elsewhere in the vicinity and at the mouth of the Rhône, Greek pottery and Etruscan ceramics of the seventh century B.C. have been recovered. For example, at Saint-Blaise the recovery of East Greek pottery has led investigators to suggest the existence of a Greek trading site there before the establishment of Massalia (Rolland 1951, 47, 59–73, 207; Boardman 1964, 224; Benoit 1965, 170).

Foundation of Massalia

During the period 800–500 B.C. many cities throughout the Greek world sent out shiploads of persons to begin new settlements on the shores of the Mediterranean and Black Seas. The reasons for colonization were various and included population pressure in the homeland, desire for new lands to farm, interest in acquiring metals needed throughout the Greek sphere, need on the part of Greek cities to find sources of wheat for importation, and surely also the desire for adventure (Dunbabin 1948; Wasowicz 1966; Boardman 1973).

Massalia was founded by Ionian Greeks from the city of Phocaea on the coast of Asia Minor (on the foundation see Wackernagel 1930; Clavel-Lévêque 1974; Momigliano 1975 for three different perspectives). During the seventh century B.C. the cities of Ionia began developing extensive trade networks throughout the Mediterranean, largely to bring in grain and metals which were not locally available in sufficient quantities (Roebuck 1959, v, 20–21). As part of this growing commerce the Ionian cities established a number of colonies beginning in the last quarter of the seventh century B.C., most of them trading posts established to obtain products from the hinterlands. Around 600 B.C. Ionian colonies were founded in France, Spain, Egypt, and the Pontus. Ionia exported such materials as wine, olive oil, pottery, and silver, and imported grain, metals, and luxury goods of various kinds (Roebuck 1959, 103).

Ancient writers indicate the date of the founding of Massalia with reference to various events in the history of the Mediterranean area (Wackernagel 1930, 2130–2131); the date suggested is *c.* 600 B.C. The archaeological dating evidence corresponds closely to the literary: Greek pottery on the site begins *c.* 600 B.C. (Villard 1960, 80).

The city was ideally situated to benefit from the Rhône waterway, the largest river connecting the Mediterranean with central Europe. Massalia was far enough away from the mouth to avoid silting, yet close enough to control traffic flow between the river and the sea. The Phocaeans who established the colony surely must have known about products available from lands up the Rhône; the location of the city suggests this, and the evidence of the seventh-century Greek pottery in the vicinity indicates that the area was known by Greeks. Massalia was also well sited on the trade routes from the eastern Mediterranean to Spain, an important source of metals. Benoit argues (1965, 31) that one major reason for the city's foundation was the Phocaean's interest in Spanish metals (also Roebuck 1959, 94–104; Langlotz 1966, 16–17).

Massalia did not possess good agricultural land. Strabo writes (IV 1.5) that wheat could not be grown in the vicinity; the vine and olive were the only crops which prospered in the hot, dry, rocky environment. During medieval times too, Marseille needed to import quantities of grain in order to feed its populace (Villard 1960, 111 n. 3). This lack of good

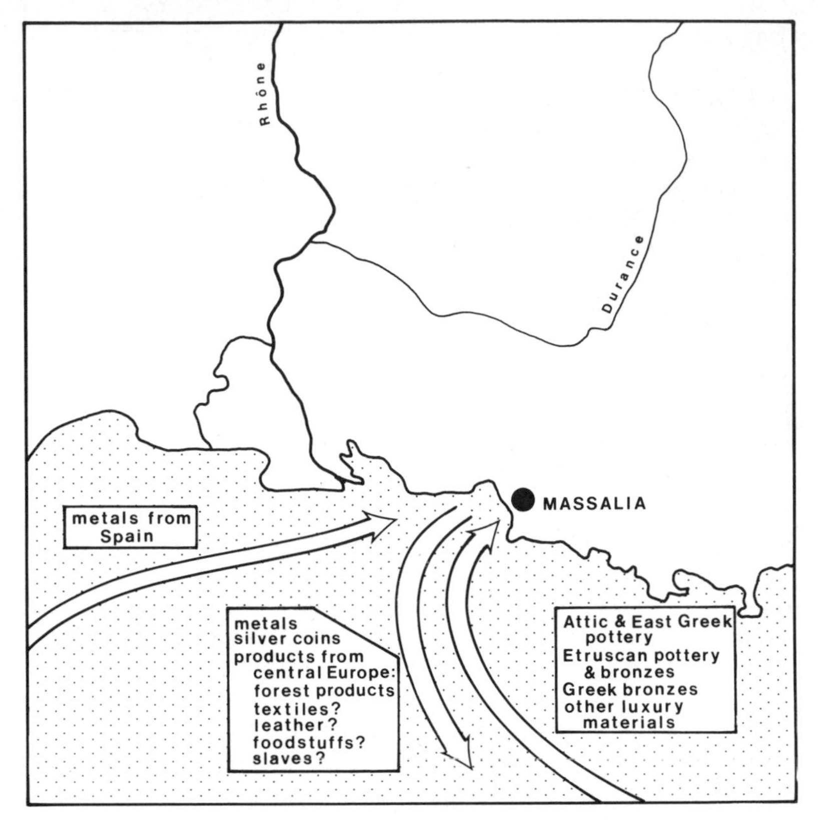

Fig. 3.12. Model representing Massalia's commercial relations with other parts of the Mediterranean world during the sixth century B.C.

agricultural land underscores Massalia's principal activity as a commercial city, in contrast to the Greek colonies established elsewhere near good fields for growing grain (Dunbabin 1948).

Massalia's commerce in the sixth century B.C.

It will be convenient to consider Massalia's commercial activity in terms of three spheres of interaction: the greater Mediterranean, the coastal and inland regions of southern France, and west-central Europe. The three spheres were interdependent: products were traded both within and between spheres.

Massalia and the Mediterranean (fig. 3.12). During the first half of the sixth century B.C. East Greek pottery is particularly abundant at Massalia (Benoit 1965, 152–153, 162–163, 186); Phoenician material occurs during the sixth century B.C. as well (Benoit 1965, 56–66). The abundance of pottery from the eastern Mediterranean suggests that traders from different parts of the Mediterranean world frequented Massalia, and that sailors from the colony traded at many foreign ports (Wackernagel 1930, 2147, records inscriptions, from different parts of Greece, which bear names of Massaliotes). After the mid sixth century B.C. Attic pottery is well represented at the site.

The city's most important commercial contacts in the western Mediterranean were probably with central Italy and Spain. Evidence for interactions with Etruscan centers includes much Etruscan *bucchero* pottery and Etruscan wine amphorae at Massalia and at other sites on the coast and in the lower Rhône valley (Benoit 1965, 33 fig. 3). A number of sunken cargo ships carrying Etruscan amphorae and fine pottery have been found off the coast of southern France at Antibes, Agde, and Grau-de-Roi (Benoit 1956*b*; 1965). The recovery of early Massaliote silver coins in Etruria (Villard 1960, 123–124; Benoit 1965, 43) and in southern Italy (Benoit 1965, 42) further underscores the city's commercial relations with that peninsula.

Massalia's relations with Iberian centers probably revolved around the peninsula's metal deposits. Tin, silver, iron, copper, and high-quality bronze have all been cited in connection with Iberia's commerce during the sixth century B.C. Massalia probably served as a transfer point for metals from Spain being shipped eastward (Jannoray 1955, 287; Roebuck 1959, 95; Benoit 1965, 191; Langlotz 1966, 16–17). Trade in metals leaves little archaeological evidence (see Piggott 1977), but interaction between Massalia and Spanish sites is indicated archaeologically; for example, Massaliote coins of this period are represented at several sites on the Iberian coast (Benoit 1965, 43).

Massalia and southern France (fig. 3.13). Since the commercial relations between the colony and surrounding areas probably depended largely upon natural products which do not survive in the archaeological record, much of the picture must be hypothetically reconstructed by extrapolation from later periods of Marseille's history. Clear evidence of relations between Massalia and the surrounding areas is pottery – Massalia's own and imported – found at numerous southern French sites. Since Massalia was the principal port of southern France and offered the best harbor facilities, it is likely that most of the East Greek, Etruscan, and other pottery which came into the area after 600 B.C. arrived at Massalia and was traded from there to the smaller settlements around the colony (Benoit 1965, 51–56; Py 1968, 70). Among the most common ceramics in the areas around Massalia are amphorae, both Massaliote and Ionian (Benoit 1965, 179–186). Benoit (1965, 100, 191, 217) argues that the colony was founded in part for the purpose of exploiting natural resources of the coast of southern France (see also Jannoray 1955, 301), as well as to engage in commerce with Spain and inland areas of central Europe.

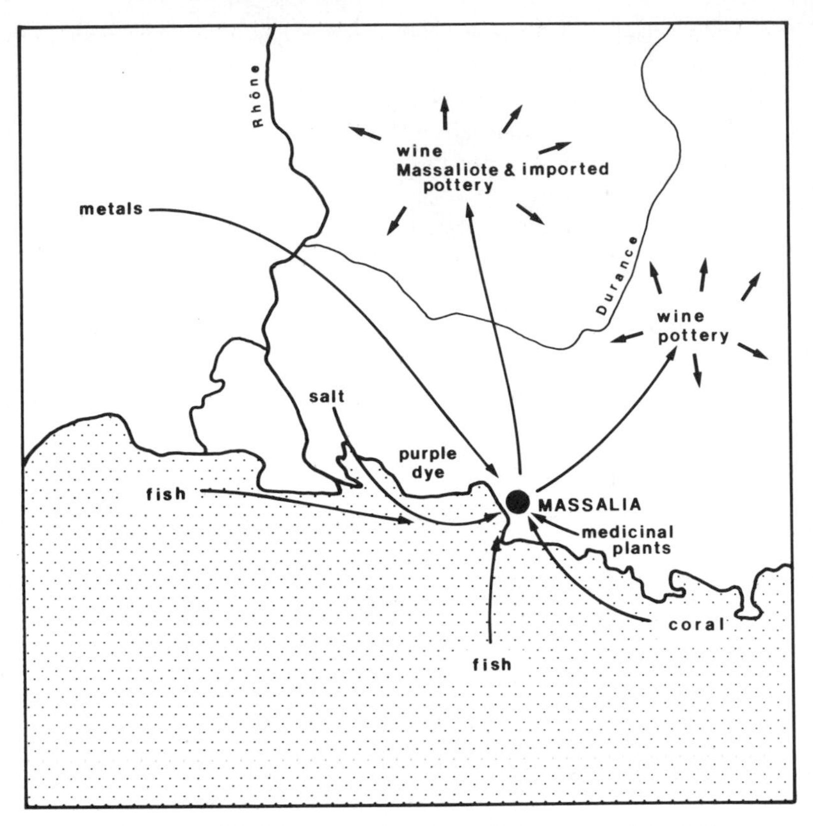

Fig. 3.13. Model representing Massalia's commercial relations with coastal and inland areas of southern France.

He suggests that, in exchange for pottery and other materials, Massalia was acquiring a wide variety of products of the area, some of which were unavailable or in short supply in other parts of the Mediterranean world and thus constituted valuable export products. According to Benoit's thesis (1965, 195–211), coral, purple dye, resin, medicinal plants, salt, and perhaps cork were available in the vicinity of Massalia and in demand in parts of the East Mediterranean and the Italian peninsula. Benoit (1965, 192–195) suggests that Massalia was obtaining mineral resources – tin, gold, silver, lead, copper, and iron – from the mountains of southern France for trade.

Massalia surely traded wine to communities in southern France. Most of the non-local pottery found at the various sites consists of vessels intended for wine transport (amphorae) or mixing and drinking wine (kraters, jugs, bowls). Greeks brought the vine with them when they settled at Massalia; Strabo mentions its presence (see p. 61). As early as the sixth century B.C., wine probably constituted an important export product from the city (Py 1968, 71; Lepore 1970, 23).

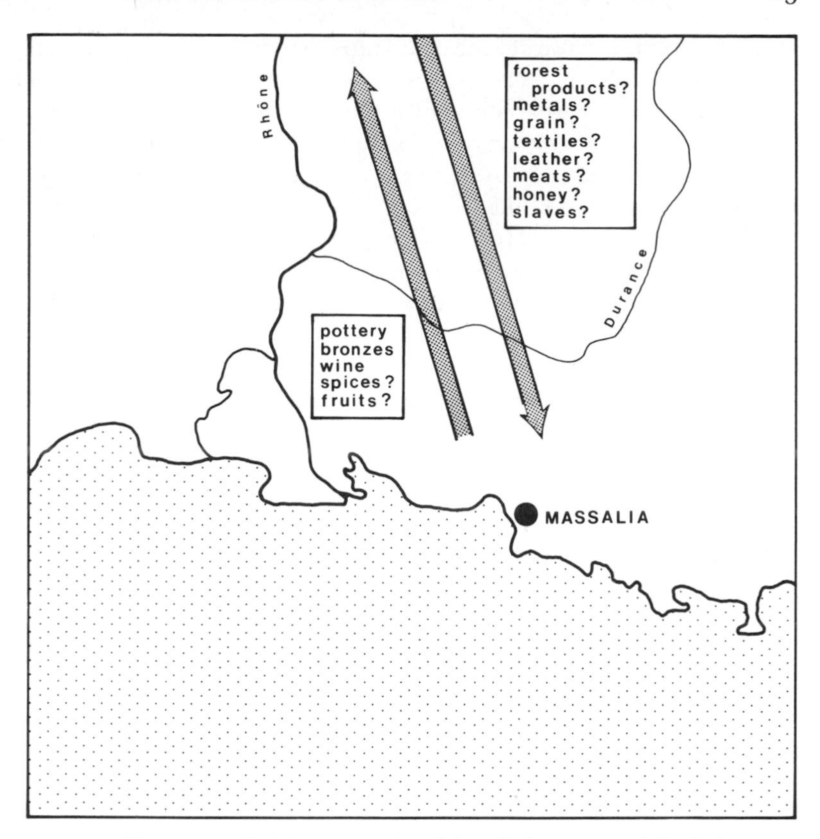

Fig. 3.14. Model representing Massalia's commercial relations with west-central Europe.

Massalia and west-central Europe (fig. 3.14). For the problem of interactions between Greek Massalia and west-central Europe, all of the archaeological evidence is in west-central Europe. The objects from the Mediterranean world which have been recovered in Late Hallstatt contexts have been enumerated above (pp. 16–18).

Wine was surely brought to west-central Europe from Massalia, though no trace of the beverage has yet been identified in the Late Hallstatt finds. (Inside some Etruscan bronze vessels found in Early La Tène contexts in central Europe remains of resin additives to wine have been identified (Déchelette 1913*b*, 123–124; Jacobsthal 1944, 142).) All of the Greek pottery in west-central Europe consists of forms used in the Greek world in connection with wine; most of the bronze vessels were also associated with wine drinking in their lands of manufacture – trefoil-mouth jugs and *Schnabelkannen* for pouring wine, kraters for mixing it.

Massalia, like most parts of the Greek world, produced wine (Strabo IV 1.5; Pliny *Nat. Hist.* XIV 8); viticulture probably arrived with the

Phocaeans. Exportation of wine constituted one of the mainstays of Greek commercial success in many parts of the Mediterranean world (Seltman 1957, 131). Many barbarian peoples with whom the Greeks came into contact delighted in drinking wine once the Greeks had introduced it. Diodorus (v 26) and Dionysius (XIII 15.16) tell of the absence of the vine in central Europe and of the bringing of wine to central European Celts by merchants from the Mediterranean world. According to Diodorus they were willing to exchange at the rate of a slave for a jar of wine.

Since there is no real archaeological evidence for wine in Hallstatt central Europe, beyond the vessels used in its transportation and consumption (and it has not been proven that the amphorae from Massalia carried wine to central Europe, or that the Attic drinking-bowls ever held wine at the Late Hallstatt settlements), the question of the scale of wine trade is a difficult one. The 'maximal view' of Late Hallstatt wine trade from Massalia sees wine as the main object of commerce as far as west-central Europeans were concerned and the basis of interaction between the areas during the sixth century B.C. (Villard 1960, 158; Piggott 1965, 195; Py 1968). Most of the literary references to the transport of wine overland mention skin wine bags (Dionysius XIII 15) and wooden casks (Strabo v 1, 8) but not ceramic amphorae, which are very heavy for the amount of wine they hold. The first two types of containers would rarely survive in the archaeological record. It is possible that a great many wagon loads of wine were carried to west-central Europe from Massalia during the sixth century B.C., and the Massaliote amphorae from eastern France and southwest Germany may be just a very small portion of the transport vessels used.

The 'minimal view', on the other hand, would suggest that the relatively small numbers of Attic pottery vessels and Massaliote amphorae in west-central Europe indicate that only small quantities of wine ever arrived and that wine constituted a rare and extravagant luxury for the richest individuals in Late Hallstatt society. Compared to Etruscan sites such as Vulci and Greek colonies such as Massalia and Spina, the quantities of Attic pottery found at Mont Lassois, the Heuneburg, and the other central European sites are very small. If the amount of imported pottery bears any direct relation to the quantity of wine brought in, then very little was imported into central Europe (Driehaus 1966).

Whatever the quantities involved, wine and its equipment made up an important cultural part of the interactions between central Europe and Greek southern France. Wine is not just a beverage; in the Greek world of the sixth century B.C., as in the Roman world and in medieval Europe, wine was closely tied to social ritual and to religious behavior (Seltman 1957). In Late Hallstatt Europe, wine probably brought with it from Greek Massalia not only the fine Attic pottery for its preparation and consumption but also ideas concerning its use (see Kossack 1964).

Besides the surviving imports and wine we do not know what might have been exported from the Mediterranean world to west-central Europe: olive oil is one possibility (Benoit 1965, 202–203). In connection with the transportation of wine from Italy to central Europe, Dionysius (XIII 15) also mentions oil and figs. Other fruits such as oranges and dates may have been brought to central Europe, as they were in medieval times (Braudel 1972, 220), as may spices.

We have no clear evidence of materials carried the other way. In other parts of the Greek world textual evidence indicates that Greek merchants obtained from non-Greek peoples a wide range of products, such as grain, timber, fish, salt, hides, slaves, gold, amber, wax, pitch, resin, and honey (Polybius IV 38, 1–5; Minns 1913, 438–441; Semple 1931; Finley 1959; 1962). Such products were often in short supply in Greek cities, but most of them usually leave no trace in the archaeological record.

Greek cities of the eastern Mediterranean were always searching for sources of metals to supply their growing industries (Roebuck 1959). The trade in tin has been much discussed in relation to Massalia's interactions with eastern France during the Late Hallstatt Period (Villard 1960, 137–161; Piggott 1977). Classical texts from well after the sixth century B.C. mention tin trade routes overland across France to the Mediterranean coast. Strabo (IV 1, 14) cites a route between Britain and the mouth of the Seine, and from there overland via the Seine, Saône, and Rhône valleys to the Mediterranean. Several investigators (Carcopino 1957; Joffroy 1962, 129–136) suggest that Mont Lassois may have been a transfer point for this trade between the Seine and Saône rivers, and thus enabled duties to be collected on the goods passing through. They argue for this function on the basis of the later texts and the quantity of Greek imports at Mont Lassois and Vix. Cary (1924), however, thinks that the textual evidence indicates that such an overland route did not come into use before the third century B.C.

Massalia participated in the metal trade in the western Mediterranean, dealing in tin as well as other metals (see pp. 61–63 above). Trade in metals leaves little or no archaeological evidence. But the absence at Mont Lassois of any finds pointing to the supposed British origin of the tin, along with Cary's argument for a late date for the beginning of the overland trade route, cast doubt on the idea of such a traffic (Hatt 1958, 152; Piggott 1977). Another consideration brings into question the proposed role of Mont Lassois in tin trade. The Hohenasperg in Württemberg and the rich graves around it (pp. 29–30, 34–36) date to the same decades as Mont Lassois and Vix. Grafenbühl and Vix contain extraordinary Mediterranean luxury objects of roughly similar character, suggesting that the interactions between Greeks at Massalia and central Europeans at Mont Lassois and at the Hohenasperg, respectively, were probably of similar character (Zürn 1970, 118–119). The apparent similarity of the two situations would suggest that the same model for interaction with Massalia should apply to both sites. Yet neither tin nor any other single resource can be identified as the basis of the Hohenasperg's relations with Greek southern France.

Several authors have suggested that the exportation of iron from Hallstatt west-central Europe to the Mediterranean may account for the wealth evident at the Late Hallstatt centers (Powell 1958, 94; Pittioni 1966). Again, no archaeological evidence supports this thesis. And as Villard (1960, 158 n. 5) points out, iron ore is fairly plentiful in Mediterranean lands and would probably not have been difficult for Massaliote Greeks or other Mediterranean peoples to obtain.

Throughout history many coastal areas of the Mediterranean have needed to import grain from abroad (Semple 1931, 344; Hasebroek 1933; Cary 1949, 246, 257; Braudel 1972, 219, 570–606). Wheat importation by Greek cities in the eastern Mediterranean from the Pontic areas and from Egypt during the sixth century B.C. is well documented in the ancient texts and underscores the general need for grain at the time (Minns 1913, 438–441; Roebuck 1950; 1959, 116–130; Will 1962, 57). Massalia lacked good arable land (see p. 61). The amount of commercial and building activity in evidence at sixth century Massalia (Villard 1960, 92) bespeaks a substantial population requiring sustenance. Proximity to the Rhône waterway meant relatively easy transport of bulk materials such as grain, and Benoit (1965, 92) has suggested that lands in the Rhône delta and in the lower Durance valley served as sources for Massalia's grain supply.

Sizable grain storage facilities at the site of Le Pègue on the eastern edge of the Rhône valley to the north of the Durance–Rhône confluence may relate to grain storage for shipment south (Lagrand and Thalmann 1973, 108). Le Pègue has yielded quantities of Massaliote amphorae as well as Attic and other Greek pottery of the same types as those common to Massalia and Hallstatt west-central Europe. Grain from rich agricultural lands further north could also have been transported easily down the Saône–Rhône river system. Evidence of regular shipments of grain from Egypt and south Russia to Greece and the Aegean shows that such distances over water were no problem. During the later Middle Ages grain from Burgundy was shipped to Marseille (Braudel 1972, 219), and central and northern Gaul provided an important source of grain for Roman Italy (Cary 1949, 246, 257). During the sixth century B.C. Massalia may have imported grain from inland France to feed its population; whether or not any such imported grain was trans-shipped to other Mediterranean ports is difficult to assess with the information available at present.

During the last century B.C. large quantities of salted pork and woolen garments were brought from the Celtic areas of eastern France to Rome and other parts of Italy (Strabo IV 3. 2; IV 4. 3). As Déchelette (1913*b*, 149–150) suggests, such goods may have been traded southward during earlier periods of the Iron Age as well. Pigs (as well as cattle) were abundant at most Late Hallstatt settlements, as the animal bones recovered indicate (Gerlach 1967, 3–5; Jankuhn 1969, 76; Bökönyi 1974, 211–212; Kimmig 1975*b*, 58), and formed an important part of the central-European diet. Meats may have been exported southward as part of the interactions with Massalia. Salt was being produced and traded on a large scale at this time (see p. 43 above), and some of this production may have been stimulated by the need to preserve meats for trade. Other domestic-animal products, such as leather and cheese, may have been important in this respect also (see Strabo IV 6. 9–10; V I. 8 on exports of the southeast Alpine region – an environment not unlike central Europe – at a later date).

Fine woolen garments were being manufactured in central Europe during the sixth century B.C. (Hundt 1970), and some may have been traded south to Massalia (on trade in textiles in and around the Mediterranean, see Semple 1931, 674–680; Jankuhn 1969, 100). Textiles produced in central Europe were being exported to centers in the Mediterranean world during the Roman Period (Strabo IV 4. 3).

Besides such products which would have been produced within the agricultural economy of Early Iron Age central Europe, a number of natural products from the forests may have played an important part. Among the forest products sought after by Greeks in barbarian lands were timber (for shipbuilding, furniture manufacture, and a variety of other purposes), pitch, resin, wax (all largely for shipbuilding purposes), and honey (Semple 1931, 261–296). Such materials were available in abundance in central Europe (Kossack 1959). Items such as timber could have been floated down the Saône–Rhône river system to Massalia. Products of smaller bulk could have been transported either by water or by land. The central European forests also harbored a variety of animals whose furs and skins may have been export products for the trade with Greek Massalia.

We do not know whether or not slavery existed in central Europe during the Early Iron Age (see Peschel 1971). It is possible that central European centers were supplying slaves to the Greek world at this time (Finley 1959).

Evidence of all these possible export products would generally not survive in the archaeological record. All may have been involved in the trade system, but at present we cannot prove which were and which were not. Our best model for trade here can be formulated from contemporary accounts of Greek–barbarian trade elsewhere and from accounts of trade during later periods in the Marseille–central Europe area (Jullian 1908; Braudel 1972). The most apropriate model for sixth-century Greek trade with west-central Europe is one which involves not one or two but many different materials in demand at Greek cities in the Mediterranean world. Three points can be cited in favor of this model.

None of the site complexes in west-central Europe yielding rich Greek imports shows any evidence of a specialized resource which might have formed the basis for interaction with Massalia. Tin ingots at Mont Lassois or large weaving complexes at the Heuneburg, for example, might provide such evidence.

Secondly, literary evidence from south Russia, an environment in many respects comparable to the area of our concern (Wasowicz 1966), indicates that an entire range of products was obtained by Greek colonists settled on the Black Sea coasts, including grain, timber, fish, salt, hides, slaves, gold, wax, honey, amber, and drugs (Polybius IV 38, 1–5; Minns 1913, 438–441). Though the literary documentation here post-dates the sixth century B.C., archaeological evidence for Greek activity during that century suggests that similar interactions were taking place at that earlier time.

Thirdly, Benoit demonstrates that Massalia's interactions with coastal and interior southern France during the sixth century B.C. were probably based on a wide variety of mineral and organic products. If the city's commerce with these areas was so broad, a similar pattern would be likely for its relations with west-central Europe.

Industry and commerce in the sixth and fifth centuries B.C.

Information about the organization of industry and commerce in the principal trade items present in west-central Europe provides additional data concerning the character of interactions between Late Hallstatt Europeans and western Greeks.

Attic pottery. The great quantities of Attic pottery recovered at archaeological sites throughout the Mediterranean world have led some investigators to hypothesize a large-scale industry producing it. It is the extraordinary preservation of this pottery that makes its presence in such abundance deceptive. In a study of the numbers of vase-painters working in Athens, Cook (1959) concludes that only some 100–125 were active at any one time. Taking account of others involved in the industry (obtaining clay, making and firing vessels, selling the finished products), Cook estimates that some 400–500 persons were probably working in the Attic pottery business at one time. Out of a total population of *c.* 150000–250000 in Athens around 500 B.C. (Cook 1962, 124), 500 persons involved in the fine pottery industry is relatively few. Representations of potters' workshops on the vases themselves also suggest that the pottery industry was a small-scale affair. There is no evidence to suggest that workshops employed more than 15–20 workers (see Richter 1923, 64–83, 87–105; Will 1958, 154; Noble 1965, xiii–xiv; Webster 1972, 8–9, 41).

Athens was an important center of commerce, and merchants from all parts of the Mediterranean world came to the city to exchange their wares

(Hasebroek 1933, 60; Finley 1973, 134). Trade in Athenian pottery was not restricted to Athenian merchants; Greeks from other cities carried cargoes of Attic pottery, and so very probably did non-Greek merchants (Cook 1959, 116; 1972, 272). Attic workshops did not usually produce vases for specific foreign customers (Cook 1959, 116–117). Traders probably purchased pottery directly from the workshops (Cook 1962, 62; 1972, 272; Webster 1972, 296); the merchants were primarily independent individuals working for their own livelihood, taking on goods where available and exchanging them for others when interested customers could be found (Hasebroek 1933, 4; Cook 1959, 117).

Despite the impressive quantities of Attic pottery found on many non-Greek sites, such as the 935 Attic black-figure vessels recovered at the city of Vulci in Etruria (Hus 1971, 87–88, n. 1), trade in this respect was probably of little economic significance to the cities concerned compared to movement of bulk products such as grain, timber, textiles, hides and furs, oil, metals, and wine (Will 1958, 157–159; Cook 1972, 276). Frequent mention is made in ancient literature of these bulk goods as trade items, but not of fine pottery (Will 1958, 157). Attic painted pottery was a luxury; particularly in non-Greek lands, it is found only associated with other luxury materials. Cook (1959, 121) compares the importance of Attic pottery in the context of other contemporary commerce to the porcelain trade of the twentieth century and its relation to modern trade as a whole.

The presence of Attic pottery at a site outside Greece indicates that the inhabitants of the site liked the pottery and were in contact with traders who had access to it. Its presence does not tell anything about the nationality of the traders, since it was popular and traded by all, nor about an individual community's relations with Athens (see Vallet 1950; Villard 1960; Reim 1968 on Attic pottery at central European sites).

Although the presence of Attic pottery in west-central Europe is important for the problem of interaction, the quantities are so small compared to those at sites such as Spina and Vulci in Italy that Attic pottery can hardly be considered a major factor in regular trade between west-central Europe and Massalia. Even the quantities recovered at Marseille are small compared to the Italian finds. Villard (1960, 33) records 272 Attic vessels at Marseille for the period 525–500 B.C.

Greek bronzes. Although archaic Greek bronzes, including those from west-central Europe, have been much studied, in comparison to Attic pottery relatively little is known about the place and date of manufacture of individual specimens. Hence less information is available on the organization of the bronze industry than for Attic pottery.

The ancient literature provides some information about the ownership and circulation of luxury bronze objects. The commissioning of individual vessels is sometimes mentioned. Concerning the bronze vessel which the

Lacedaemonians wished to present to Croesus, Herodotus (I 70) writes 'they made a krater of bronze'. When a Samian ship returned from Tartessos with a great cargo of silver, the sailors spent a tenth of their profits 'and made therewith a bronze vessel, like an Argolid cauldron, with griffins' heads projecting from the rim all round,' which they dedicated at the temple of Hera (Herodotus IV 152). Such instances illustrate why extraordinary bronze vessels were sometimes made: as gifts to powerful allies or as dedications.

Textual evidence suggests that exchange was not the predominant mechanism of circulation. Tripods and kraters, often exceptionally large or made of silver or gold, are frequently mentioned as dedications at Greek sanctuaries, offered by both Greeks and non-Greeks (e.g. Herodotus I 14–15, 92), and as gifts presented to powerful friends or allies:

> the Lacedaemonians had sent to Sardis to buy gold, with intent to use it for the statue of Apollo which now stands on Thornax in Laconia; and Croesus, when they would buy it, made a free gift of it to them.
>
> For this cause, and because he had chosen them as his friends before all other Greeks, the Lacedaemonians accepted the alliance. So they declared themselves ready to serve him when he should require, and moreover they made a krater of bronze, graven outside round the rim with figures, and large enough to hold twenty-seven hundred gallons, and brought it with the intent to make a gift of requital to Croesus (Herodotus I 69–70).

The Greek tripods and kraters in rich burial associations on the borders of the Greek world (see p. 53 above) probably changed hands through such gift-giving between powerful individuals in Greek and non-Greek societies (Fischer 1973).

Etruscan bronzes. For Etruria of the sixth and fifth centuries B.C. we have no direct textual evidence concerning the manufacturing or circulation of finished goods. Greek and Roman writers refer to the high quality of Etruscan bronze work and cite its popularity in Greece and Rome (references in Dennis 1883, I, 48–50). The huge number of bronze objects recovered in Etruscan cemeteries and elsewhere in the ancient world indicates a substantial output of the industries.

Etruria is rich in metal ores (Cary 1949, 123; Minto 1955, 292; Cambi 1957); archaeological evidence for the mining of copper and tin during this period has been studied in the area of the 'Metal Mountains' around Campiglia Marittima (Minto 1955, 298–305). Little is known about the circulation of unworked metal between Etruscan cities, though that of finished products is well documented (Camporeale 1969).

Greeks and barbarians: textual evidence

Little historical documentation is available relating to the contacts between Greek Massalia and the non-Greek peoples around the city, and none of the sources applies directly to west-central Europe. Several legends concerned with the foundation of the colony describe alliances and battles between Greeks and the natives, but it is unclear whether any of these tales has its basis in historical reality (literature in Wackernagel 1930, 2131; see also Momigliano 1975, Chapter 3). Evidence provided by documents dealing with other parts of the contemporary Greek world gives some idea of how western Greeks and central Europeans might have interacted with one another.

Archaeologists and historians working on the Mediterranean world of the sixth and fifth centuries B.C. have barely begun to tackle systematically the problems of culture contact (Humphreys 1967, 384–386). No comprehensive study of references in the ancient literature to interactions between Greeks and other peoples exists (but see Knorringa 1926). A few specific instances from the ancient sources will be cited here. Interactions between Greeks and non-Greeks were probably often of similar character in different parts of the ancient world: central Europe, Etruria, Iberia, and south Russia. The textual evidence and the similarity of archaeological contexts containing Greek imports in the different regions suggest further similarities in the nature of the interactions (Boardman 1973).

Herodotus provides important information about transmission of cultural elements between Greeks and other peoples. He notes that some peoples were eager to adopt Greek products and customs while others were not. The Egyptians had no interest in borrowing elements from the Greek world (Herodotus II 83). In the land of the Scythians, one nobleman was severely punished when it was discovered that he secretly wore Greek dress and practiced Greek customs (*ibid.* IV 75). The archaeological evidence, however, suggests that the Scythians had no reservations about importing Greek objects such as pottery and bronzes (Hoving 1975).

As one means through which barbarians became familiar with Greek objects and customs, Herodotus (IV 75) describes the visits to Greek cities by the Scythian Anacharsis. By observing Greek life first-hand, Anacharsis learned the use of objects of material culture and was introduced to certain Greek rituals, some of which he adopted upon his return home. In the West it is possible that central Europeans visited the city of Massalia and there learned of wine drinking, fine pottery, Greek sculpture, and other aspects of Mediterranean life.

Barbarian peoples also became familiar with Greek culture through the presence of Greeks living and working among them. Pliny records the emigration of Demaratus from Corinth to Etruria in the seventh century B.C.; he set himself up at Tarquinia and began manufacturing clay statuary. Archaeological evidence in Etruria attests to the presence of Greek potters working there (see Boardman 1973, 198–199). Perhaps Greeks lived and worked at sites such as the Heuneburg and Mont Lassois in west-central Europe (see Dämmer 1978, 55). The clay brick wall at the Heuneburg may have been built by a Greek, and the fast-turning potter's wheel may have been introduced into southwest Germany by a Greek potter.

Two important points emerge from the ancient literature about the circulation of luxury goods between Greek and non-Greek peoples. First, many special objects such as tripods, giant kraters, and vessels of gold and silver, are often mentioned as gifts presented to chiefs or kings for the purpose of making an alliance, securing a friendship, or establishing trade relations. Such gift-giving occurs frequently in the *Odyssey* (see Fischer 1973) and the same process is described in the fifth century B.C. by Herodotus (III 20). The same mechanism is also documented in a wide range of historical and ethnographic contexts (Sahlins 1965; Mauss 1967). Some of the exceptional objects in west-central Europe such as the Vix krater, the tripods of La Garenne and Grafenbühl, and the Grächwil hydria, probably arrived in central European hands in such a way.

Secondly, many ancient sources demonstrate the priority of 'political' over 'economic' considerations in commerce between Greeks and non-Greeks. In studying the circulation of materials between west-central Europe and Massalia it is unrealistic to imagine the exchange of 'equivalent' amounts of Greek and central European products. The relatively small quantities of Greek pottery and bronze objects recovered in Late Hallstatt contexts cannot be interpreted to indicate that Massalia never received much central European material. Herodotus (I 163) provides an instructive example of the importance of political over material (or economic) considerations. The king of Tartessos gave a great amount of wealth to the Phocaeans, apparently for no other reason than friendship:

> The Phocaeans so won this man's friendship that he first entreated them to leave Ionia and settle in his country where they would; and then when he could not persuade them to that, and learnt from them how the Median power was increasing, he gave them money to build a wall round their city therewith. Without stint he gave it; for the circuit of the wall is of many furlongs, and all this is made of great stones well fitted together.

At a later period a king in Macedonia provided timber to Greeks for building; as noted by Finley (1962, 26–27), the king fixed the price of the wood, or gave it to the Greeks, as he saw fit. For the Greeks the essential task was to please the king in order to obtain desired favors (this might be accomplished by giving him special gifts).

When actual exchange of goods is mentioned, the rate often appears odd to modern minds. For example, central Europeans exchanged slaves at the rate of a slave for a jar of wine, according to Diodorus (v 26).

These patterns of interaction between Greeks and non-Greeks are not only characteristic of that historical context but are common to interactions involving traditional societies. To illustrate the regularity of these patterns in contact situations, a few examples will be cited here from historical and ethnographic contexts demonstrating the same mechanisms which Herodotus and other ancient writers describe for Greek–barbarian interactions.

As Herodotus tells of Scythians' visiting Greek cities and learning Greek ways, Firth (1929, 451) describes visits of Maori chiefs from New Zealand to Australian cities where they encountered European culture. In both cases, the effect of such visits was the opening up of one culture to elements from the intrusive cultural system. This pattern of chiefs' visiting centers of other cultures often played a major role in the transmission of information between societies.

The residence of foreign craftsmen and merchants in commercial centers is also a common phenomenon. Roman writers record the activity of Roman merchants living and plying their trades in Germanic territory (Tacitus, *Annals* II 62; *History* IV 15; Caesar, *Gallic War* I 39, IV 2–3). This situation is difficult to recognize archaeologically in most instances; the activity of Greek potters in Etruria is exceptional (see p. 74). Historical sources frequently show that neighboring societies were interacting much more than the material evidence would suggest.

As far as the circulation of luxury goods between societies is concerned, much evidence on mechanisms is available in ethnographic and historical sources. Giving of gifts in the form of precious objects to chiefs and kings in order to gain favors of a political or economic kind is well documented (e.g. Lopez 1945; Sahlins 1965; Mauss 1967; Cipolla 1970).

The priority of 'political' over 'economic' matters in the circulation of goods between societies is well illustrated by several instances of trade between European merchant groups and parts of Africa and Asia during the sixteenth and seventeenth centuries. A good example is provided by Arnold (1957, 168) in discussing European trade with Dahomey during the latter century. The exchange transaction was completely regulated by the king and his agents, and the king set the prices, or rates of exchange, at the time of each transaction, as he saw fit. In such a context one can easily imagine the effect of a pleasing gift to the king on the rate of exchange in a particular transaction.

Depending upon the quality of relations between the chief or king and the other party, rates of exchange can vary considerably. Even in cases when the exchange is not directly under chiefly or royal control, rates often seem absurd to modern sensibilities. Diodorus' example has been cited. Lurie (1959) shows how small amounts of copper could buy vast quantities of local produce from North American Indians. In New

Zealand during the contact period, 150 baskets of yams and eight pigs were exchanged for one musket, and in another instance five slaves for one musket (Firth 1929, 453). A gun could be exchanged for five oxen, and an axe for one ox, among the Herero in Africa (Gibson 1962, 623–624). Similarly, patterns of exchange between Greeks based at Massalia and Late Hallstatt central Europeans probably did not operate according to the economic principles with which modern Westerners are directly familiar.

3.5 *Models for the contact and interactions*

The different kinds of data discussed in this chapter provide information about the nature of interactions between Hallstatt Europe and Greek southern France. Archaeological evidence in west-central Europe shows several significant features. First, all of the materials imported from the Mediterranean world are luxury goods, as far as surviving substances are concerned. Many of the objects such as the tripods and the Vix krater are of special value and significance in their lands of origin, as suggested by the workmanship and by the contexts in which they are found in Greece and elsewhere.

Secondly, the archaeological evidence suggests that only the elite in west-central European society benefited directly from the results of contact with the Greek world. Almost all of the imports are found in burials which are exceptionally rich in local products. Several imported objects often occur together in graves, as at Grafenbühl and Vix.

Besides being restricted to a very small segment of the Late Hallstatt population, the imports are concentrated at a few major settlement complexes in west-central Europe. The great majority of Greek and Etruscan luxury objects found in Hallstatt central Europe occur at the Heuneburg, the Hohenasperg, and Mont Lassois.

Finally, the archaeological evidence indicates that the elite in Late Hallstatt Europe admired many aspects of Mediterranean culture and were eager to adopt those elements into their own cultural system. The presence of Greek and Etruscan objects in the wealthiest graves suggests that the central European elite held Mediterranean luxury goods in high regard. Imitation of bronze vessel forms and of pottery shapes and decoration is further evidence of the interest of Early Iron Age central Europeans in Mediterranean material culture, as are the clay brick wall at the Heuneburg and the stele at Hirschlanden.

As argued above, commerce between traditional societies usually operates according to principles different from those governing modern market trade (Belshaw 1965). In both the ancient literature and historical and ethnographic sources are numerous examples of exchanges such as gift-giving between members of different societies. This mechanism serves a variety of purposes for the giver and results in different kinds of institutionalized interactions for the societies involved.

Drawing on these different kinds of evidence, an attempt is made here to formulate a model for the contact between the traders based at Massalia and Hallstatt central Europeans and for the kinds of interactions between the groups which developed from the initial contacts. To judge from the chronology of the imports, it would seem that, after about 550 B.C., interactions were occurring on a regular basis at the Heuneburg, the Hohenasperg, Mont Lassois, and perhaps at other sites not yet fully investigated.

At least three different kinds of archaeological evidence indicate that the interactions were taking place at the person-to-person level, as opposed to transmission of trade goods through middlemen. The Heuneburg clay brick wall, the Hirschlanden statue, and the fast-turning potter's wheel, all imply the transmission of specialized information from one individual to another, wherever this transmission may have taken place and whoever the individuals involved may have been.

Reviewing relevant literary evidence from the ancient historians, Fischer (1973, 455–456) suggests that certain of the imports were 'political gifts' from Greeks to potentates in central Europe. Several objects stand out from the rest as unique pieces, manufactured for a special purpose. These include the Vix krater, the Vix diadem, the Grafenbühl sphinxes, and the Grächwil hydria; the Grafenbühl tripod and La Garenne tripod and cauldron are also of special character because they belong to a class of objects employed in Greek society as gifts and dedications (*ibid.*, 455 n. 69). Such objects are likely to have been made on special order and would not have circulated in regular commercial channels (Piggott 1965, 195; Fischer 1973, 455), as did wine-bearing amphorae and Attic pottery. The distinction between unique, highly ornate objects on the one hand, and more common types on the other (amphorae, Attic pottery, and the Etruscan jugs and basins) is important, because different kinds of imports probably passed from Mediterranean merchants to central Europeans through different mechanisms (see p. 8 above). It has been suggested that the Vix krater, the Grächwil hydria, and the Grafenbühl sphinxes were produced specifically for non-Greek, barbarian taste (Kimmig 1958, 85; 1964, 472 n. 15; Jucker 1966, 121–123; Herrmann 1970, 26–27). The Vix krater, the largest archaic Greek bronze vessel known, finds parallels in non-Greek contexts: the enormous krater made for the Lydian king Croesus (Herodotus I 70) and the large volute krater painted on the wall of the Tomb of the Lionesses at Tarquinia (Ducati 1937, pl. 2).

Two examples of political gift-giving from Herodotus are instructive. One is the case of the huge krater made for Croesus by the Lacedaemonians (p. 72 above). In another instance:

> Cambyses. . .sent [an embassy] to Ethiopia. . . bearing gifts, to wit, a purple cloak and a twisted gold necklace and armlets and an alabaster box of incense and an earthenware jar of

> palm wine... [The embassy came to the king of the Ethiopians and delivered this message:] 'Cambyses king of Persia, desiring to be your friend and guest, sends us with command to address ourselves to you; and he offers you such gifts as he himself chiefly delights to use' (Herodotus III 20–21).

Upon receiving a gift, a person incurs with it an obligation to the donor (Sahlins 1965, 208; Fischer 1973, 447). In the two instances quoted by Herodotus, one party gives a gift – something of exquisite workmanship or special value – to a powerful individual from whom the party wishes some concession or privilege.

If the Vix krater and perhaps the diadem, the tripod and carvings from Grafenbühl, the Grächwil hydria, and the La Garenne tripod and cauldron were gifts given by Greeks to central European chiefs, what was the purpose of the gesture? The purpose may have been to establish relationships between Greek merchants and central European chiefs by means of which Greeks could obtain the products they sought from west-central Europe. Finley (1962) has called attention to the essential role of relations between Greek traders and non-Greek potentates in instances in which Greeks sought natural products in barbarian lands. The same principle is illustrated in later contexts in studies by Arnold (1957), Hanks (1957), Cipolla (1970), Odner (1972, 645), and Duby (1974, 56).

Once a central European chief received Mediterranean luxury objects as gifts and became favorably disposed toward his donors, how might the interaction have proceeded? A pleased chief might turn over to Greek merchants quantities of whatever products they sought as a return gesture; Herodotus' example of the Tartessian king's giving Phocaeans enough money to build a city wall sugests that a barbarian potentate's generosity should not be underestimated. A likely possibility is that once friendly relations were established, a formal system of exchange was instituted between the chief and Greek merchants, along the lines of the administered trade defined by Polanyi (1957, 262) and documented for historical Africa by Arnold (1957). In such a system the exchange of goods takes place at the approval of the chief at times, places, and rates set by him. Some such arrangement existed between Greek traders at Naucratis and the Egyptian king at about this same time (Herodotus II 178). Perhaps through a system of administered trade central European products such as forest resources, metals, meats, textiles, and slaves were exchanged for luxury goods from the Mediterranean world such as Attic pottery, wine, Etruscan bronze vessels, and coral.

The restriction of the possession of Mediterranean luxury imports to the elite in Hallstatt Europe, as the grave evidence shows, would support the notion of administered trade as portrayed by Arnold. The chief and his immediate supporters were the beneficiaries of the luxury goods brought in, and diffusion to society at large was strictly limited to such divisible substances as coral.

The success of Greek efforts to obtain products in west-central Europe depended primarily upon the power of Late Hallstatt chiefs over the resources and upon Greek ability to win the favor of those chiefs. Gifts such as those cited above would have gained the favor of a barbarian chief, particularly if there was a prospect of more of the same. Once the central-European chiefs were positively disposed toward Greek merchants seeking their goods, it was simply a matter of working out the details of exchange transactions.

4
Contact and culture change:
end of the Early Iron Age

The ways in which cultural systems, or societies, are affected by contact with other cultural systems depend upon a variety of factors. These can be divided into two groups: (1) the content of the cultural systems in contact (including the subsystems and their component elements comprising the cultural systems and the ways in which they are interrelated); (2) the nature and circumstances of contact and interaction (including the location at which interaction takes place, the individuals involved from each society, and the interests of each party in the interactions).

The nature and circumstances of interaction strongly affect the changes occurring in both societies (Barnett *et al.* 1954). Some of the variables of concern here are the types of individuals involved (merchants, chiefs, craftsmen), numbers of persons taking part in interaction situations, location of interaction, and length of time during which interaction takes place. The number of different combinations is infinite, and each factor plays an important role in determining the kind of impact that interaction will have on a society. Recent studies show that even today administrators and social scientists are often unable to predict the effects which contact may bring about in a society, so complex are the interrelations between the elements of a cultural system (see examples in Spicer (1952) and Walker (1972)). Models which archaeologists might develop for study of prehistoric contexts are simplistic in the extreme, but more complex models are beyond the informative capabilities of present archaeological evidence.

Until now this study has dealt with primarily static issues. In this chapter, contact between west-central Europeans and Mediterranean peoples will be considered in terms of its relation to cultural changes in west-central Europe. Three main questions will serve to focus this discussion. What changes were occurring during the Late Hallstatt Period in west-central Europe? What role was played by the interaction between central Europeans and Mediterranean peoples? Why did the interactions affect central European cultural systems the way they did?

4.1 *Changes in the Early Iron Age cultural system*

In accordance with the aims of this chapter, the Early Iron Age cultural system must be characterized not in static descriptive terms but in the context of the dynamic interrelations of its subsystems. Culture viewed as a system consists of an infinite number of subsystems (p. 4 above) which are in a state of continuous change (Linton 1936, 296; Clarke 1968, 103–104). They are models defined by the investigator for studying cultural change (Renfrew 1972, 22–23). Four such subsystems are of principal concern here: circulation (transmission of materials and services between persons and groups); manufacturing (manufacturing activities at all levels of organization); settlement (location, size, and organization of settlements); and social (social, including political, organization). Subsystems are interrelated in such a way that any change in an element in one subsystem will result in corresponding changes in all others such that the dynamic equilibrium of the total system is maintained (Clarke 1968, 50–51). If equilibrium is not maintained the cultural system disintegrates.

In order to make clear the nature of the changes in the four subsystems during the Early Iron Age, a brief description will be presented of the character of each subsystem during the Early and Late Hallstatt Periods. These descriptions are necessarily schematic and general, and synthesize a large amount of archaeological data.

Early Hallstatt (roughly 800–600 B.C.)

The best source of information about the subsystems is Kossack's study (1959; 1972) of the Hallstatt Period in southern Bavaria. His results are comparable to those of regional analyses of southwest Germany (on Württemberg see Rieth 1938; Kimmig and Hell 1958; Neuffer 1974) and will form the basis of this discussion.

Circulation subsystem. Most of the objects recovered in Early Hallstatt contexts are made of locally available materials, with the important exception of the bronze objects. Substances which occur frequently in Late Hallstatt southwest Germany such as amber, coral, glass, and gold (see pp. 41–46 above) are rare in Early Hallstatt contexts. Early Hallstatt communities in Württemberg and in neighboring areas engaged in local exploitation and working of materials; little interaction with regions beyond the communities' boundaries is evident (Kossack 1959, 69–77).

Manufacturing subsystem. The vast majority of objects in Early Hallstatt contexts were manufactured locally, viz. pottery, bronze jewelry, bronze and iron swords. Except on some pottery, ornamentation and stylistic variation is minimal and there is little evidence for developed crafts specialization compared to the following period. Distributions of specific types of objects also suggest that most were produced locally (Kossack 1959, 114–115).

Settlement subsystem. Although, from central Europe, little evidence is available relating to the character of Early Hallstatt settlements, analysis of well-researched cemeteries provides information about settlement patterns. Kossack (1959, 86) calculates that throughout southern Bavaria during this period settlements were small, generally occupied by some 30 or fewer inhabitants. He assumes that all dead were buried in the same manner, that each cemetery was used by one settlement, and that each settlement used just one cemetery. In our present state of knowledge these assumptions cannot be proved correct, but they cannot be disproved either. The character of the few Early Hallstatt settlements known from southwest Germany indicates that Kossack's suggestion about the size of the sites is applicable there (Garscha and Rest 1938; Rieth 1938, 143–144; Schröder 1963, 24). Early Hallstatt settlements might be best characterized as farmsteads or hamlets, perhaps occupied by extended family units (Kossack 1959, 86; 1972, 92).

Social subsystem. The best evidence for social organization comes from the graves. Small cemeteries are characteristic of the Early Hallstatt Period: in many, one or two graves contain a bronze or iron sword and a greater number of, sometimes more highly ornate, ceramic vessels than the majority of burials (von Föhr 1892, 37–40; Kossack 1972, 90; Neuffer 1974, 2–5 with fig. 1). These Early Hallstatt sword graves are not concentrated in particular regions or around specific settlements, but occur throughout central Europe in cemeteries of plain graves (Rieth 1942, map 1; Kossack 1972, 90, 92). The character of the sword graves, all of which are quite similar in the wealth of their burial assemblages (Kossack 1972, 90), does not suggest great social distance between the individuals buried in them and those buried in the other graves. The men buried with swords can best be regarded as headmen of hamlet communities, all of which were roughly equal in size, economic importance, and political power (Kossack 1972, 92).

Late Hallstatt (roughly 600–450 B.C.)

In all four subsystems different patterns are apparent in southwest Germany during the Late Hallstatt Period. The discussion here will focus on the Heuneburg; patterns at the Hohenasperg and Mont Lassois are similar.

Circulation subsystem. During the Late Hallstatt Period foreign substances are well represented in southwest Germany, particularly at the centers but also in cemeteries removed from them (pp. 43–46 above). Whereas west-central European communities of Early Hallstatt times had few apparent commercial interactions with outside areas (except for the importation of copper and tin), the communities of Late Hallstatt times had access to a range of Mediterranean luxury goods as well as other materials circulating in central Europe, including amber, coral, glass, and gold.

Manufacturing subsystem. Finds at the Heuneburg provide evidence for a variety of crafts industries. Molds have been recovered which were used in the production of bronze earrings (Bittel and Rieth 1951, pl. 11 no. 5) and bronze bracelets (Schiek 1959, 120–121). An oven for melting bronze for casting has been uncovered among the settlement structures, and remains of the casting process attest to bronze-working on the site (Gersbach 1971, 78). Fragments of sheet bronze found may relate to an industry in bronze vessels and ornaments (Kimmig 1975*b*, 58). It is likely that fibulae, bronze vessels, and bronze and iron daggers were manufactured at the centers and exported from them into the countryside. The quantities of these products in the settlement deposits and cemeteries at the Heuneburg, together with the evidence of bronze-working at the site and the lack of evidence for that industry at the smaller settlements which have been partly excavated, suggest that production of such objects was concentrated at these centers (Mansfeld 1973; Kimmig 1975*a*, 206–207). The same is probably true of the gold neck rings and other ornaments of this metal. Coral was brought to the Heuneburg and there cut into various ornaments (p. 26). As further excavation is carried out both at the centers and at other settlements in Late Hallstatt central Europe the patterns of manufacturing and circulation of finished goods will become clearer.

During the Late Hallstatt Period a variety of new fine-crafts industries appear, including those in gold jewelry (Paret 1941–1942), in bronze vessels (Dehn 1965; 1971; Hawkes and Smith 1957, 191–198), in ornamental daggers, in lignite and jet carving, and in coral cutting. The development of these industries during the Late Hallstatt Period is closely connected with the rise of an elite group expressing its social status in the rich burials near the centers. At this same time the character of much of the pottery indicates the emergence of an industry specializing in this material (Torbrügge 1968, 100).

Settlement subsystem. During the Late Hallstatt Period a number of large settlement complexes like the Heuneburg appeared for the first time. Associated with the Heuneburg are 11 exceptionally large tumuli containing up to 25 graves each and some 50 smaller mounds also containing multiple burials (fig. 3.2). Many more tumuli probably existed there at one time. The settlement deposits at the Heuneburg also indicate a community of very different character from those represented by the known Early Hallstatt sites. In the fully excavated southeast corner of the site have been found several phases of substantial rectangular buildings placed close together filling the entire area (Gersbach 1971, foldouts 1–6; 1975; 1976, foldouts 1–2). Sites such as the Heuneburg, the Hohenasperg, and Mont Lassois must be considered more of the character of towns than of villages; several investigators have argued that some such sites represent an early form of urban centers in Europe (discussion in Kimmig 1969; Hensel 1970; Neustupný 1970).

Additional evidence for changes in the organization of settlement units and in cultural life as a whole is provided by the patterns of weapons in the graves. There is, in the Late Hallstatt Period, a notable increase in the number of weapons in graves (particularly spearheads) which may relate to the arming of larger numbers of fighting men and their organization into infantry units for group warfare (Kossack 1959, 93–99; Frey 1976, 176; P. S. Wells 1978, 225–226). Such organization of combat troops into larger units can be understood in terms of growing centralization of population, economic activity, and political power at the Late Hallstatt centers.

Social subsystem. The Late Hallstatt rich graves are concentrated at the centers, in contrast to the Early Hallstatt sword graves which are scattered around the countryside in small hamlet cemeteries. In two important respects the grave goods of the Late Hallstatt rich graves differ from those of the Early Hallstatt sword graves.

During the later period a much greater quantity of luxury goods was available. These included Greek and Etruscan objects and the fine crafts products of local industries – gold jewelry, bronze vessels, ornamental daggers, fibulae, and wagons. During the early period these items were rare in central Europe.

Secondly, Late Hallstatt rich graves are more richly outfitted in comparison to plain graves of that period than Early Hallstatt sword graves are in comparison to plain graves of the early period. Comparison of, on the one hand, the grave goods of the Sternberg sword grave (von Föhr 1892, 37–40; Neuffer 1974, 2–5 with fig. 1) with those of the burials at Zainingen, and, on the other, of the burial assemblage in the Grafenbühl central grave with the goods in the secondary graves in that tumulus, suggests that differentiation in grave inventories increased substantially during the Early Iron Age. This increase in the differentiation of grave wealth must be viewed in conjunction with changes in settlement size and character. At the centers of Late Hallstatt, instead of small hamlet and village settlements, there are large settlement complexes with dense occupations, concentration of material wealth, specialized industries, and active contacts with Mediterranean civilizations. The rich graves around the Heuneburg and the Hohenasperg are very different

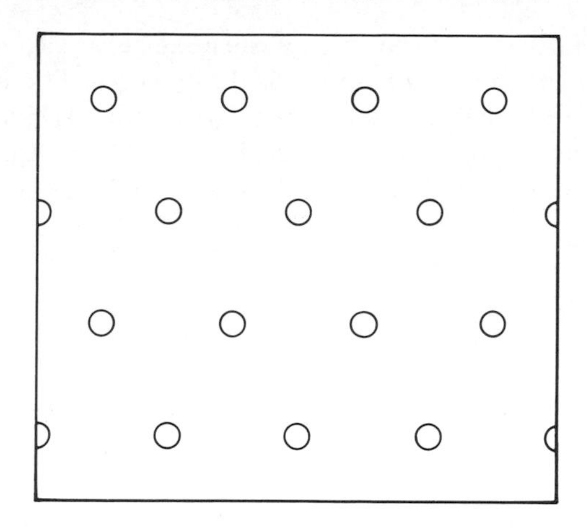

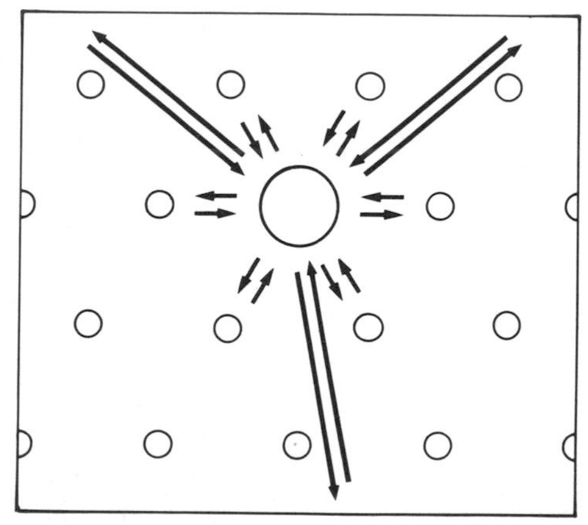

Fig. 4.1. Model representing the major differences in the cultural landscape of Württemberg in Early and Late Hallstatt times. *Top*: In the early phase, the evidence indicates small hamlet-like settlements of roughly equal size and economic importance scattered across the countryside. *Bottom*: The emergence of a few major centers in the Late phase changed the pattern. At these sites were concentrations of population, material wealth, industrial and commercial activity, and probably political power. The centers served as foci for long-distance commerce and developed intensive exchange systems with the smaller settlements in their regions, trading manufactured and imported goods for foodstuffs and raw materials.

in character from Late Hallstatt burials elsewhere in Württemberg, and they suggest a concentration of political power and social status at these centers. As size and complexity of settlements increase, there is more room and more need for status differentiation and for the emergence of higher statuses. As the centers developed during Hallstatt D, higher status positions evolved than could exist in the small hamlet and village organized Early Hallstatt cultural system (Shennan 1975, 283; Gall and Saxe 1977). During the course of Hallstatt D the process of differentiation was operating continuously: Hallstatt D1 rich graves such as Hohmichele Grave 6 and Vilsingen are less wealthy and distinct from other graves than are the Hallstatt D2 and D3 burials such as Grafenbühl and Vix.

Culture change

A wide range of types of transformations can occur in cultural systems (Kroeber 1948, 386–444). Changes are for the most part in the nature of replacements of elements by new ones (Linton 1936, 279–280). Subsystems are restructured by such replacements, and new patterns emerge in the cultural system (Barnett 1953, 9). New objects, processes, and ideas cannot simply be added to a cultural system, but must be integrated into the whole.

Culture is in a constant state of change (Linton 1936, 296); subsystems are interrelated in a state of dynamic equilibrium such that every subsystem is constantly changing, and the nature of the interactions between subsystems is always changing; subsystems are continuously readjusting to the changed states of the other subsystems in such a way that the cultural system as a whole survives (Clarke 1968, 50–51, 103–104). If they cannot adjust to ongoing changes, the system breaks down.

> As cultures and their parts actually live, thrive, decay, and alter, and as they influence one another, these several processes (persistence, invention, loss, change), which in the abstract seem so neat and distinctive, are found to manifest themselves in association and interwoven. All of them are often at work at once, so that the same phenomenon may be seen as an example of two or three of them. This constant interrelation of processes is characteristic of culture (Kroeber 1948, 344).

Is it possible to explain why certain kinds of culture changes occur? The answer is not clear (see opinions expressed in essays in Renfrew 1973 and Hill 1977). Many social scientists now take the view that any specific event or major change in culture has not one or two but a whole series of causative factors (e.g. Bloch 1953, 191; Carr 1961, 89; Renfrew 1972, 476). Culture is made up of a theoretically infinite number of interacting subsystems, and every subsystem is actively involved in any culture change. In most cases no one subsystem can be singled out as causing the change (see Renfrew 1972, 15–26, 476–485).

In the present study our interest is in the interactions between central Europeans and Mediterranean peoples, and it is in terms of these interactions that an explanation of the observed changes will be offered. We can view the establishment of the trade port at Massalia around 600 B.C.

and Greek demand for a variety of central European products as the principal factor which 'kicked off' the sequence of changes in central European cultural systems. Conditions (political, economic, commercial, technological, demographic) in central Europe had to be such that members of the societies there were able and willing to respond to the Greek initiatives. But I wish to argue that it was the Greek interest in central European products that first started the sequence of profound changes. The observed changes (rise of centers, emergence of a materially rich elite, growth of local trade networks) could not have taken place had not the preconditions already been set, but without the triggering effect of Greek interest in central European products the changes would not have occurred as they did. The systemic aspect of the change processes was essential; positive feedback (the multiplier effect: see Renfrew 1972) was instrumental in carrying forward the changes.

Changes in Late Hallstatt central Europe

The cultural systems of Early Hallstatt times were organized on a local level with primarily non-specialized manufacturing, little interregional circulation of materials (except copper and tin), and a low degree of social stratification. No hierarchy of settlements is discernible. During Late Hallstatt times the cultural systems were organized on different principles. Much of society's activities were organized around a small number of centers at which industry and commerce were carried on to a degree unmatched by other sites of the period. Manufacturing was specialized and finished products distributed to small settlements around the centers. Commerce extended to distant parts of Europe. Social stratification was highly developed, with a small number of high-status individuals associated with each center.

The major difference in the organization of cultural life during the Early and Late Hallstatt Periods is in the degree of centralization of social, industrial, commercial, and demographic aspects. Late Hallstatt centers served as collecting, manufacturing, and redistributing sites in their territories. No evidence has yet been identified for the collection of foodstuffs and organic raw materials from the countryside, but the archaeological evidence for distribution of bronze objects, gold, glass, coral, and amber from the centers to the surrounding areas suggests that some such products were circulating in the opposite direction.

Social anthropologists have emphasized the importance of systems of redistribution for the organization of cultural systems as a whole (Polanyi 1959; Fried 1960; 1967; Service 1962; Sahlins 1963; Earle 1977). Service and Sahlins distinguish between 'tribes' and 'chiefdoms' largely on the basis of the extent to which redistribution is the main principle of economic organization (implying the existence of centers). According to their argument, in tribes redistribution is minimal, major centers do not exist, and the cultural system is characterized by numerous small settlement units of roughly equal political status and economic importance. Tribes have chiefs, but these personages are generally only of local importance within the villages. In chiefdoms, major centers exist, around which are smaller settlements. Centers serve as loci of redistribution of goods and services and as seats of political power and social status. Persons of highest rank (Sahlins 1963, 169, calls them 'paramount chiefs') preside over the activities at the centers and over lesser officials in the territories influenced by the centers.

Some of the features defined by social anthropologists as characteristic of centrally organized societies are clearly recognizable in the archaeological record of Late Hallstatt Württemberg: (*a*) Development of refined and specialized crafts industries (see Service 1962, 148; Sahlins 1963, 171; Trigger 1974, 100). (*b*) Emergence of an elite at the centers, contrasting with the relatively undifferentiated village social organization (Service 1962, 149–150). (*c*) Organization of major public labor projects (Service 1962, 170; Sahlins 1963, 171; Trigger 1974, 100). The wall systems at the Heuneburg, including the clay brick wall, certainly required substantial investment of labor energy, as did the exceptionally large tumuli around the Heuneburg and the Hohenasperg. (*d*) Increase in the size of settlements (Service 1962, 148). (*e*) Existence of a network of local chiefs under the paramount chief to coordinate the activities of society at the local level (Sahlins 1963, 160). The graves which contain some elite objects such as gold neck rings, daggers, or bronze vessels, but are not of the same degree of wealth as the richest burials around the centers and are located in the countryside away from the centers, such as Vilsingen, Kappel, Dusslingen, and Baisingen (see Zürn 1970, 122 on these last two), may well be those of lesser chiefs representing the paramount chief's authority in the countryside (Zürn 1970, 122–128; Frankenstein and Rowlands 1978).

4.2 *Analysis of the Greek/central-European interactions*

As we have seen, a variety of Mediterranean cultural elements (imported objects, imitated forms, and adopted technical information) appear in the context of the Late Hallstatt cultural system. In order to consider the effects of the introduction of these elements into west-central Europe I have adopted a framework proposed by Rogers and Shoemaker (1971, 18–19) involving five variables in contact situations: the source of the introduced elements, the channels through which they are introduced, the messages transmitted, the receivers of the messages, and the effects on the cultural system of the introduction of the new elements.

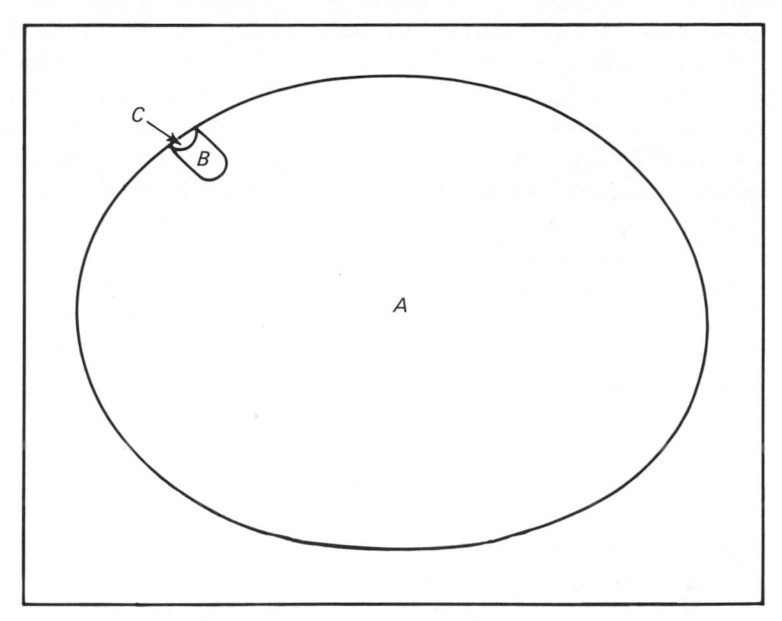

Fig. 4.2. Model illustrating the point that whole cultures do not come into contact, but only parts of them do. *A* represents a culture, in the anthropological sense (in this case Greek culture in the sixth century B.C.). *B* represents one site of that culture (the city of Massalia). *C* represents that part of the culture at that site with which a specific outside group comes into contact.

Source

Most of the Mediterranean imports in Late Hallstatt west-central Europe arrived via Massalia and the Rhône valley (see pp. 59–60 above), though their places of origin include Athens, the Near East, Greek southern Italy, Etruria, and southern France. Cultural systems are not brought into contact, but only parts of them (fig. 4.2); the parts which are, depend upon the nature and purpose of the contact (Linton 1940, 496–497; Barnett *et al.* 1954; Curtin 1975, 5). If contact was limited to interactions between Greek explorers and merchants in west-central Europe, then the only aspects of Greek culture with which central Europeans would have come into contact would have been the objects brought to them from the south, and the behavior and material culture of the explorers and merchants. Furthermore, Greek traders would have been unlikely to have dispensed all of their 'cultural information' to central Europeans; only those parts of their cultural system would have come into play which bore some direct relation to the purpose of the interaction – to the obtaining of central European products for Greek consumption and trade.

If some central Europeans visited Greek southern France they would have been exposed, superficially at least, to a wider range of elements of the western Greek cultural system, specifically those elements present at Massalia. Unless some central Europeans actually settled in Massalia for a time (which they may have done), it is unlikely that Massaliote culture would have had a very profound effect on them. Similar instances in other contexts (see pp. 73, 75 above) suggest that such visits in centers of foreign cultural systems do not in themselves usually effect significant cultural changes; in the two textually documented examples cited, the main effect of the visits was to whet the visitors' appetites for luxury goods from the host culture.

Greek artisans may have been working in Late Hallstatt central Europe (p. 74 above). They would have brought with them only a part of Greek culture and it is unlikely that they as individuals would have had any profound influence upon central Europeans beyond the introduction of certain technical innovations.

Interactions between Late Hallstatt Europe and Greek southern France are documented archaeologically over about a century, from early finds at Hohmichele Grave 6 and Vilsingen to late ones at Grafenbühl and the Heuneburg settlement. Since central European culture was changing during this century (as was western Greek culture), and the process of interaction was itself generating change, the source of cultural elements altered in character during this period. Initial contact may have been in the form of Greek explorers and traders visiting west-central Europe, or central Europeans visiting Massalia. Later, more regular patterns of interaction were probably established, and the growing familiarity of each party with the other surely affected the impact of interaction on changes in both cultural systems. At the end of the century of interaction the Vix and Grafenbühl graves, both outfitted with a series of extraordinary luxury goods from the Mediterranean world, suggest the interest of powerful and wealthy parties in the Greek sphere in the maintenance of friendly relations with central European chiefs.

Channels

Three main mechanisms have been suggested here for the bringing of cultural elements from the Mediterranean world to west-central Europe. Explorers and traders from Massalia may have traveled to central Europe bringing gifts for Hallstatt chiefs and arranging exchanges to obtain desired products. As interactions became more regular, this mechanism may have become an established institution like the administered trade described by Arnold (1957; also Hanks 1957; Odner 1972, 645). The result was the introduction of a variety of imported objects from the Mediterranean world.

Central Europeans may have visited Greek Massalia and there learned something of western Greek life and become desirous of some attractive elements of that culture, such as fine pottery, bronze vessels, and wine. They may have arranged to have supplies of them brought regularly to west-central Europe, perhaps through a mechanism such as administered trade.

Greek or other Mediterranean artisans may have worked in west-central Europe and introduced certain technical features to Europe north of the Alps.

Messages

Messages are the elements or pieces of cultural information transmitted between one cultural system and another. Three kinds of messages have been identified here: imported objects, adapted forms and motifs, and technical information.

Imports. Among the imports, a distinction must be made between those objects which are common in the Mediterranean world and those which are rare. Well represented in the Greek and Etruscan spheres are bronze boss-rimmed bowls, trefoil-mouth jugs, *Schnabelkannen*, Attic painted pottery, and ceramic amphorae. Rare in the Mediterranean area are objects represented by the Vix krater, the Vix gold diadem, the Vix *phiale mesomphalos*, the La Garenne tripod and cauldron, the Grafenbühl tripod, the Grafenbühl sphinxes, the Grächwil hydria, and the Eberdingen-Hochdorf cauldron. (It is difficult to know how common silk, represented in Hohmichele Grave 6, was in the Mediterranean world, since its recovery may be only a fortunate case of preservation: see Wild 1970, 12–13.)

Other materials which do not survive in the archaeological record were surely brought to central Europe as well, and may have played important parts in the commercial interactions. Wine was certainly traded; other luxury consumables such as olive oil, spices, fruits, and drugs may have been traded up the Rhône valley too, as they were during medieval times (Braudel 1972, 220).

Forms and motifs. Central European craftsmen imitated and adapted the shapes and decorative patterns of many of the imported objects. Among the most apparent adaptations are two distinct forms of bronze vessels (pp. 57–58 above) and shapes and decorative patterns on Late Hallstatt pottery (p. 58 above).

Technical information. The know-how to produce wheel-made pottery and to use the lathe, to construct the brick wall at the Heuneburg, and to sculpt the Hirschlanden stele was transmitted from the Mediterranean world to west-central Europe.

In relation to the imported objects and the new technical information brought to central Europe, the question must be asked why these particular elements were transmitted from the Mediterranean world and not others. Why are a few kinds of Etruscan bronze vessels represented, but not the many other contemporary forms (see Neugebauer 1943)? When the potter's wheel and techniques of stone sculpture are evident, why are not other techniques such as that of casting bronze figurines? Why is a brick wall present, but no trace of stone architecture?

Also puzzling is the absence of Massaliote silver coins in central Europe, although these were minted in large quantities from about 530 B.C. and have been found all over the southern French littoral and in the lower Rhône valley (Rolland 1949). Since the last quarter of the sixth century B.C. appears to have been the time of greatest interaction between Massalia and west-central Europe, it is especially significant that not a single coin from the Greek city has been found there.

Only a very small portion of Greek and Etruscan material culture is represented in central Europe. Those elements that are present did not arrive by accident, but through highly selective processes, the nature of which is unclear. Greek traders and explorers traveling to central Europe may have played a part in selecting the objects to bring north with them; and central Europeans visiting Greek southern France may have selected particular elements which struck their fancy.

The very small range of Greek and Etruscan objects and technical information from that part of the world represented in Late Hallstatt Europe suggests that the interactions were not in the form of frequent meetings by large numbers of individuals from either or both cultural systems. It suggests rather that interactions were limited to small groups of persons, and that meetings took place for specific and well defined purposes. If large segments of the societies had been in frequent contact, this fact should be reflected archaeologically by the presence of large numbers of jewelry items, coins, and other small finds which might have changed hands. The limited range of Greek and Etruscan goods in central Europe is consistent with a model of well organized and closely controlled interactions in which the parties involved knew ahead of time what to expect.

Receivers

The archaeological evidence indicates that only a small number of persons in central Europe received what the Mediterranean world had to offer. Luxury imports are restricted to a small number of graves, and imports, imitations of imports, and other evidence of interaction are all concentrated at the few large settlement complexes.

It has been suggested above that the chief at each center oversaw interactions with Greeks and maintained tight control over contact situations. The model proposed is one of administered trade, whereby the ruler strictly regulates the time, place, and circumstances of interaction. Incoming goods, in this case imports from the Mediterranean world, were

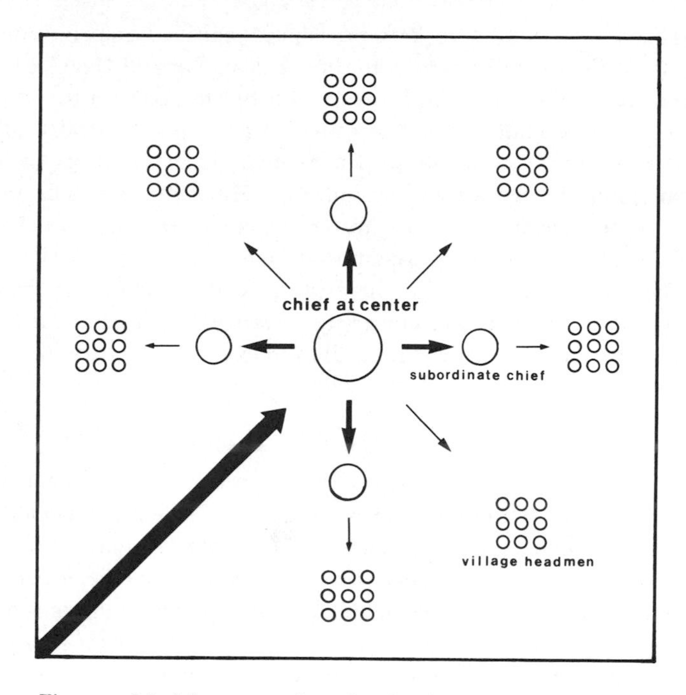

Fig. 4.3. Model representing the circulation of Mediterranean imports in west-central Europe. All materials were brought from the Mediterranean world to one of the centers. The chief directed the trade arrangements. He and others at the center retained some of the imports (particularly exceptional pieces such as those in the Grafenbühl and Vix graves). The chief passed some objects, such as the various bronze jugs, on to his subordinate chiefs at smaller communities. Some of the divisible imports – coral and amber – were passed to local headmen in the countryside, probably partly directly from the center and partly through the intermediary of the subordinate chiefs. The dissemination of the various Mediterranean products was thus controlled by the chief at each major center, and circulation of the materials followed the lines of the sociopolitical hierarchy of the system.

brought directly to the chief, and he kept or redistributed them as he saw fit. Some luxury imports were distributed to the chief's immediate subordinates, including members of the elite group at the centers and local representatives of authority in the countryside (Frankenstein and Rowlands 1978). Less valued materials were distributed more widely (amber, coral) and appear in small quantities in graves of non-elite individuals throughout west-central Europe (fig. 4.3).

Chiefs in Late Hallstatt society appear not to have been interested in adopting western Greek culture *per se*, but only in acquiring some of its material accoutrements. There is no evidence in central Europe of interest in Greek writing or stone architecture, for example.

The receivers of Greek imports and cultural information during Hallstatt D1 were different from those during D2 and D3. Great changes were taking place in central Europe during the sixth century B.C. In the rich graves of Hallstatt D1 no object is present of a kind described in Greek literature as a gift presented to a chief or king. In Vix and Grafenbühl, both dating to around or slightly after 500 B.C., imports of such types do occur – the giant krater in Vix, the tripod in Grafenbühl – as well as a variety of other exceptional items. Judging from the character of the imports the chiefs at the end of the Late Hallstatt Period were considerably more powerful and important than those at the beginning of that period, at least as far as the Greeks were concerned.

4.3 *Effects in central Europe*

When a new element is brought from outside into a cultural system, in order for it to be adopted it must replace some element already present (Spicer 1952, 91). As a new element is adopted systemic readjustments must occur in different subsystems such that the new element becomes integrated with the other elements. Use of imported bronzes and of Greek painted pottery by the elite at the centers had repercussions on local bronze and pottery industries. Vessels from the Mediterranean world began arriving in west-central Europe during Hallstatt D1, and during D2 and D3 both bronze and ceramic containers of Mediterranean origin became increasingly numerous at the centers. The arrival of these imported vessels into the hands of the Late Hallstatt elite may have contributed to a decline in the value of locally made fine pottery. The richest Early Hallstatt graves, such as the Sternberg, are characterized by the number and size of finely ornamented ceramic vessels of Alb-Salem, or Alb-Hegau, type, as well as by long swords (von Föhr 1892, 37–40; see Torbrügge 1968, 100). Similar vessels, though often smaller and less ornate, constitute standard grave goods in Early Hallstatt burials throughout Württemberg (Zürn 1957*b*).

With the beginning of Hallstatt D1 the fine Alb-Salem (Alb-Hegau) pottery gradually disappears from the rich graves; it is replaced by imported bronze vessels (Vilsingen, Kappel in Baden) and their imitations (Hohmichele Grave 6) along with some modestly ornamented local pottery. In the course of the Late Hallstatt Period, Alb-Salem (Alb-Hegau) pottery ceases to be used in the plain graves as well (Spindler 1975*a*) and is replaced by very simple ceramic vessels or by bronze jewelry (Neuffer 1974, 8). The introduction of Greek and Etruscan bronze and pottery vessels into the cultural system at the beginning of Hallstatt D1 may have contributed to this change in the popularity of pottery as a grave good, particularly among the elite and later among the populace (for a similar case see Clarke 1976, 471–472). The decline in the use of pottery as a grave good (Table 1) had repercussions in other subsystems, particularly those concerned with the pottery industry.

Table 1. *Numbers of ceramic vessels in graves at Early Iron Age cemeteries in Württemberg*

	Typological period of cemetery
Zainingen: 34 cremation graves	Hallstatt C
Mean 7.56	
Median 6	
Mode 5	
Range 25	
Tannheim: 21 inhumation graves	Hallstatt C/Early D
Mean 5.1	
Median 2	
Mode 2	
Range 20	
Magdalenenberg: 122 inhumation graves	Hallstatt D1
Mean 0.71	
Median 1	
Mode 1	
Range 4	
Mühlacker: 42 inhumation graves	Hallstatt D1–D3
Mean 0.05	
Median 0	
Mode 0	
Range 1	

Before Hallstatt D1 bronze vessels were rare in west-central Europe. The few specimens dating to the Urnfield and Hallstatt C Periods are widely separated from one another geographically and chronologically (von Merhart 1952). The arrival of Etruscan bronze vessels beginning during Hallstatt D1 stimulated an active local industry producing imitations (see pp. 57–58 above). Growth of such a new industry involved other changes in the system, such as an increased demand for bronze and development of a new specialized craft industry.

Direct effects of the introduction of wine are difficult to assess, since there is no good evidence concerning the quantities involved or distribution of the beverage in central Europe. If regular supplies of wine were available to the elite, the drink probably replaced some other beverage such as beer. Introduction of the potter's wheel may have contributed to the specialization of the pottery craft in Late Hallstatt Europe.

The introduction of the technique of building with clay bricks and that of sculpting the human figure in the round appear to have had little effect on the Hallstatt cultural system as a whole. The Heuneburg wall and the Hirschlanden stele are isolated phenomena, and the Mediterranean techniques apparent in the production of each are not in evidence in any other artifacts yet recovered. After Period IV at the Heuneburg the Late Hallstatt occupants reverted to the traditional earth-and-timber wall structure, like the defensive systems preceding the brick wall.

The archaeological evidence indicates that interaction took place between central Europeans and western Greeks over a period of roughly a century. Contact maintained over such a long period must have some purpose for both parties concerned. Polanyi's assertion (1957, 260–261) that trade is a specific activity, carried out for the procurement of certain products, can be applied to interaction in general: if members of two cultural systems interact over a period of time, there must be specific reasons for their doing so. For the western Greeks based at Massalia, interaction with central Europeans resulted in an availability of a variety of natural and manufactured products which were in short supply in Mediterranean coastal lands. Why did central-European chiefs want Greek and Etruscan bronzes, pottery, and brick walls?

Borrowing of elements from a foreign cultural system is done first by individuals, not by societies (Barnett 1953, 39, 61, 97–98). Individuals borrow elements from outside for two general reasons: out of curiosity or the desire for things new and different, and in expectation of gaining some advantage through the borrowing (Linton 1940, 470; Foster 1962, 147–148). The first seems to be a universal human characteristic; the second requires further discussion. Both were probably involved in the case under consideration here.

The advantages which Late Hallstatt chiefs may have expected to gain can be characterized by the terms prestige and power. The desire for prestige can act as a strong force in determining human behavior (Herskovits 1952, 122; Foster 1962, 148). Prestige can be gained in a variety of ways depending upon the values and means available in a societal system. One is acquiring objects associated with a foreign group of high status in the eyes of one's compatriots. Foreign objects often have *per se* high prestige value (*ibid.*, 148). The objects of Greek and Etruscan origin which occur in Late Hallstatt contexts were high status items. Find contexts and literary evidence indicate that they were all luxury goods in the Mediterranean world (pp. 52–57 above); in central Europe they occur only in association with local elite luxury materials.

Both by their possession of ornamental luxury objects of foreign origin, and by their visible association with Mediterranean cultural systems (having a brick wall constructed; drinking wine, perhaps with a drinking ritual partly borrowed from the Greeks (Kossack 1964); perhaps wearing foreign clothes such as the silk in Hohmichele Grave 6), members of the Early Iron Age elite probably gained in prestige within their own cultural system. Gain in prestige is generally accompanied by other gains, as in the realm of social status and political authority (Herskovits 1940, 19).

Lurie (1959) illustrates how Powhatan made use of the presence of the early American colonists in order to gain prestige among his followers and thereby to increase his political power. Cipolla (1970) describes how, in seventeenth-century China, mandarins gained in prestige and status as they obtained gifts of fine mechanical clocks from Europeans seeking favors and privileges. Chiefs, kings, and other figures of authority adopt new elements – material objects, behavior patterns, or ideas – if the adoption improves or protects their position (Rogers and Shoemaker 1971, 361). For this reason the Late Hallstatt chiefs may have taken up objects and behavior patterns from the Mediterranean societies. As they saw the positive effects of such adoption of exotic foreign goods, they would have become all the more eager to maintain the relationship with western Greeks which enabled them to acquire such materials and would have done all they could to assure their supply of Mediterranean luxury goods. The strong desire on the part of the chiefs to maintain contact with the south and to acquire the luxury products from the Mediterranean societies had important effects on the Hallstatt cultural system as a whole.

4.4 *Systemic change in Hallstatt Europe*

Chiefs play central roles in the economic organization of their societies (pp. 7–8 above). They manage the economic system and act as collectors, accumulators, and redistributors. In all social systems chiefs and kings are permitted a certain latitude in their behavior as long as their people do not feel they are taking disproportionate advantage of their position (Murdock 1949, 84; Hocart 1936, 197–209, 214–215; Firth 1965, 235).

In order for the Hallstatt chiefs to assure a continuous supply of bronze vessels, fine pottery, wine, and the rest – which they did maintain – they had to keep providing the Greek traders with what they wanted. As the central figures in the economic systems of their societies the chiefs were in a position to do so (Sahlins 1960*a*, 409; 1972, 135). Some materials sought by Greeks were probably natural products which required collecting in central Europe: furs, pitch, resin, wax, honey. Others were probably produced at the settlements: leather, textiles, meats. Slaves, if they existed in the system, would have been captured in warfare and raids. Before Greeks established the trade port of Massalia and expressed interest in products of central Europe, it is likely that little surplus was being produced there. The Early Hallstatt settlement pattern was one of scattered farmsteads and hamlets carrying out more or less the same subsistence and local manufacturing activities (pp. 81–82 above). While some inter-village commerce existed (bronze, or its constituents, had to be imported), the distribution of both locally made objects and the rare foreign materials suggest that aside from metals the settlement units were materially independent of one another.

In order to supply Greek traders with products they sought, central European chiefs had to organize the production of surpluses for export. Chiefs in traditional societies can increase the productive activities of their groups by providing incentives for members' greater application to production (Sahlins 1960*a*, 409; 1960*b*; 1963, 291–293; Firth 1965, 191, 232). With the initial cooperation of their households and close relatives, they can provide more and greater feasts and other redistributive ceremonies, and can distribute special goods to members of the society as rewards and incentives for production. In the Late Hallstatt case such goods may have included both centrally manufactured objects such as fibulae and glass beads, and imported materials such as amber and coral.

We have no evidence regarding the quantities of materials transported from central Europe to Massalia, but they must have been substantial for Greek interest to have been maintained throughout the sixth century B.C. and for Greeks to have provided such gifts as the Vix krater and the Grafenbühl tripod and sphinxes in order to ensure the supply. When interaction is carried on over a period of time, the generation of the products sought by the interacting societies becomes increasingly important to the group supplying them because through their production and trade desired foreign goods become available (Linton 1940, 493). Changes effected in the economic subsystem in order to produce larger surpluses of the trade goods bring about changes in other subsystems. Studies by Firth (1929, 476–482) and Rogers (1964) provide instructive examples of how the desire on the part of an outside group for specific resources stimulates profound economic changes in a cultural system to increase production of those resources; the economic changes are accompanied by changes in the societies' division of labor, settlement patterns, group size, and social structure. Changes surely occurred throughout the Early Iron Age cultural system as a result of the chief's efforts to increase the surpluses of those products sought by the Greek traders.

In order to increase the amount of natural products (furs, pitch, resin, wax, honey) collected, a chief would have had to engage more individuals in the task of collecting and to stimulate those already involved in collecting to devote more time and energy to the task. The catchment area exploited by some communities would have been expanded. Expansion of the area would have necessitated the development of communication and transportation systems by which materials could be brought together for shipment south. Not every hamlet became a central collecting point for products destined for the Mediterranean world. Some Early Hallstatt headmen were able to respond to the Greek initiative because of their leadership and organizing abilities and their relations with supporting individuals and groups, and others were not (see Sahlins 1963). As the former group of headmen developed an expansive system for collecting natural products, other local leaders with less initiative or ability to rally widespread support would have become involved in the collection process too by organizing collection on a more local level; their communities would have then become satellites to the emerging centers (Frankenstein and Rowlands 1978, 76–77).

Intensification of mechanisms for collecting materials can lead to the development of collecting centers. The more extensive and intensive the collection process, the more important centers become. The growth proceeds through positive feedback – the more collection grows, the more important centers become; as centers expand in scale and activity, they make possible greater collection.

In order to increase the quantities of locally produced materials (textiles, leather, meats) to trade, a Hallstatt chief had to stimulate a greater degree of specialization in production. Individuals removed from the pool of subsistence producers to join the ranks of such specialists would have had to be sustained by the products of a larger number of those devoting their time to subsistence activities. Like the collection of natural materials, the production of goods in surplus quantities can thus also lead to the development of centers. In farmsteads and hamlets every family is a food-producing unit and provides most needed finished products (except metals). Specialization can only be maintained where a large population is available, such that specialists can depend upon others to provide basic food and clothing. The growth of a site's role as a center and the development of craft specialization are mutually reinforcing processes.

In terms of the model advocated here, a hamlet headman or village chief, responding to the interest of Greek traders in central European products, may have stimulated more intensive collection and production activities by his community. As the members of the community began to collect and produce more, specialized roles became increasingly important and, as specialization increased, efficiency in collection and production also increased. The village would have become a local center of collection and production. Such a village may have developed into a center such as the Heuneburg. Other surrounding communities, whose headmen were less able to rally the cooperation of large numbers of individuals, would have become subordinate to the more active chief and participated in the collection and production of that growing center (Frankenstein and Rowlands 1978, 76–77).

As a few sites began to emerge as centers, other changes occurred in the cultural system. As a result of the increased communication and movement of goods involved in the intensification of collection, circulation of a range of goods increased during the Late Hallstatt Period. For the first time in Württemberg amber, coral, gold, and glass appeared in quantity, particularly at the centers but also in many plain graves in the countryside. The abundance of these materials in the rich graves at the centers and the scattered finds of them in graves throughout Württemberg suggests a growth in redistribution from the centers which may be a

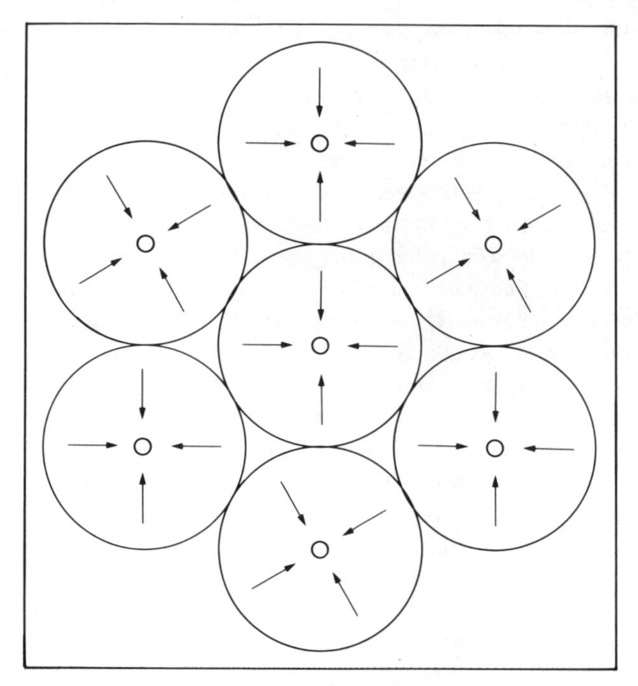

Fig. 4.4. Model representing the economic self-sufficiency of Early Hallstatt communities in Württemberg. The small circles represent settlements, the large circles the territories in which communities raised crops, pastured livestock, and collected various needed materials. Each community was largely independent economically, except for the procuring of metals.

reflection of the chiefly distribution of valued goods as rewards and incentives for surplus production. Thus the circulation of a variety of materials, many not directly related to the interactions with the Mediterranean world, but playing a part in the production scheme, began to circulate throughout the region (pp. 38–46 above).

As the Heuneburg and other centers were developing, relations between communities in west-central Europe were changing. When all settlement communities were of roughly the same size and equal importance in the economic and social systems, each was more or less independent of the others. Some interaction took place, but during Early Hallstatt times there is little archaeological evidence for specialization at specific settlements (aside from metal production). During the Late Hallstatt the centers and the surrounding villages became interdependent (figs. 4.4, 4.5). Centers depended on the smaller settlements for materials they collected and produced for export south to Greek Massalia and probably for agricultural products to support specialist craftsmen, merchants, and administrators. The smaller settlements depended upon the centers both for imported luxury substances (amber, coral) and for products manufactured at the centers (bronze rings and fibulae, iron weapons,

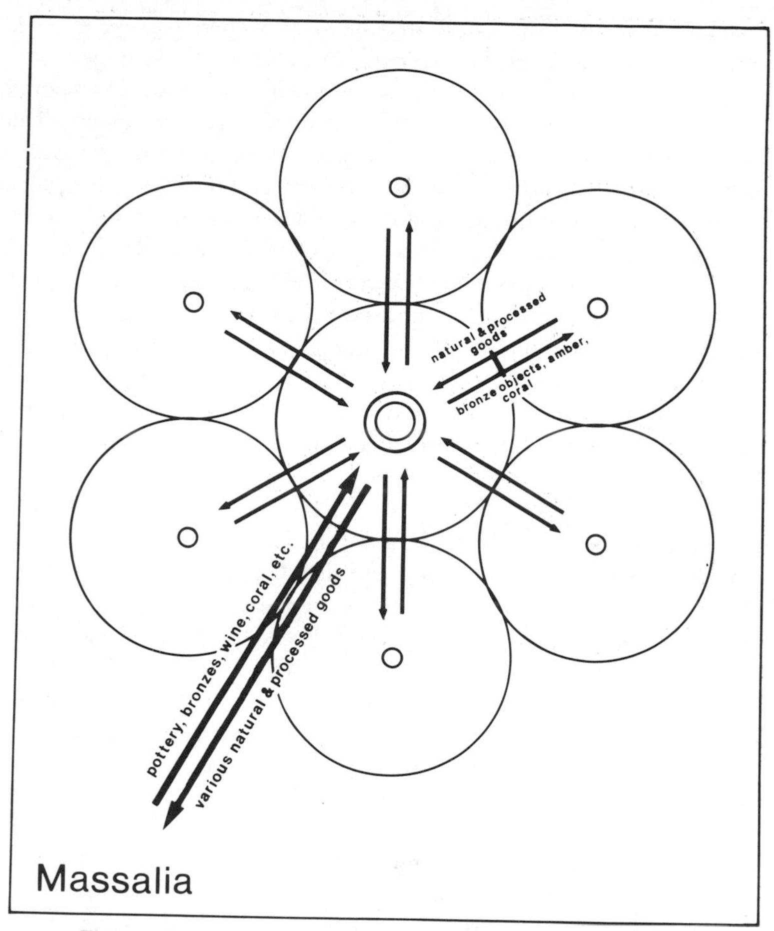

Fig. 4.5. Model representing inter-community interaction during the Late Hallstatt Period in Württemberg. The centers now served as commercial foci, importing from the smaller surrounding communities a variety of foodstuffs and natural and processed goods. In exchange the centers provided the smaller settlements with manufactured goods (particularly metal objects) and imports from the Mediterranean world (some bronze vessels, coral and amber). All communities were now tied into the large-scale production–distribution system centered at sites such as the Heuneburg. It was to maintain the commerce in luxury goods with the Greek world that the chiefs at the centers organized this economic network.

glass beads). Whether the transfer of goods between centers and villages occurred as tribute and redistribution, as direct exchange, or through some other mechanism is a question beyond the scope of this study, but one which might be examined through analysis of the increasing number of well excavated cemeteries and settlements.

The circulation, manufacturing, and settlement subsystems have been mentioned; changes in social organization occurred as well. As some settlement units developed into centers, the chiefs at them gained in status and power. They remained at the center of the economic subsystem, and as that subsystem became more developed through expanded collection and specialized production, they became more powerful. As Gall and Saxe (1977) argue, when a cultural system grows in complexity, more cultural energy must be expended on organization and administration; the latter increase may be of a geometric nature (*ibid.*, 262). The reflection of this greater expenditure of energy necessary at the Late Hallstatt economic centers is apparent in the rich burials – they are in exceptionally large tumuli (requiring extra labor to construct) and contain both fine local crafts products (indicative of new specialized industries) and exotic luxury goods from distant cultural systems (implying elaborate political and commercial networks extending over great distances).

The special developments of the Late Hallstatt Period in west-central Europe ended some time during the first half of the fifth century B.C. Imports stopped arriving into Württemberg around 475 B.C. (Dehn and Frey 1962), and very few graves were richly outfitted after that date (the grave at Kleinaspergle is an exception in both respects). The fine-crafts industries declined in their productivity, and at the Heuneburg the intensity of production and trade dropped sharply.

As I have argued elsewhere (Wells and Bonfante 1979), the end of the special cultural development of the Late Hallstatt Period in west-central Europe may have come as the result of the end of Greek interest in the products of central Europe. Around 500 B.C. there is good evidence for a rapid increase in Greek trade in other parts of the border lands of the Mediterranean, such as at the Head of the Adriatic (Vallet 1950; Alfieri and Arias 1958; Zuffa 1975) and on the Black Sea coast (Wasowicz 1966; 1975). The Po Plain and neighboring regions of northern Italy and Yugoslavia, and the south Russian lands, are environments which could have been producing in surplus the same products sought by Greeks in central Europe, and the upswing in Greek commercial activity in these regions may have led to the end of the active commerce between Massalia and central Europe. The reasons for the change in the sources of materials sought by the urban centers of the eastern Mediterranean are not immediately apparent; they may have had to do with relative ease of transport, with political relations between the groups involved in the trade, or with terms of exchange.

I argue above that it was the importation of the luxury products from the Mediterranean world that first led the chiefs in Hallstatt central Europe to stimulate greater surplus production for export and enabled them to continue to increase the productive capability of their communities. The imported luxury goods provided means of rewarding cooperation and encouraging further loyalty and effort, both in the stimulation of production of export goods and in the maintenance of other institutions in the cultural system such as the fine-crafts industries producing gold neck rings and bracelets, ornate daggers, and bronze vessels for the chiefs and for their subordinate leaders in the smaller settlements around the centers. When the commerce with Greeks in southern France ceased, this flow of luxury goods stopped, both exotic objects such as bronze vessels and ivory carvings, and unfinished divisible materials such as coral and probably amber. Since the cultural system in the Late Hallstatt Period had become dependent upon the regular influx of these Mediterranean products, when they stopped arriving the system had to readjust to their absence. In terms of settlement size and activity, differentiation of burial inventories, and production of specialized crafts items, the organization of cultural life in the period following the flourishing of the Heuneburg and other centers was more similar to that of the Early Hallstatt than to that of the Late Hallstatt Period (Liebschwager 1972; also Bittel 1934).

5
The nature of the contact:
beginning of the Late Iron Age

5.1 *Patterns in the archaeological evidence*

For examination of contact and change in west-central Europe during the Early La Tène Period, the evidence from the Saarland will be considered, because the greatest concentration of Mediterranean imports occur there and the region is relatively well known archaeologically (Haffner 1976). Although much of the literature on the Iron Age suggests that the patterns of Mediterranean imports and rich graves are similar in Late Hallstatt and Early La Tène contexts, there are profound differences which indicate further changes in the interactions with the Mediterranean world.

No evidence in the Saarland during Early La Tène times indicates the existence of centers similar to the Late Hallstatt Heuneburg, Hohenasperg, and Mont Lassois. Settlements of such character have not been found, nor have groups of rich graves associated with specific habitation sites been identified (see Driehaus 1965; Schindler 1968, 136–141). All of the Mediterranean luxury goods in the Early La Tène Saarland occur in graves. Burial practices resemble those of the Late Hallstatt – inhumation under a tumulus, usually with several graves in each mound. The kinds of burial goods are also similar: bronze fibulae and ring jewelry, occasional iron weapons, and in the richest graves gold jewelry, wheeled vehicles, and bronze vessels from the Mediterranean world. Different is the style of ornament on locally made objects; they are decorated with motifs of the La Tène tradition instead of Hallstatt ones.

Settlements

The paucity of information about settlements in the Saarland can be attributed both to the lack of systematic effort to locate and excavate sites and to the nature of those that are known (Haffner 1966*a*, 28; Schindler 1968, 10). Fortified hilltop settlements, as well as unfortified lowland sites, have been identified (Haffner 1976, 148, 410–411), but very few of either type have been investigated. Those which have been partly excavated have yielded sparse archaeological remains compared to the cultural materials recovered at the Heuneburg and other Late Hallstatt settlements.

Cemeteries

Two kinds of burial sites in Hallstatt Württemberg were discussed: large tumuli around major settlement centers, and cemeteries not associated with centers. In the Early La Tène Saarland, the graves which contain bronze vessels from Mediterranean workshops, gold jewelry, and wheeled vehicles are not concentrated around particular settlements but are situated throughout the region (Schindler 1968, 139 fig. 57; Haffner 1976, map 10). On the basis of the locations of the Early La Tène rich graves with respect to fortified hilltop settlements, some investigators have argued for associations between the rich graves and the habitation areas (Schindler 1968, 136–141; Haffner 1976, 152–153). The situation is very different from Late Hallstatt Württemberg, however. As far as the present evidence indicates none of the fortified settlements has more than one or two rich graves associated with it, and none of the hilltop sites has been shown to have been a permanently occupied town-like settlement with dense population and concentrated industrial production such as has been found at the Heuneburg. The distribution of the rich graves alone makes apparent the difference in the organization of Early La Tène society in the Saarland from that of the Late Hallstatt in Württemberg.

The kinds of objects included in graves are similar in the two contexts. In the rich graves in both are Mediterranean imports (mainly bronze vessels), gold jewelry (especially neck and arm rings), weapons (daggers in Late Hallstatt, short-swords in Early La Tène), and wheeled vehicles (four-wheeled wagons in Late Hallstatt, two-wheeled carts or chariots in Early La Tène). Like the plain graves of the Late Hallstatt, those of La Tène A contain primarily bronze ring jewelry (mostly neck and arm rings) and fibulae. The cemeteries of plain graves are of roughly the same size as those of Late Hallstatt Württemberg.

Seven richly outfitted graves and three plain grave cemeteries will constitute the sample for consideration here. The cemeteries were all excavated in recent years, and most of the tumuli were undisturbed at the time of investigation. Most of the rich graves have not fared as well; they were found sometime during the last century in the course of railroad construction or agricultural work. In most cases only subsequent excavations could be conducted by qualified persons in order to study the structure of the burials, generally after most of the grave goods had been removed. Many objects are known to have vanished before being studied, and many more surely disappeared without being heard of. Only Reinheim was investigated in the twentieth century; it is the single rich

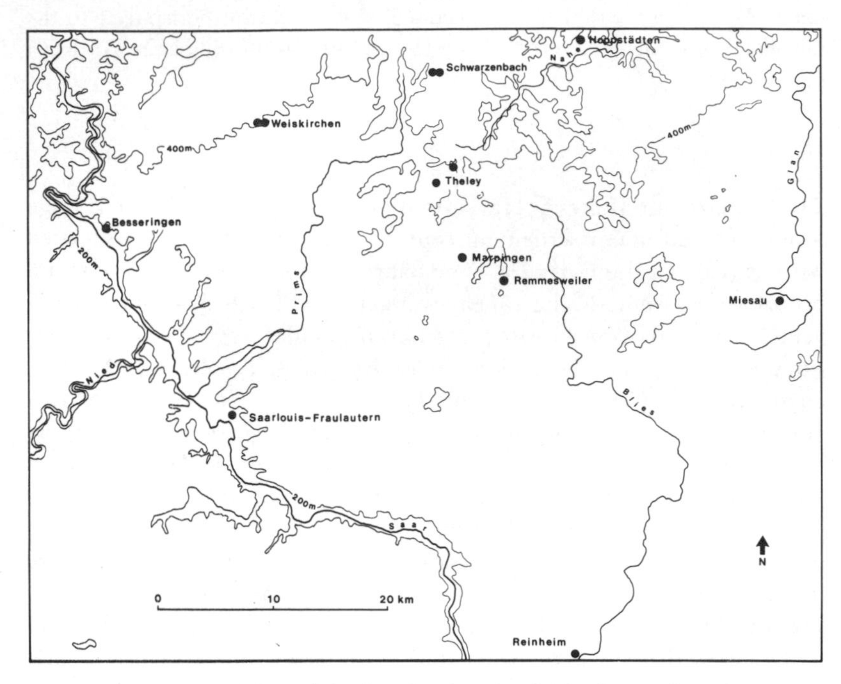

Fig. 5.1. Map of the Saarland and neighboring regions showing sites discussed.

Fig. 5.2. Bronze belt hook with coral inlay from Weiskirchen I. Width 6.6 cm.

Fig. 5.3. Bronze *Schnabelkanne* from Weiskirchen II. Height 42.5 cm.

Early La Tène burial in the Saarland which provides a full picture of the structure and inventory of such a grave.

Besseringen. In the course of very unsystematic digging in 1858 and 1863, remains of a wooden two-wheeled vehicle with metal parts, a hollow gold ring with cast ornament, and a bronze *Schnabelkanne* were recovered in the town of Besseringen. Burned bones and ashes were found in the bronze vessel (Haffner 1966*b*).

Weiskirchen I. In the process of digging soil from a mound in 1851 a farmer came upon a packing of stones and remains of a wooden burial chamber.

Fig. 5.4. Bronze stamnos from Weiskirchen II. Height 40 cm.

Beneath the stones he found a bronze *Schnabelkanne*, a piece of gold leaf ornament on iron backing, a bronze belt hook ornamented in Early La Tène style and with coral inlay (fig. 5.2), an iron short-sword in an iron sheath with sheet bronze sheath covering, three iron spearheads, a large iron knife (*Hiebmesser*), a mask fibula with enamel inlay, and two bronze coupling rings with coral inlay (Haffner 1966*c*).

Weiskirchen II. This tumulus, close to Weiskirchen I, was opened in 1866. Inside the mound, surrounded by stones, were found a bronze *Schnabelkanne* (fig. 5.3), a bronze stamnos (fig. 5.4), a gold leaf band ornamented with a row of impressed sphinxes, and an iron short-sword with bronze sheath with three sheet gold rosettes decorating the chape (Haffner 1966*c*).

Schwarzenbach I. In 1849 a farmer uncovered fragments of a bronze vessel while ploughing. Digging further into the ground he found the remains

Fig. 5.5. Gold openwork covering for a bowl from Schwarzenbach I. Diameter 12.6 cm.

of a burial chamber in a tumulus of earth, and inside it fragments of a bronze *Schnabelkanne*, a bronze amphora, the gold leaf covering for a bowl (fig. 5.5), and some other gold leaf fragments including mask ornaments, perhaps remains of drinking horns (Frey 1971*b*, 85) (Schindler 1966).

Schwarzenbach II. After the discovery of gold in Schwarzenbach I, many tumuli in the area were dug into (Schindler 1966, 217). From this second Schwarzenbach mound, close by the first, were recovered (of the recorded finds) a bronze vessel resembling a *Schnabelkanne* with a cast figure as the handle (containing burned bone fragments) and a gold arm ring with three pairs of human heads ornamenting it. Iron weapons have been mentioned in connection with the grave but it is unclear whether they belonged to it (Gerhard 1856, 195; Jacobsthal and Langsdorff 1929, 26; Schindler 1966).

Theley. The Fuchshübel tumulus at Theley was excavated in 1835 and 1836 by the Antiquities Club of St Wendel; excavation procedure and publication (1838) were remarkably good for the time. Inside a wooden burial chamber was a two-wheeled vehicle with bronze and iron parts on which the deceased had been laid. On one arm was a plain hollow gold ring, on one finger a ring of gold wire. Next to the body were two iron spearheads. A *Schnabelkanne* and some animal bones and teeth were also found in the chamber (Haffner 1966*d*).

These six rich graves were found before 1880. Only Theley was excavated in systematic fashion. Plans or detailed descriptions of the grave contents are lacking. It is likely that some objects were overlooked in the graves, and some are known to have disappeared quickly after discovery. Usually only six or eight objects survive from the rich graves found during the last century, and they are usually large metal objects easily identified. By contrast every rich Early La Tène grave excavated since 1930 has yielded not only large objects – bronze vessels, bronze and iron weapons, and gold jewelry – but also quantities of beads, gold threads and buttons, and other ornaments (see for example the rich graves from Worms-Herrnsheim on the middle Rhine (Schaaff 1971) and Dürrnberg-Hallein in Austria (Penninger 1960)).

Reinheim. The Reinheim grave was found in the course of sand quarrying operations in 1954 and was systematically excavated. A chamber of oak wood within a burial mound contained an inhumation burial. Among the grave goods were 2 bronze bowls, a gold leaf-covered bronze jug with tube spout, a gold neck torc ornamented with figures, an open gold arm ring similarly ornamented, a closed gold arm ring, an ornamented and a plain gold finger ring, 2 decorated bands of gold leaf (drinking horn mounts), 3 gold leaf rosettes (from a vessel), 2 gold plaque fibulae with iron and coral parts, a bronze fibula with human and animal heads, a bronze fibula in the form of a rooster with coral and bone ornament, a bronze mirror with a figural handle inlaid with coral, 2 small bronze pendant male figures, a glass bracelet, 16+ glass beads, a lignite bracelet and fragment of a second, a shale ring, several stones of different kinds worked into different forms, 2 fragments of jet, an amber pendant in the form of a foot, 17 amber beads, 5 amber spacer beads, a handle-shaped amber object 8.8 cm long, and textile fragments identified as linen (Keller 1965; 1970).

Theley. The Theley cemetery, comprising 18 tumuli, is located about 4000 m southwest of the rich burial in the same community (Haffner 1964). Fourteen of the mounds have been excavated, yielding a total of 37 definite burials; other possible graves are represented by stray finds in the mound fill. Of the 37 graves only 1 contained no grave goods. Seven contained only pottery. The other 29 contained some metal objects. Weapons were found in 8 graves, of which 3 had 1 spearhead; 2 contained a spearhead and a sword; and 3 contained 2 spearheads (all spearheads and swords are of iron). Bronze arm rings were the most common grave good, occurring primarily in pairs. Most graves contained one ceramic vessel, while some had two or three.

None of the Theley graves contained any gold object, a bronze vessel, or a wheeled vehicle. Copper and tin constitute the only substances which had to be brought in from outside (unless the copper was locally produced – Schindler 1968, 24–88), with the possible exception of 13 glass beads in Grave 3 in Tumulus XVIII. No amber, coral, lignite, or jet are represented.

Miesau. Miesau is located just across the boundary between the Saarland and the Rhineland–Palatinate, but since its graves belong to the same material culture group as those from the Saarland, it will be included here. The cemetery consists of 19 tumuli, 11 of which have been excavated. Twenty-four intact or slightly disturbed graves were found, ranging in date from Late Hallstatt through Early La Tène; most are contemporary with the series of rich Early La Tène graves (Engels and Kilian 1970, 168).

Of the 24 graves, six contained no surviving goods. One contained only pottery. The other 17 had in them metal objects. Three had iron weapons, in one case a sword, in two instances large knives (*Hiebmesser*). Bronze bracelets were the most frequent grave goods, occurring most often in pairs. As at Theley, at Miesau there were no finds of gold, bronze vessels, or vehicles. No glass beads, amber objects, lignite, or jet were recovered. Only metals in the graves had to be imported from outside.

Saarlouis-Fraulautern. The grave goods at this cemetery are of the Late Hallstatt tradition rather than in the Early La Tène style; the cemetery is probably contemporary with the Early La Tène sites of the region (see pp. 13–14 above; Pauli 1978, 437). It consists of 8 tumuli, 6 of which have been excavated; a total of 84 graves were found (Maisant 1972; 1973).

Twenty-eight of the 84 graves contained either no surviving goods or only a pebble. Another 11 contained only pottery. The other 45 had metal grave goods, but no weapons occurred. As in Theley and Miesau, bronze bracelets were the most common grave goods, most frequently occurring in pairs. Like Theley and Miesau, the Saarlouis-Fraulautern cemetery contained no gold objects, no bronze vessels, and no vehicles. Amber and coral were absent, but glass beads were found in 2 graves – 4 in Tumulus III, Grave 3 and 1 in Tumulus VI, Grave 1 – and a pair of jet bracelets were recovered in Tumulus VI, Grave 7.

Circulation of materials

In the graves of the Early La Tène Period in the Saarland (and those of the latest Hallstatt phase which is largely contemporary – see pp. 13–14 above) are several substances which do not occur in the area. As in Württemberg, all of the basic nesessities for a comfortable settled existence were available to Iron Age inhabitants of the Saarland. Iron and copper were probably produced locally (Driehaus 1965; Schindler 1968); tin had to be imported. The foreign materials represented in the Early La Tène graves are the same as those discussed above in Late Hallstatt Württemberg, but the distributions are somewhat different.

Source in Saarland	Iron, copper
Source in central Europe, but not Saarland	Tin (?), lignite, jet, gold (?), salt
Source outside central Europe	Amber, coral

Iron. The Saarland has long been a major source of iron in central Europe. Evidence for local smelting dates back to the Hallstatt Period (Haffner 1971; 1976, 160, 293; Schindler 1968, 89–146; 1976). Several investigators believe that iron production and trade played an important role in the economic life of the Early La Tène inhabitants of the Saarland and the Rhineland–Palatinate (Driehaus 1965; Pauli 1978, 441, 461).

In Early La Tène graves bronze is still more abundant than iron. Only weapons (swords, spearheads, *Hiebmesser*) and knives are consistently made of iron. These objects are frequent in the rich burials but rarer in the others. In a few instances iron replaces bronze as the metal for jewelry.

Copper. Schindler (1968, 24–88) has discussed the nature of copper deposits in the Saarland and the evidence for copper mining during different periods. There is as yet no direct evidence for mining and smelting during the La Tène Period; however, on the basis of the location of Iron Age and Late Bronze Age settlements and hoards with respect to copper deposits it has been suggested that copper was being mined, smelted, and combined with tin to make bronze. (See Schindler 1968, 85–88, on analyses of ore deposits and of bronze objects from the area.)

Tin. For tin the same problems arise as for the Late Hallstatt context in Württemberg (p. 41 above). No archaeological evidence from the Saarland aids in the identification of the tin source areas.

Lignite. In the three cemeteries and seven rich graves considered the lignite objects are one bracelet and a fragment of another in the rich burial at Reinheim. Since the other rich graves were not well excavated, lignite objects may have been overlooked; the absence of lignite at Miesau, Theley, and Fraulautern, all well investigated, is more significant. (Of other Early La Tène rich graves in the middle Rhine area, only Worms-Herrnsheim (Schaaff 1971) contained lignite – in the form of a leg ring.)

Lignite does not occur naturally in the Saarland, nor in the greater middle Rhine area (see map, Rochna 1962, 73 fig. 5). The objects at Reinheim and Worms-Herrnsheim most likely came from southwest Germany. Rochna's distribution map shows seven finds of lignite in the middle Rhine area, six of them in Late Hallstatt contexts. Since both the forms and the composition of the objects are the same as lignite finds in southwest Germany, it is very probable that the middle Rhine objects are imports from the area.

Jet. In the graves considered, jet occurs in the form of two small fragments in Reinheim and as two bracelets in Tumulus VI, Grave 7 at Saarlouis-Fraulautern. Other objects of jet in the Early La Tène rich burials have not been reported. Like lignite, jet does not occur in the Saarland or in bordering territories. Rochna's map shows no jet finds of the Hallstatt period in the middle Rhine area. The jet at Reinheim and Saarlouis-Fraulautern, like the lignite, is probably an import from the Swabian Alb of Württemberg.

Gold. Among the plain graves considered here there is no trace of gold. Objects such as the small gold earrings and gold wire spirals which occasionally appear in plain Late Hallstatt burials in Württemberg are not represented in these Early La Tène graves. The rich graves almost always (by definition) contain large gold objects. Elaborate figure-ornamented neck rings occur in Besseringen and Reinheim; bracelets in Schwarzenbach II, Theley, and Reinheim (two); finger rings in Theley and Reinheim (two); a gold leaf covering for a bowl in Schwarzenbach I; drinking horn mounts in Weiskirchen II and Reinheim; gold leaf ornamental fragments bearing masks in Weiskirchen I and Schwarzenbach I; three rosettes on the chape of the scabbard in Weiskirchen II; and gold plating on a fibula in Reinheim. Gold objects in these graves (which are representative of gold in all Early La Tène rich burials) can be regarded in two main groups: jewelry (neck, arm, and finger rings) and ornament for a variety of metal objects, particularly drinking vessels and weapons.

The source of the gold in the Early La Tène context is unclear. Local sources of the gold are possible, but at the present state of research impossible to confirm (Hartmann 1978, 607–608).

Salt. The Late Hallstatt salt-producing sites of eastern France (p. 43 above) also come into question for the Early La Tène Saarland. Schindler (1968, 83–85) argues that salt production and trade played an important part in the industrial and commercial activity of the Saarland region during the Iron Age.

Amber. Among the sites considered amber occurs only in two of the rich graves. In Weiskirchen I an amber button or knob is on the gold leaf-covered iron piece. The Reinheim grave contained numerous amber objects (p. 110 above). Among other rich graves of the middle Rhine area Schwabsburg contained an amber knob on a gold leaf-covered iron object similar to that in Weiskirchen I (Lindenschmit 1904, 362, pl. 2 no. 12); Kärlich Grave 4 had in it six beads (Günther 1934, pl. 2 nos. 6, 7); Dürkheim contained two flat beads (Sprater 1928, 111 fig. 122).

Coral. Coral appears in two of the rich graves discussed and is not represented in the three plain grave cemeteries. In Weiskirchen I, coral inlay appears on the bronze belt hook, on the bronze and iron sheath, and on the two bronze coupling rings. In the Reinheim grave, coral ornament is present on two plaque fibulae of gold-leaf covered iron, on the rooster fibula, and on the hands of the figure forming the handle of the bronze mirror. In rich graves elsewhere in the middle Rhineland, coral appears as inlay on the lead ring from Laumersheim (Kimmig 1950) and as inlay on fibulae from Altrier (Thill 1972, 490) and Thomm (Dehn 1940, pl. 13 no. 5). Since the coral in Early La Tène contexts occurs as inlay in locally made La Tène objects, the substance was almost certainly imported from the Mediterranean in its natural state and worked into desired forms in central Europe, as it was at the Late Hallstatt centers (p. 44 above).

Glass. Of the rich graves only Reinheim contained glass objects: an arm ring, 16+ beads, and 2 small rings. No glass objects are recorded from any other middle Rhine area rich graves, from the Saarland or elsewhere; such small items as glass beads may well have gone unnoticed during excavations of the last century.

Several glass objects occur in the plain grave cemeteries examined. At Theley, 13 glass beads were found in Tumulus XVIII, Grave 3. At Saarlouis-Fraulautern Tumulus III, Grave 3 contained 4 beads. And Tumulus VI, Grave 1 of the same cemetery held 1 bead.

Materials from outside the immediate region are less well represented in the Early La Tène Saarland than in Late Hallstatt Württemberg, if the small number of sites examined here are representative. (It would be interesting and valuable to conduct a full study of these substances in all recorded graves in the two contexts to make a thorough comparison.) Gold occurs in abundance in the rich graves in both contexts; it is represented in three of the seven plain grave cemeteries in Late Hallstatt Württemberg, but in none of the three Saarland cemeteries examined. Amber too is restricted to the richest graves in the Early La Tène Saarland, while in Late Hallstatt Württemberg it is present in at least one grave in all seven plain grave cemeteries. Coral appears in three of the plain grave cemeteries in Württemberg, but only in the richest burials in the Early La Tène Saarland. Lignite and jet, well represented in plain graves in Late Hallstatt Württemberg, are represented by only a single pair of bracelets in one grave at Saarlouis-Fraulautern. Glass is present, though not in abundance, in some of the plain grave cemeteries examined in both contexts.

New patterns in the evidence

Like the Late Hallstatt Period in Württemberg, the Early La Tène in the Saarland is marked by the appearance of large numbers of luxury objects from the Mediterranean world. In the Early La Tène context the imports are almost exclusively of Etruscan origin. The only Greek objects in the greater middle Rhine area are the Attic kantharos from Rodenbach, two Attic kylikes from Kleinaspergle, and a sherd of Attic pottery from a pit at Urmitz-Weissenthurm. No Greek or Etruscan object has been found in a Late Hallstatt context in the middle Rhine area, though the earliest La Tène contexts known contain Etruscan bronzes.

The Kleinaspergle grave is of particular importance. It is associated with the Hohenasperg, along with Grafenbühl and Römerhügel; but unlike those two and the other surrounding rich graves (pp. 34–36 above), the objects in Kleinaspergle are of Early La Tène character. The grave contained a rich assemblage of gold and bronze objects ornamented in classic Early La Tène style along with an Etruscan stamnos and two Attic kylikes (one red-figure, one black-polished) dating around 450 B.C. (Jacobsthal 1944, 136). Since Kleinaspergle is not one of the earliest of the Early La Tène graves (see Megaw 1970, catalog), its presence at the Hohenasperg suggests that the Late Hallstatt center continued in importance while the Early La Tène ornamental tradition was developing in the middle Rhineland. As a rich La Tène grave at a Hallstatt settlement complex, Kleinaspergle is an anomaly – all other known rich Early La Tène graves in west-central Europe are located in areas where there are no rich, import-containing graves of the Late Hallstatt Period.

No series of rich burials comparable to those in Late Hallstatt Württemberg precedes the appearance of the wealthy graves of the Early La Tène Period in the Saarland. These Early La Tène rich graves, characterized by Etruscan bronze vessels, ornate gold jewelry, finely crafted local bronze containers, and two-wheeled carts or chariots, appear as a new phenomenon in the Saarland and neighboring parts of the middle Rhine area. Some graves of the preceding period containing four-wheeled wagons and bronze situlae stand out from the majority of burials (Haffner 1976, 404–405), but they are very different in character from both the Late Hallstatt rich graves in Württemberg and from the Early La Tène rich graves in the Saarland.

No centers comparable to the Heuneburg or the Hohenasperg have been found in the Saarland dating to either the Late Hallstatt or Early La Tène Period. Excavations carried out on fortified hilltop sites similar topographically to the Hallstatt centers of Württemberg have yielded no evidence of such dense permanent occupation. In contrast to the concentrated distribution of Late Hallstatt rich graves around the centers, the Early La Tène wealthy burials are scattered across the middle Rhine area from Basse-Yutz, near Metz, France, in the west to the Rhine, and from Koblenz in the north to Saarbrücken in the south (Driehaus 1965, 37 fig. 3). The rich graves are somewhat more densely concentrated in the northern part of the Saarland than elsewhere, but there too no particular grouping around specific sites is apparent.

5.2 *A model for the social structure*

The rich graves of the Early La Tène Saarland bear certain similarities to those of the Late Hallstatt in Württemberg; e.g. the kinds of materials found in the two contexts. Yet there are important differences. In the Late Hallstatt context, Vix and Grafenbühl far surpass all other Late Hallstatt graves in their wealth of exotic imported objects, many of rare and precious materials (gold, ivory, amber). Among the Early La Tène rich graves no such extraordinary burials have been found. Particularly significant is the presence in Late Hallstatt rich graves (Vix, Grafenbühl, Grächwil) of exceptional objects probably made specifically for barbarian taste (see p. 77 above). In the Early La Tène rich graves all of the imports are objects which were also used as grave goods in their lands of origin (see below).

As noted above, no centers comparable to those of the Late Hallstatt context have been found in the Saarland. The evidence suggests a settlement pattern of individual farmsteads and hamlets or very small villages (Haffner 1976, 148–149). No large cemeteries have been found to suggest a substantially larger population, such as that at the Heuneburg.

Both the richness of the graves and the number and distribution of burials indicate a society in the Early La Tène Saarland organized very differently from that of Late Hallstatt Württemberg. If the communities were that much smaller than the Hallstatt centers, then the status and power of the leaders of those communities were proportionately less (Shennan 1975, 283; Gall and Saxe 1977). The individuals buried in the rich graves were probably headmen or chiefs of only very local significance. There is no evidence to suggest that one chief was substantially wealthier or more powerful than any other, nor do any settlements stand out as larger or more active in industry or trade than others. Craft specialization existed, particularly in the production of luxury goods for the elite: gold jewelry, bronze vessels, and ornate bronze jewelry and weaponry. At present, it is difficult even to speculate on the location and organization of those specialized industries; without the existence of centers it is unclear where the products would have been made.

Among the Early La Tène rich graves, although different degrees of wealth are apparent in the burial assemblages, no groupings of graves on the basis of wealth have been identified as they have for the Late Hallstatt context (pp. 49–50 above). In place of the structured hierarchy managing the complex economic and social systems of the Late Hallstatt cultural system in Württemberg, in the Early La Tène situation we see a decentralized, dispersed, economic and social organization with local chiefs of roughly equal status exercising their authority in small communities.

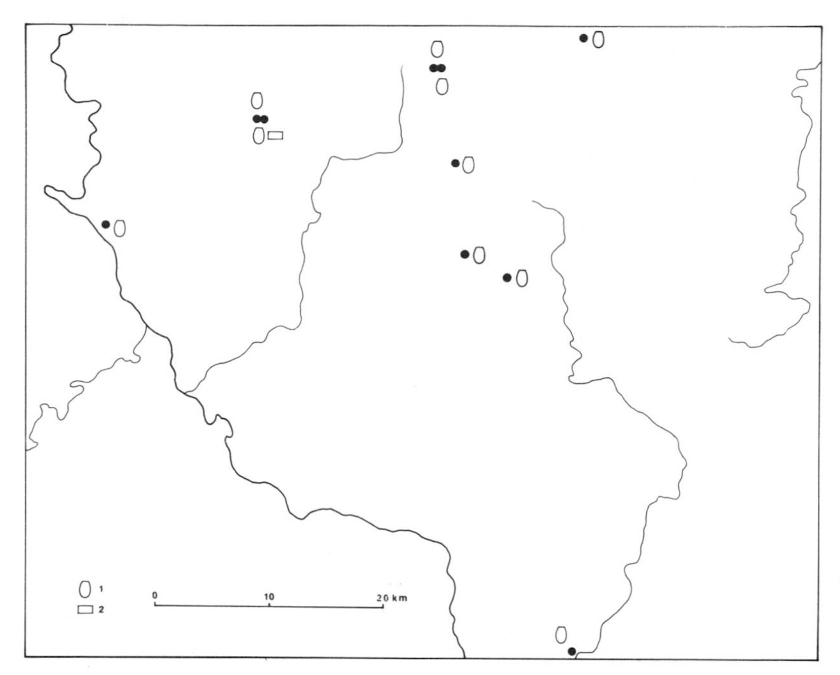

Fig. 5.6. Map showing distribution of luxury imports in the Saarland (for sites compare fig. 5.1). 1-bronze vessels; 2-other (gold band). The map indicates the presence of each category in each grave, but not the quantity.

5.3 *The evidence for contact*

In the Early La Tène Saarland there is evidence for importation of objects from the Mediterranean world and for imitation of forms and motifs, but not of the transmission of technical information from the south into central Europe.

Imports

Distribution. Fig. 5.6 shows locations of Mediterranean luxury imports in the Saarland and neighboring parts of the Rhineland–Palatinate. Comparison with the map of imports in Late Hallstatt Württemberg (fig. 3.10) reveals the difference in the patterns of occurrence. In Württemberg the imports are concentrated at the Heuneburg and the Hohenasperg; in the Saarland they are distributed throughout the area.

Context. In the Saarland and other parts of the middle Rhineland, Mediterranean luxury products occur in graves, usually in those distinguished by their wealth in local products as well. There are important exceptions to this general pattern, however. A review of the literature dealing with the circumstances of discovery and excavation in the middle Rhineland of Early La Tène graves which contained imports suggests that only the following six graves were fairly well reported, at least as far as objects larger than beads and small ornaments are concerned (only two of these graves are in the Saarland): Altrier, excavated in 1970 by Thill (Thill 1972); Hillesheim, excavated in the late 1920s by the Trier Museum (Steiner 1929); Marpingen, excavated in 1960 by Schindler (Schindler 1961); Oberwallmenach, excavated in 1934–1935 by Koch (Polenz 1971); Reinheim, excavated in 1954 by Keller (Keller 1965); and Urmitz-Weissenthurm, observed and later excavated by Koenen between 1900 and 1905 (Koenen 1906). In the case of all the other Early La Tène graves in the middle Rhineland containing imports, it is unclear to what extent the finds now present constitute a complete inventory; in many cases we know that grave goods disappeared immediately or shortly after discovery (see e.g. Lindenschmit 1870, vol. 2, part 2, text to pls. 1, 2; 1881, vol. 3, part 3, text to pl. 2; Steiner 1930, 167).

These six graves provide a good picture of the range of material wealth present in graves which contained an imported object from the Mediterranean world. Reinheim is by far the richest, with large quantities of gold and amber, various rare objects of bronze including one of the few Early La Tène mirrors known, and a range of materials such as glass, coral, and lignite. Altrier, Hillesheim, and Marpingen do not approach Reinheim in quantity or rarity of their grave goods, yet all three contained an Etruscan bronze vessel and a small amount of gold (in each case only one type of gold object). Urmitz-Weissenthurm contained no gold but an Etruscan bronze jug, a locally made bronze situla, and a two-wheeled vehicle. The most poorly outfitted of the six, Oberwallmenach, contained an Etruscan *Schnabelkanne* as the only grave good; it served as a cremation urn. Thus of these six graves, one is very rich, one very poor, and the others, while distinctly better outfitted with unusual objects that most Early La Tène graves, are considerably less wealthy than most of the Late Hallstatt graves in Württemberg which contained Mediterranean imports.

The other Early La Tène graves containing imports in the middle Rhineland show a similar pattern. Rodenbach and Dürkheim are exceptionally richly outfitted (comparable to Reinheim); Besseringen, Weiskirchen I and II, Schwarzenbach I and II are richer than most. The other graves containing imports are poorer than these in terms of the amounts of gold and special local objects. Since none of these graves was well observed at the time of opening, and in many cases disappearance of objects is documented, the discussion, in concrete terms, of degrees of burial wealth is difficult at best.

Character of the imports. The range of kinds of imports in Early La Tène contexts is much more limited than in Late Hallstatt. Among rich graves in the middle Rhineland three categories of imports can be distinguished: bronze vessels (all Etruscan), Greek pottery (vessel at Rodenbach, sherd at Urmitz), and the gold leaf band in Weiskirchen II.

Bronze vessels. In the Saarland the following vessels are believed to be of Etruscan origin: *Schnabelkannen* in Besseringen, Weiskirchen I and II, Schwarzenbach I and II, Theley, Marpingen, and Remmesweiler; stamnos in Weiskirchen II; amphora in Schwarzenbach I; two bowls in Reinheim.

In both Late Hallstatt and Early La Tène contexts bronze vessels are the most common kind of Mediterranean import in graves. In Late Hallstatt west-central Europe a total of 24 bronze vessels of Greek and Etruscan manufacture have been found in graves. Among these, 13 different types are represented. Eight types occur only once: the Vix krater, Vix rimmed bowl, Hochdorf cauldron, Grächwil hydria, Hatten trefoil-mouth jug, Conliège amphora, and the bowl and pyxis from Kastenwald. The best represented form in Hallstatt contexts is the boss-rimmed bowl, which occurs seven times.

In Early La Tène west-central Europe a total of 45 bronze vessels of Etruscan origin appear in graves. Only six different types are represented. Three occur just once: the Dürkheim tripod, Schwarzenbach amphora, and Ferschweiler kyathos. The best represented form is the *Schnabelkanne*, occurring 23 times. (Several *Schnabelkannen* have been recovered in graves in southwest Germany and eastern France which cannot be assigned to either the Late Hallstatt or the Early La Tène Period (Frey 1957, 236); these vessels are not included in the present discussion.)

	Late Hallstatt	Early La Tène
Total vessels	24	45
Types represented only once	8 (33%)	3 (7%)
Type best represented: number present	7 (29%)	23 (51%)

Two very different patterns are evident. In the Late Hallstatt context a wide range of different bronze vessel types are represented. In the Early La Tène graves over half of the total number are of a single type: the *Schnabelkanne*. Forty-two of the 45 Etruscan bronze vessels are one of three forms (*Schnabelkannen*, stamnoi, basins). A greater degree of standardization is apparent in the selection of vessels brought from the Mediterranean world during Early La Tène times.

SCHNABELKANNEN. Twenty-three of the 45 imported bronze vessels found on the middle Rhine are *Schnabelkannen*. (On the origin, chronology, and variation of this vessel form see Jacobsthal and Langsdorff 1929; Neugebauer 1943; Szilágyi 1951–1952; Frey 1955; Bouloumié 1968; 1973.) The greatest concentrations of these vessels occur in Etruscan contexts, and all of the features point to Etruscan manufacture (Neugebauer 1943).

Less certain are the chronological end-points of production. Etruscan bronze vessels cannot be dated with the accuracy of Attic painted pottery, and the chronology of the various forms is still being worked out. On the basis of the few datable grave groups in the Mediterranean world, Frey (1955, 29 n. 48) suggests a beginning date of *c.* 525 B.C. The end of production may lie around 400 B.C. (Bouloumié 1968, 399).

Stylistic and distribution evidence points to the city of Vulci as the source of the majority of *Schnabelkannen* (Neugebauer 1943, 237; Bouloumié 1968, 459). Unclear is whether Vulci was the only Etruscan city which manufactured the vessels, or whether other cities, particularly Tarquinia, Falerii, and Bisenzio, might have produced *Schnabelkannen* as well (Bouloumié 1968, 459).

Schnabelkannen occur in considerable numbers in central Europe and in Italy (fig. 5.7). The greatest concentration outside Italy is in the middle Rhineland; small numbers occur in Marne, scattered around central France, and in Bohemia and Austria. In Italy most occur in Etruria, at Bologna, and around Ancona. Jugs looking like *Schnabelkannen* are shown on an architectural terracotta from Velletri being used to pour wine into drinking bowls (Kossack 1970, 162 fig. 15). In Veneto in northeastern Italy a bronze belt hook from the Carceri cemetery at Este bears a scene of a server holding a *Schnabelkanne* and handing a drinking bowl to a reclining banqueter (Frey 1969, pl. 67 no. 18).

At Vulci, the city of origin of at least the majority of these vessels, six well-documented grave groups contain *Schnabelkannen*: Tomba a cassone (Jacobsthal and Langsdorff 1929, 16–17); Grave 34 (Gsell 1891, 81–83); Grave A (Pellegrini 1896, 286); Osteria Graves 45, 47, 50 (Frey 1955, 29–30 n. 48). Of these six graves, three contain two *Schnabelkannen*, three contain one. In addition, three each contain two or more other types of bronze vessel; and five of the six contain Attic fine pottery. All six of these graves at Vulci are rich by that city's standards and by Etruscan standards in general (Bouloumié 1968, 399). It is significant that the *Schnabelkannen* are associated with other vessels connected with wine drinking: other jug forms, ceramic amphorae, ceramic drinking-bowls, dippers, and footed cups. At the city at which the *Schnabelkannen* were produced, only individuals of above-average wealth received these vessels in their graves.

STAMNOI. One Etruscan bronze stamnos has been found in the Saarland – in Weiskirchen II (fig. 5.4). Elsewhere in the middle Rhineland stamnoi occur in the graves at Altrier, Dürkheim, and Basse-Yutz (2). The

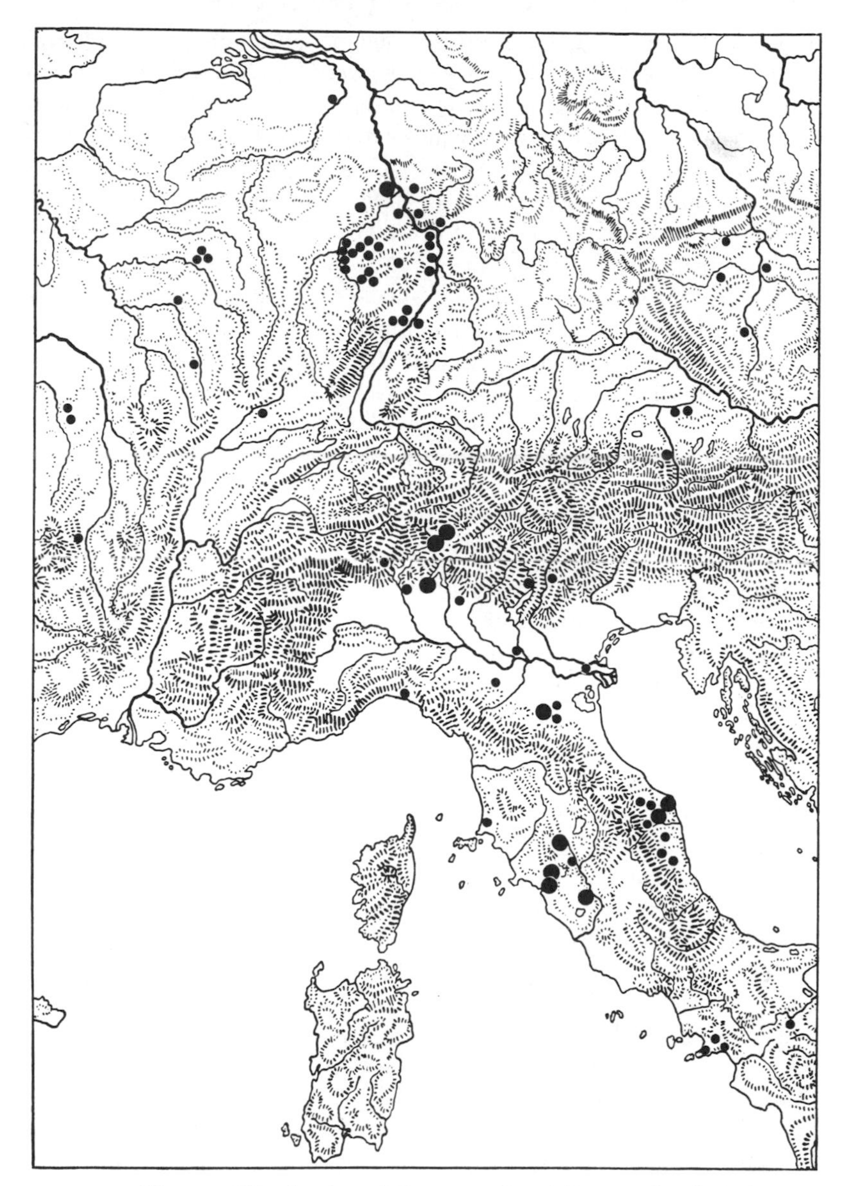

Fig. 5.7. Distribution of Etruscan *Schnabelkannen*. Small circles: 1–2 specimens; large circles: 3 or more specimens. Note concentration in the Saarland and surrounding areas.

Kleinaspergle find from northern Württemberg can be added to the group. One other stamnos has been recovered in west-central Europe, at Courcelles-en-Montagne in eastern France.

The stamnoi are not identical but share basic features of form, construction, and decoration. In the form of the handle attachments there is variation among the central European finds, and there are slight differences in overall shape. All of the central European stamnoi are Etruscan. On the basis of stylistic comparisons with other bronzes and of grave associations, they can be dated to the first half of the fifth century B.C.; Jacobsthal suggests a general dating of 475–450 B.C. for Etruscan bronze stamnoi as a whole (1944, 137), Riis more recently suggests a time of manufacture of 500–475 B.C. for the Weiskirchen, Kleinaspergle, and Dürkheim specimens (1959, 38).

Much of the evidence points to Vulci as the place of manufacture. For the Dürkheim specimen, stylistic comparison of the hippocamps on the handles with similar handles found at Vulci suggests an origin at that city (Neugebauer 1943, 244; Jacobsthal 1944, 136). For the other handles the issue is not as clear because of lack of comparable published material. Many stamnoi have been found in the cemeteries at Vulci (Beazley 1947, 248), and Riis (1941, 86) thinks it likely that all of the vessels came from workshops in that city. In any case distribution of finds and stylistic analysis point to central Etruria as the place of origin of the stamnoi. The overall distribution of the Etruscan bronze stamnoi shows two main areas of concentration, central Italy and west-central Europe.

In the Greek world (ceramic) stamnoi were used for mixing and storing wine and probably for storing other liquids as well (Philippaki 1967, xviii–xix). Only four recorded closed grave groups in Italy contain bronze stamnoi: two at Bologna, one at Spina, and one at Todi. No closed grave associations containing stamnoi are known from Vulci, where they were probably made. The Todi find (Schaaff 1969, 197 no. 13) has not yet been fully published; besides the stamnos, the grave contained a bronze stamnos-situla and a bronze basin with heart-shaped handles. The other three Italian graves contained at least 10 bronze vessels besides the stamnos, all associated with wine drinking in the Etruscan world: jugs, sieves, stamnos-situlae, mugs, small buckets, kyathoi, and basins. Each also contained Attic painted pottery of types used in drinking wine. The grave contexts suggest that bronze stamnoi formed part of the wine equipment and that they were owned and used by individuals of considerable wealth.

BASINS. In the middle Rhineland, 13 bronze basins from the Mediterranean world have been found. They were in seven graves, one of which contained one basin and six two basins each. The main formal distinction among the basins is between those with handles (two cast vertical handles with heart-shaped attachments) and those without. Five basins with handles occur (fig. 5.8), and seven without (the fragments of the second Thomm basin do not show whether a handle was present or not). In four graves (Armsheim, Hermeskeil, Rodenbach, and Zerf) the combination of a handled basin with a handle-less one occurs. In the Reinheim burial were two handle-less basins. In Waldgallscheid there was one handle-less basin.

Fig. 5.8. Bronze basin with handles from the rich grave at Rodenbach in the Rhineland–Palatinate. Diameter 35 cm.

On the basis of the bronze working and decoration, an Etruscan origin for the basins is generally accepted, and it is thought that they were made in the same workshops as the Schnabelkannen (Jacobsthal 1929, 46, 64; Jacobsthal and Langsdorff 1944, 138–139). In Italy, basins with handles with heart-shaped attachments have been found in three well-documented grave contexts: Bologna, Certosa Margherita, Tomba grande dei Giardini (Ducati 1928–1929); Spina, Valle Trebbe Grave 128 (Aurigemma 1960, I, 46–62, pls. 19–48); and Todi, San Raffaele (cited in Schaaff 1969, 197). Two handles of the type are recorded from Vulci, but without grave provenance (*ibid.*, 197). The Bologna and Todi graves contained stamnoi as well as basins and have been cited above. The Spina grave is one of the richest at that site, containing an abundance of bronze objects and Greek painted pottery. Chronology of the pottery suggests a date for the grave in the third or fourth quarter of the fifth century B.C. These three Italian burials indicate that basins occur together with wine vessels, and in graves of exceptional material wealth.

SCHWARZENBACH AMPHORA. This vessel has cast vertical handles with small Silenus figures seated at each handle base. It belongs to a small group of known bronze amphorae. An almost identical specimen was found at Vulci and is now in the Vatican Museums (Beazley and Magi 1939, I, pls. 8, 4). On the basis of stylistic comparisons of the Schwarzenbach amphora with bronze vessels known to have been produced at the workshops of Vulci, Riis (1941, 85; 1959, 38) suggests that it too was manufactured at that city, and dates the vessel to the second quarter of the fifth century B.C. (*ibid.*). Since ceramic amphorae were used largely in the service of wine, it is likely that an ornate bronze one such as the Schwarzenbach specimen was also intended for similar use.

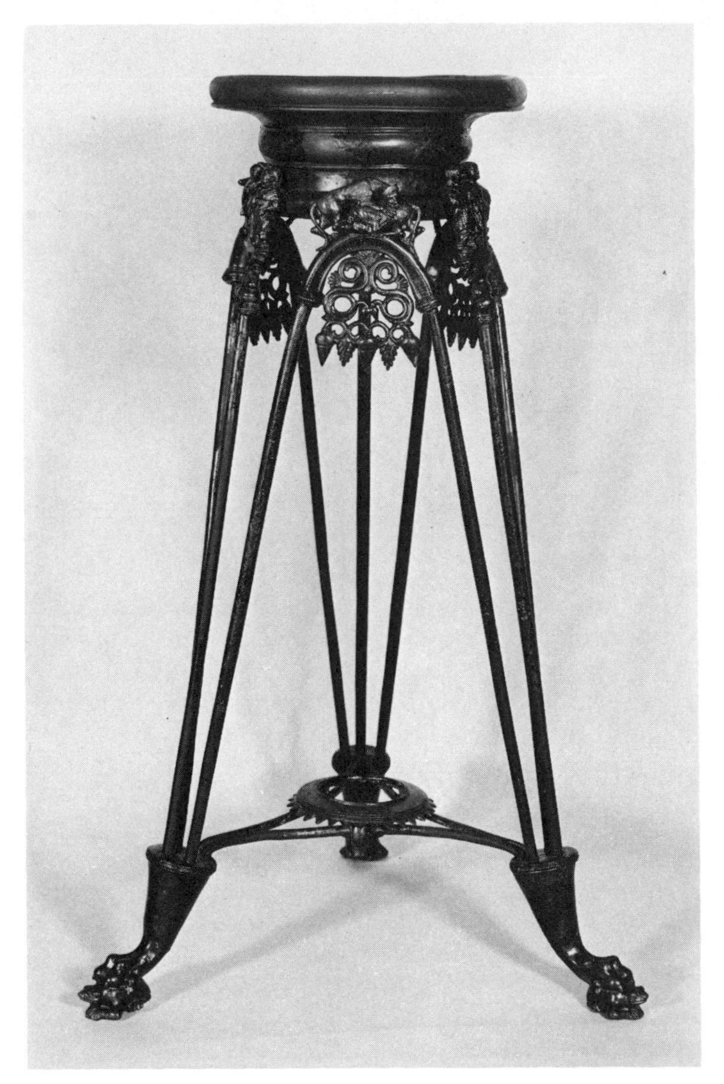

Fig. 5.9. Bronze rod-tripod from the rich grave at Dürkheim in the Rhineland–Palatinate. Height 57 cm.

DÜRKHEIM TRIPOD (fig. 5.9). Like the Greek tripods from the Late Hallstatt graves of Grafenbühl and La Garenne, the Dürkheim tripod is a rod-tripod (Riis 1939). Riis places it with 14 others in a series designated the 'ornate Etruscan group'. Of the 15, the sites of discovery of 13 are known. Eight (or nine, see Neugebauer 1923–1924) come from the cemeteries at Vulci, and another two were found elsewhere in Etruria. The other three come from Spina, the acropolis at Athens (fragment), and Dürkheim. The concentration of finds at Vulci and the close stylistic connections between the tripods and other bronzes found there and ascribed to the local bronze industry make an origin at that city very likely (Neugebauer 1943, 208). On the basis of stylistic comparisons and grave associations Riis (1939, 24) dates the group to the period 540–470 B.C.

Of the 13 tripods of known provenance, only three besides Dürkheim come from documented grave groups; none of these comes from Vulci: Todi (Savignoni 1897, no. II, 293; Riis 1939, no. 5); Falerii (Savignoni 1897, no. XI, 291 n. 3; Riis 1939, no. 14); Spina, Valle Trebbe Grave 128 (Aurigemma 1960, I, 46–62; pls. 19–48; Riis 1939, no. 10). Spina, Valle Trebbe Grave 128 has been mentioned in connection with the bronze basins; this grave contains a great wealth of bronze vessels and Attic painted pottery. The Todi grave, while not as richly outfitted as the Spina one, contains a rich inventory of bronzes, two ceramic vessels, and several items of jewelry. Finds reported from the Falerii grave do not give an impression of great wealth, though Attic painted pottery is present as well as a bronze figurine.

FERSCHWEILER KYATHOS. Kyathoi occur frequently in Etruscan graves which contain other bronze vessels and Attic painted pottery. Since the objects are small and only simply ornamented if at all, they appear to have been a minor item among the vessels. Information on distribution of finds of kyathoi is not readily available. Specimens similar to that at Ferschweiler occur in Etruscan burials of the same character as those containing the other imports in west-central Europe: *Schnabelkannen*, stamnoi, basins, and tripods. Vulci Grave A contained a kyathos, a *Schnabelkanne*, two basins, and a variety of other finds (Pellegrini 1896, 286). Spina, Valle Trebbe Grave 128, mentioned above for its rod-tripod and basin, also had four bronze kyathoi as well as a rich assemblage of Attic painted vessels and other bronzes. At Bologna, three kyathoi occur in the Tomba della Anfore Panatenaiche in the Arnoaldi cemetery, along with several painted Attic vessels, a bronze stamnos, and a number of other bronze objects (*Notizie degli scavi* 1882, 133–134). The specific function of the kyathos was apparently that of a small dipper (hence the high handle) which could be lowered into a large-mouthed vessel of wine in order to remove small quantities.

Greek pottery. No finds of Greek pottery have been reported in Early La Tène contexts in the Saarland. In the neighboring Rhineland–Palatinate two Greek ceramic vessels have been found, one in the rich grave of Rodenbach and one in a 'settlement pit' at Urmitz-Weissenthurm. At Rodenbach, an Attic red-figure kantharos was found in a grave also containing a *Schnabelkanne*, a bronze canteen, two bronze basins, an iron sword and three spearheads, gold jewelry, and other items. The vessel dates to the middle or second half of the fifth century B.C. (Jacobsthal and Langsdorff 1929, 25; Howard and Johnson 1954, 191–192; Dehn and Frey 1962, 204).

The find at Urmitz-Weissenthurm consists of a single sherd of Attic red-figure pottery from a pit thought to belong to a settlement (Jacobsthal 1934, 17); the piece has been dated by Jacobsthal to 460–450 B.C.

Also associated with Early La Tène materials are the two Attic kylikes from the rich grave of Kleinaspergle in north Württemberg; one is red-figure, the other black polished. Both date to around 450 B.C. (Dehn and Frey 1962, 204). In eastern France two finds of Attic pottery associated with Early La Tène objects are recorded: one is the red-figure kantharos in the grave at Courcelles-en-Montagne dating to the middle or second half of the fifth century B.C.; the other the red-figure kylix in the Marne rich grave of Somme-Bionne, dating to 430–420 B.C. (Dehn and Frey 1962, 204).

For the Early La Tène Period, as for the Late Hallstatt, the Attic painted pottery associated with native materials provides the most precise source of data for establishing the absolute chronology. The earliest date for any of the Attic pottery in the middle Rhineland is 460–450 B.C. suggested for the Urmitz-Weissenthurm sherd; all of the middle Rhineland and eastern French grave finds of Attic pottery date within the period 450–400 B.C., providing a *terminus post quem* of 450 B.C. for those graves.

Weiskirchen gold leaf band. The gold leaf cylinder from Weiskirchen II is unique. It is 3 cm wide and 4.7 cm in diameter. Around the middle of the band is a row of ten seated sphinxes with horned helmets in relief (Jacobsthal 1944, 136, 140; pl. 254*d*; Haffner 1976, pls. 15, 1). Opinions vary as to whether it is Etruscan (Jacobsthal 1944, 140; Megaw 1970, 70) or East Greek (discussion in Megaw 1975, 24). It may have been an ornament on a drinking horn (*ibid.*); the size and shape compare closely with those of the pair of sheet gold bands from Reinheim (Keller 1965, pl. 14). Gold ornaments for drinking horns are relatively common in Early La Tène rich graves (Mariën 1962; Jacobsthal 1944, 167; Haffner 1976, 46–50).

Imitation of Mediterranean elements

Most significant of the archaeological evidence for the adaptation of Etruscan styles and forms to central European tastes is the development of the Early La Tène art style. Early La Tène ornament is a new phenomenon in central Europe and represents a major departure from the artistic traditions of Urnfield and Hallstatt times (Jacobsthal 1944, 158; Megaw 1970; Frey and Schwappach 1973; Pauli 1978, 455). The Early La Tène style of ornament developed in the middle Rhineland, where the majority of the Etruscan imports have been found.

Components from several artistic traditions besides that of the native central European Hallstatt have been identified in Early La Tène art, among them Etruscan, Greek, Scythian, and Persian (Jacobsthal 1944,

Fig. 5.10. Gold arm ring from the grave at Rodenbach. Diameter 6.7 cm.

155–160). Stylistic analysis of the human and animal heads and floral motifs on gold and bronze jewelry (fig. 5.10), bronze vessels, and weapons from Early La Tène workshops often points to one of these artistic traditions as the source of particular traits. Recent studies have shown the rich abundance of Eastern imports and elements (borrowed traits) in Etruria during the Orientalizing Period of the seventh century B.C. The Greek and Eastern elements in Early La Tène art are most likely to have reached west-central Europe via the products of Etruria. Eastern Greek, Scythian, Persian, and other artistic traditions are represented in Etruria at this time, both by objects imported from the East (such as metal vessels) and by stylistic elements and decorative motifs adopted and integrated by Etruscan craftsmen into the local artistic milieux (see Maxwell-Hyslop 1956; Brown 1960; Johansen 1971).

Several objects from central Europe provide additional information about the impact of Etruscan material culture on that of the Early La Tène. Three bronze jugs from west-central Europe are based on the *Schnabelkanne* form but are richly ornamented with Celtic masks and animal heads; one is from Kleinaspergle (fig. 5.11) and two are from Basse-Yutz (Jacobsthal 1944, nos. 381*a*, *b*; see also the Dürrnberg jug from Austria, Megaw 1970, no. 72). Clay versions of the *Schnabelkanne* were also manufactured in west-central Europe (Schindler 1974, 37–39). Less like the *Schnabelkanne* in the form of the spout yet derived from that

Fig. 5.11. Bronze vessel based on the *Schnabelkanne* form, from Kleinaspergle (see pp. 35–36). Height 37 cm.

Etruscan form are the jugs with tube-shaped spouts from Reinheim and Waldalgesheim (Jacobsthal 1944, no. 387), both of which are engraved with elaborate La Tène linear ornament and have an animal figure perched on top of the lid (on this group see Dehn 1969).

The first bronze mirrors in central Europe appear during the Early La Tène Period; specimens have been found in the Reinheim burial, at Courcelles-en-Montagne in eastern France (Déchelette 1913*b*, pl. 32 no. 1), and at Hochheim on the Main (Jacobsthal 1944, no. 373). A connection between these objects and the flourishing Etruscan industry in bronze mirrors (Beazley 1950) is very likely.

Two-wheeled vehicles frequently occur in the Early La Tène rich graves, never four-wheeled wagons as in the Late Hallstatt context. Such two-wheeled carts or chariots are well represented in Etruria. One was found in a side chamber of the Regolini-Galassi tomb at Cerveteri

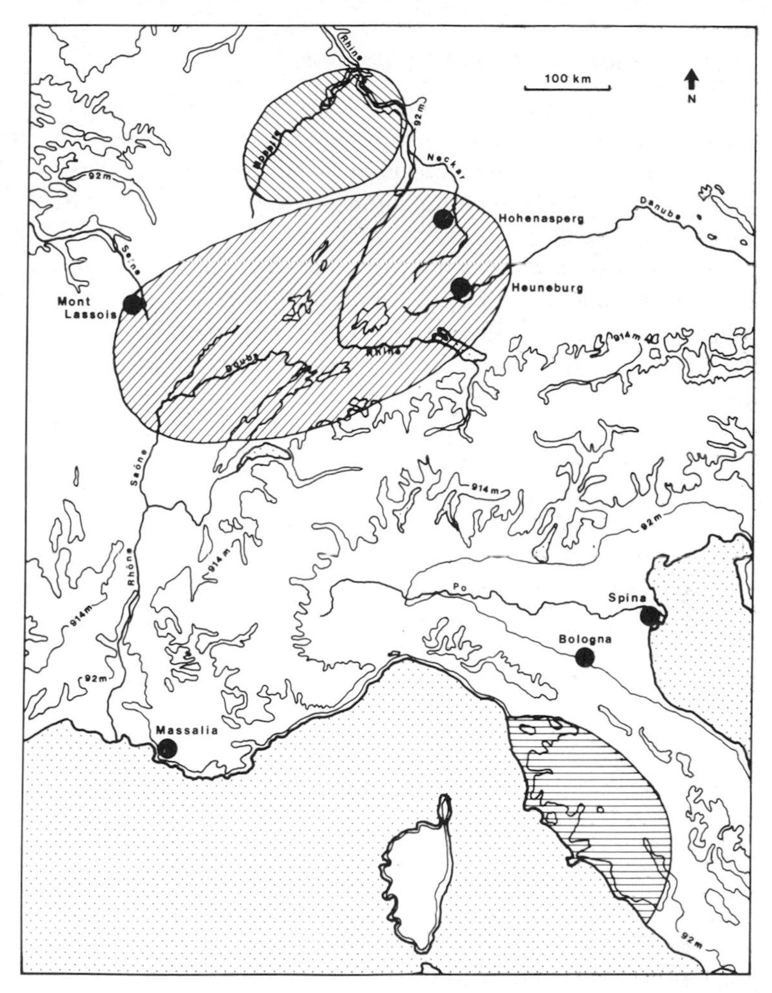

Fig. 5.12. Map showing the parts of west-central Europe and the Mediterranean world most directly involved in interactions. *Top shaded area*: the Saarland and environs, the region yielding the most evidence for interactions with Etruscan Italy during Early La Tène times. *Middle shaded area*: Baden–Württemberg, east-central France, and northwest Switzerland, the region yielding the most evidence for interactions with Greeks based at Massalia during Late Hallstatt times. *Bottom shaded area*: Etruria, the center of Etruscan civilization. Just north of Etruria across the Apennines are the fifth-century commercial cities of Bologna and Spina.

(Boethius 1962, 48 fig. 4*a*), another at Monteleone (Heurgon 1964, pl. 14). Representations of such vehicles appear on grave stelae at Bologna (Scullard 1967, pl. 92). (For further discussion of features of Early La Tène material culture indicating derivation from Etruscan Italy see Jacobsthal 1944, 155–160, and von Hase 1973.)

5.4 *Etruscan and central-European interactions*

Etruscan activity in Italy, including both Etruria and the Po Plain, was different in important respects from Greek activity in southern France. The interactions between Etruscans and central Europeans were probably correspondingly different from those between Massaliote Greeks and central Europeans.

The Etruscan imports of the Early La Tène Period probably arrived in central Europe across the Alps. None of the Etruscan vessel types which appear in the La Tène rich graves has been found in Provence or in the Rhône valley. Among the Greek objects (Attic pottery in particular) which do occur in the Rhône corridor and its environs, a sharp fall-off in numbers of finds is evident around 500–480 B.C., suggesting that Massalia's activities inland in France declined at that time (see p. 102 above). Archaeological evidence suggests that commercial interactions between Etruria and Massalia also declined markedly by about 500 B.C. (Benoit 1965, 43).

Both archaeological and historical evidence points to northern Italy as the immediate source area for the Etruscan bronzes in central Europe. All of the types in the Early La Tène graves – *Schnabelkannen*, stamnoi, basins, kyathoi, the rod-tripod – are represented at sites in the Po Plain, particularly at Bologna and Spina. Many *Schnabelkannen* have been found in the southern areas of the Alpine passes leading toward west-central Europe (fig. 5.7).

The Po Plain 600–400 B.C.

Two events in the historical tradition are of special importance here; both concern the peopling of the Po Plain during this period. One is the expansion of Etruscan civilization across the Apennines sometime around 530–520 B.C., the other the arrival of central Europeans (Celts) into the Po Plain.

Livy writes (V 33) that the Etruscans, whose home was in present-day Tuscany, in central Italy, expanded their territory northward into the Po Plain, and 'added the same number (of cities) beyond the Apennines, sending over as many colonies as there were original cities, and taking possession of all the transpadane region (except the angle belonging to the Veneti who dwell about the gulf) as far as the Alps.' Polybius states (II 17) that the Etruscans at one time held dominion over the rich plains of the Po, drawing from them part of their abundant resources.

The crossing of the Apennines mentioned by Livy probably took place during the last decades of the sixth century B.C. (Bloch 1968, 35; Mansuelli and Scarani 1961; Mansuelli 1960, 70; Chevallier 1962*a*; Scullard 1967, 198–199). The dating evidence is primarily archaeological. In the cemeteries at Bologna there appears in the last third of the sixth century B.C. an abundance of objects of Etruscan manufacture. These include bronze vessels of various kinds and are identical to grave goods found at the major Etruscan cities in Tuscany, such as Vulci, Cerveteri (ancient Caere), and Tarquinia. Archaeological evidence for the presence at the end of the sixth century B.C. of Etruscans or, if not ethnic Etruscans, persons 'Etruscanized' with respect to their grave assemblages, also occurs at Spina in the Po delta (Alfieri and Arias 1958, 160) and at Marzabotto (Mansuelli 1960), just south of Bologna in the foothills of the Apennines.

Bologna was the most important locus of Etruscan presence in the Po Plain. Even before the evidence for Etruscanization of the area around 530–520 B.C., Bologna was exceptional for its concentration of population, industrial activity, and commerce (Chevallier 1962*a*, 104; Mansuelli 1960, 69; Scullard 1967, 22–23). During Villanovan times the bronze industry at Bologna reached a high stage of development relative to other parts of Italy, and the quantities of bronze in Villanovan graves there attest to the material wealth of the area's inhabitants. Trade with Etruria is indicated by the presence in graves at Bologna of metal and glass objects from Tuscany (Chevallier 1962*a*, 104).

The location of Bologna is important: it is situated on the boundary of the Po Plain and the Apennines, on the natural route running along the northern edge of the Apennines from Rimini to Milan, later the Via Emilia of the Romans. Bologna is also located at the head of an important passage through the Apennines connecting the Po Valley with Tuscany.

Archaeologically the first phase of Etruscan Bologna (Felsina) is marked by the appearance, around 520 B.C., of graves in the Certosa cemetery which look very much like Etruscan graves in Tuscany with respect to grave inventories and structures (Zannoni 1876–1884). The ethnic identity of the individuals buried in these graves is unclear; in any case Etruscan material culture became dominant at Bologna around 500 B.C.

Outside of Spina, Marzabotto, and Bologna, there is little archaeological evidence for the presence of Etruscans or of Etruscanized native north Italians (Mansuelli and Scarani 1961, 245; Scullard 1967, 212–217; Colonna 1974). Archaeologists and historians generally regard Livy's statement about the Etruscans' founding of 12 cities in the plain as exaggeration (Bloch 1968, 35; Laviosa Zambotti 1953, 59; Scullard 1967, 198).

From the beginning of Etruscan presence in the southern part of the Po Plain at Bologna, Spina, and Marzabotto, the archaeological evidence attests to lively commercial interactions between these sites (Zuffa 1975). The trade between Bologna and Spina, and between Bologna and Etruria via Marzabotto, is well documented. At Bologna there is much Greek pottery which arrived at the port of Spina, and Etruscan bronzes, jewelry, and other items from Tuscany (Mansuelli and Scarani 1961,

248). In the cemeteries at Spina great quantities of bronzes from the workshops at Vulci in Tuscany have been found (Aurigemma 1960); these probably arrived at Spina via Marzabotto and Bologna. At Marzabotto, there is evidence for the mass production of bronze objects (Mansuelli and Scarani 1961, 247), probably for export to sites in the Po Plain. Bologna and Spina stand out from the rest of the Po Plain in the abundance of Attic pottery, Etruscan bronzes, and other Etruscan objects found in their cemeteries.

Etruscan penetration of the southern Po Plain had the effect of opening up to Etruscan consumption the riches of that river basin. Polybius, writing in the first century B.C., used only superlatives in describing the fertility of the Po lands and the richness of grain harvests there (Polybius II 14–15; see also Strabo V 1.12). Chevallier (1962*a*, 115) suggests that Etruria imported agricultural products from the Plain and perhaps salt from the marshes along the Adriatic, and in return gave Etruscan manufactured goods such as the bronze vessels and jewelry in the graves at Bologna.

Greek traders at Spina were also concerned with agricultural products of the Po Plain. Greek activity at that city was apparently aimed principally at securing grain from the Plain for transport to Greek cities (Vallet 1950, 51; Mansuelli and Scarani 1961, 265; Benoit 1965, 43). Besides grain, other agricultural and animal products such as meats and hides may have interested Greek merchants (Mansuelli and Scarani 1961, 265).

Etruscan penetration of the Apennines brought Etruscan civilization, or at least some elements of it, closer to central Europe. The dating of the early Etruscan presence in the Po Plain (cemetery finds at Bologna and Spina and the settlement at Marzabotto) corresponds closely to that of the first Etruscan objects which appear in Early La Tène contexts on the middle Rhine. Etruscan graves begin to appear shortly before 500 B.C. in the Po Plain, and the manufacturing dates ascribed to the imports in the Rhineland begin around 500 B.C. (see above). All of the Etruscan vessel types in the Rhineland are represented in the Po Plain. It is likely that the thriving commercial centers of the Plain were involved in the transmission of Etruscan bronzes northward to central Europe.

Etruscans were not the only new group to appear in the Po Plain during the period under consideration. Livy writes (V 33–34) of two phases of migration of Celts into northern Italy. The earlier occurred during the reign of Tarquinius Priscus in Rome (616–579 B.C.). According to Livy, the reason for this migration was overpopulation in central Europe; two groups of emigrants set out, one to settle in the Hercynian forests of east central Europe, the other in Italy.

Livy describes a second immigration of Celts into Italy around 400 B.C. They moved down the Italian peninsula, sacking the city of Rome in 396 B.C. The immediate reason for this immigration, according to Livy, was the allure of the wine and fruits of Italy. Livy notes that, prior to this event, wine had been brought from Italy to central Europe, thus introducing the beverage to the Celts; eager for more, they invaded Italy.

Polybius (II 17) writes that some Celts were close neighbors of the Etruscans in the Po Plain, and that in order to capture the excellent country in which the latter lived, a large army of Celts attacked suddenly, expelling the Etruscans from the Po Valley.

Some investigators have dismissed Livy's earlier migration of around 600 B.C. as fanciful popular tradition without basis in fact (e.g. von Duhn 1926). But some important recent work suggests that central Europeans were present in northern Italy by 500 B.C. (Hatt 1960, 368; Chevallier 1962*b*; Mansuelli 1960, 80; Peyre 1963; 1969; Scullard 1967, 218).

Livy suggests that the first group of central Europeans came around 600 B.C. in search of new farmland. Polybius' statement to the effect that some Celts were close neighbors of north Italian Etruscans may relate to groups which had settled in the Po Plain to farm. Bertrand and Reinach suggest (1894, 30) that Polybius was speaking of two distinct groups of Celts: one which lived peacefully with north Italians and a second which came along and attacked Etruscan settlements. In any event Livy and Polybius indicate that Celts were present in northern Italy well before the great invasion of around 400 B.C.

Several recent discoveries provide important evidence bearing on this question. At Casola Valsenio, about 20 kilometers southeast of Bologna, in a river valley in the Apennines, and at San Martino in Gattara, southeast of Casola Valsenio, small cemeteries dating to the first half and middle of the fifth century B.C. have been excavated. Some investigators argue that these contain graves of central Europeans. At Casola Valsenio were found burials containing weapons ornamented in Early La Tène style together with an Attic black-figure kylix dated to sometime between 500 and 470 B.C.; some authors have suggested that the graves are those of 'Celts' (Mansuelli 1960, 80; Scullard 1967, 218; Peyre 1969, 167–168). At San Martino 12 inhumation graves were found in a single tumulus, most containing rich assemblages of vessels, fibulae, weapons, and Attic pottery dating to the third quarter of the fifth century B.C. Bermond Montanari, the excavator (1969, 226), argues that the graves are Celtic, in part because of the location of offensive weapons at the shoulder of the deceased, a practice common north of the Alps. The practice of burying a body with sets of weapons (foreign to Etruscan custom) and the general similarity of the San Martino graves to the later Celtic burials at Dovadola makes a Celtic attribution of the San Martino burials at least a good possibility (Peyre 1969, 168; Frey 1971*a*, 374; Colonna 1974, 11).

In the cemeteries of Bologna, grave stelae depicting battles with central Europeans appear as early as the late fifth century B.C. (Frey 1971*a*, 375). Celts can be identified on the stelae by their characteristic weapons, and the stelae can be dated by chronologically diagnostic types in the graves with which they are associated.

Late Hallstatt fibulae from west-central Europe have been found in northern Italy; from the Bologna cemetery alone come six specimens (Frey 1971*a*, 376). The fibulae may have been brought indirectly through commercial mechanisms, but they may also have been brought directly by central Europeans. The graves at Bologna containing these fibulae may be those of central Europeans who settled at the commercial center of Bologna and were interred with otherwise local grave goods. The fibula types belong primarily to Hallstatt D3 of Zürn, the latest phase of the Hallstatt material tradition, beginning probably around 500 B.C. (see fig. 1.6).

Also significant here are two Early La Tène swords with ornamented bronze sheaths found in graves at the southern end of the Alpine valleys leading toward central Europe. The swords were recovered in Grave 31 at Castioni and Grave 108 at Cerinasca d'Arbedo. The closest parallels to these swords are a series recovered in the Early La Tène rich burials in the middle Rhineland and the Marne (Osterhaus 1969, 140 map fig. 3; Frey 1971*a*, 372). These two are the only ones of the group found south of the Alps, and may mark the graves of central Europeans.

The archaeological evidence, still rather sketchy though it is, combined with the information provided by Livy and Polybius about central Europeans in northern Italy, makes a Celtic presence in the Po Plain very likely during most of the fifth century B.C.

5.5 *Models for the contact and interactions*

The differences in the patterns of imports in the Late Hallstatt and Early La Tène contexts suggest a difference in the nature of the interactions between central Europeans and Mediterranean groups. Among the imports in Late Hallstatt associations is a wide variety of materials from the Mediterranean world: 13 different kinds of bronze vessels; much Attic pottery; transport amphorae; ivory, amber, and bone carvings; silk; gold jewelry (Vix diadem and perhaps the ornamental spheres from Ins and Jegenstorf). In the Early La Tène, although the number of bronze vessels from the Mediterranean world is nearly twice that during the Late Hallstatt Period, only six different types are represented. The only other imports reported are the Weiskirchen gold leaf band, the small number of Attic vessels, and the silk in the grave at Altrier.

Patterns in the occurrences of imported objects in the two contexts are also different. In both, the majority of graves containing imports have in them a single imported object, most often a bronze vessel. Among the Late Hallstatt burials, the greatest number of surviving imported objects is nine – at Vix. Grafenbühl contained five different kinds of imports; more were probably present before the grave was looted. In Early La

Tène graves the greatest number of imports is four – at Rodenbach. In the Early La Tène context there are no graves which compare with Vix and Grafenbühl in wealth of imported luxury goods. (Since the majority of rich graves known from both contexts were robbed, statistical comparison of these patterns is of doubtful significance. We can hope that more undisturbed graves will be found in the future, such as that at Eberdingen-Hochdorf, to provide a more solid basis for analysis.)

Economic and environmental differences between Greek Massalia and Etruscan Italy also suggest a difference in the nature of the interactions. Massalia was a commercial city; it was established as a trading center and owed its livelihood and prosperity to commerce. Many products necessary to the material survival of Massalia and its inhabitants were not locally available and had to be brought in. As Strabo tells us, the city had no rich agricultural lands, and had to import grain and probably other foodstuffs. Massalia probably had no forests in its immediate area, yet needed wood for the construction of buildings and ships. Lumber had to be brought from outside, perhaps from up the Rhône, as did other items needed for ship maintenance, such as pitch, resin, and tar.

Etruria was very fertile (Diodorus v 40; Livy ix 36; xxii 3) and surely did not import grain from great distances. From the time Etruscans arrived in the Po Plain around 520 B.C. (before any of the Etruscan objects in the Early La Tène graves were made), that great breadbasket was open to them. Etruria was largely covered by forest in Etruscan times (Fries 1962, 236–238; Heurgon 1964, 122–123); forest products which Greeks at Massalia may have sought in central Europe (pitch, resin, tar, wax, honey, skins and furs) were locally available to Etruscans (Heurgon 1964, 118–121, 122–123). They also had good sources of iron and copper ore and even some tin (p. 72 above).

Thus the archaeological and literary evidence suggests that Etruscans in Tuscany, and, after about 520 B.C. in the Po Plain, had access to most if not all of the natural products which western Greek traders were likely to have been acquiring in Late Hallstatt central Europe for consumption of the city of Massalia and for export trade to the eastern Mediterranean. For this reason, and because of the different patterns in the occurrence of the Mediterranean imports in Late Hallstatt and Early La Tène contexts, a model is required for the interactions that brought Etruscan bronzes to Early La Tène central Europe which is different from that proposed for the Late Hallstatt central European interactions with western Greeks.

Chevallier (1962*b*, 358) is probably correct in suggesting that, during the period 600–400 B.C., a variety of different groups of central Europeans arrived in northern Italy for a variety of different reasons. Livy's account (v 34) of the Celtic migration into Italy at around 600 B.C. suggests that some early groups may have come across the Alps in search of fertile land to settle. Polybius' remark (ii 17) about Celts' being close neighbors of

Etruscan groups in the Po Plain also intimates a settled agricultural population. In light of the natural richness of the Plain, it would not be surprising for central Europeans to settle and farm there.

Several investigators (Chevallier 1962*b*, 359; Mansuelli 1960, 80) suggest that central Europeans living in the Po area (perhaps having settled as farmers, perhaps having come originally as traders) served as intermediaries in commerce involving the shipment of Etruscan bronzes from the commercial center of Bologna northward across the Alps to central Europe. Chevallier (1962*b*, 365) proposes that Celts in Italy also took part in trade between Etruscans at Bologna and Greeks at Spina, acting as intermediaries in that network.

If Celtic agents in Italy were organizing the shipment of bronzes northward as trade goods, it is unclear why these bronzes should appear archaeologically only in the middle Rhineland and to a much smaller extent in the Marne valley and in Bohemia. In the Late Hallstatt context Greek interest was clearly directed to the major commercial, industrial, and demographic centers of west-central Europe. During the Early La Tène Period such centers were lacking, as far as we know. Why, then, should the Etruscan imports have been directed to one specific region of west-central Europe? If the bronze vessels had been trade items, what exchange goods might have been involved? As noted, most of the materials probably sought by Greeks in central Europe occurred naturally in Etruria and in the Po Plain; there is no obvious resource of the middle Rhineland which might have interested Etruscans.

Finally, if the bronze vessels arrived through a system of trade, how were they distributed in central Europe? In the Late Hallstatt context the distribution of luxury imports can be related directly to the economic system and to the social structure – the chief at each site had control of the objects and he decided how they were to be distributed among the members of his community. It is difficult to imagine that Early La Tène chiefs in the middle Rhineland were placing orders for bronze vessels with agents in Italy. Equally unlikely is a market system in central Europe through which wealthy individuals bought bronze vessels from Etruria.

Some central Europeans may have served as mercenaries in Italy during the sixth and fifth centuries B.C., though there is no direct evidence. Use of mercenaries is well documented from other parts of the Mediterranean world at this time (Cook 1962, 60; Andrewes 1967, 175, 181–182), and there was no shortage of battles and wars fought by Etruscan cities during the latter part of the sixth century and beginning of the fifth B.C. (Scullard 1967, 194–197). In this connection we can recall the prominence of weapons in the possibly Celtic graves of the fifth century B.C. in northern Italy. If some central Europeans served as mercenaries in Italy, they may have obtained Etruscan bronze vessels in return for their services. Since the *Schnabelkannen*, stamnoi, and basins were produced in great numbers, they may have constituted suitable means of payment. Some of the graves containing Etruscan bronzes in central Europe may be those of such mercenaries returned home, or of relatives of such individuals.

Groups of young men from central Europe may have gone to northern Italy during the sixth century B.C. to seek their fortunes, having heard accounts of the rich lands and cultural attractions of Mediterranean civilization. Through the interactions between central European centers of the Late Hallstatt Period and Greek Massalia, information must have spread throughout central Europe about the attractions of the Mediterranean world. If some central Europeans conceived of Italy as a land of riches and were free to leave their homes, they may have traveled there. According to Livy, this attraction was one of the motivating factors for the Celtic migrations across the Alps (pp. 132–133 above).

Etruscan Bologna was a great industrial and commercial center from about 520 B.C. on, and Spina was an international commercial city with resident Greek and Etruscan populations carrying on a large-scale trade in fine pottery, grain, and other products of the Po Plain. These rapidly expanding industrial and commercial centers of the late sixth and early fifth centuries B.C. would have provided many attractive opportunities for enterprising young men from central Europe. Some may have joined the labor force and worked in a variety of industries, on construction projects in the growing cities, or in the transportation of goods for trade. We know that foreigners were living and working in Greek cities at this time (Burford 1972, 35–36) and were participating in a variety of different aspects of the economy (Hasebroek 1933, 22–43, 101, 125; Finley 1973, 48, 79–80, 163). Other central Europeans may have set themselves up independently in the urban centers as craftsmen or merchants (as Demaratus did in Tarquinia, see pp. 73–74 above). It is likely that material wealth could have been acquired quickly by capable young men in the fast-growing urban centers of northern Italy. Indeed, through participation in the economic growth of these cities, central Europeans from the middle Rhine area may have acquired the bronze vessels which were later placed in their graves, and perhaps those of relatives, at home.

An ethnographic example which may offer some insight into the processes involved is described by Izikowitz (1951). Among the Lamet of Vietnam, many young men left their homes to work in teak forests and on plantations in Thailand. Their goal was to earn specific luxury goods of high prestige value at home, goods unavailable in their home territory. The prestige objects were bronze drums. Drums were precious to the Lamet because possession of them gave the owner prestige, and the drums could be used to pay the large bride-price necessary to acquire a rich wife (also resulting in increased prestige). If they could return home with a number of bronze drums, and make skillful use of them in social maneuvering (such as Sahlins (1963) describes for the rise of a Melanesian headman), these men could attain the highest status in the social system (Izikowitz 1951, 305). A mechanism something like this one may have been operating in the Early La Tène case.

The large number of Etruscan bronzes in the Rhineland might be explained by the development of a regular pattern of young men going to northern Italy and working in the cities there. It is clear from the archaeological evidence that there was a great deal of travel at this time across the Alps between central Europe and northern Italy (Wyss 1975). In the ethnographic example, Izikowitz (1951, 347) indicates that the period of work in Thailand became a regular feature of Lamet society; members of other societies living around the Lamet did not engage in the same activity. Perhaps only the cultural groups living in the middle Rhine area, where the majority of Etruscan objects are found, maintained the practice of working in the Po Plain, hence the absence of the imports in other parts of central Europe. This mechanism might also help to explain the wide range of wealth in grave goods associated with the imports, ranging from richly equipped graves such as Dürkheim, Rodenbach, and Reinheim to poorer ones such as Oberwallmenach and Marpingen. Some young men may have been unsuccessful at acquiring the bronzes they desired. Upon returning to central Europe different individuals would have had differing degrees of success at using their new status potential in the form of prestigious luxury goods for rising in the social status hierarchy and accumulating wealth in the form of gold jewelry, ornate bronze objects, and a chariot.

Probably more than one such mechanism was involved in the arrival of the Etruscan bronze vessels in Early La Tène central Europe. In any contact situation a variety of different mechansims operate at the same time under varying conditions and between different individuals. The model suggested here is consistent with the archaeological and historical evidence in central Europe and in northern Italy. I do not suggest that this mechanism was necessarily the one involved but that, until more data become available, it provides a consistent and constructive way of looking at the evidence and of accounting for the patterns observed.

6

Contact and culture change

beginning of the Late Iron Age

6.1 *Changes in the cultural system*

Since the nature of the interactions in the Late Hallstatt and Early La Tène cases was different, we can expect the results of those interactions to have been different in terms of culture change in central Europe.

Circulation subsystem. A small quantity of materials of foreign origin occurs in graves of the Late Hallstatt Period in the Saarland, including glass beads, lignite jewelry, and very rarely gold (Haffner 1965, 11; 1966*a*, 29; Schindler 1968, 62–65). No substantial increase occurs in the quantities present in the plain graves at the start of the Early La Tène Period. The rich graves contain Etruscan bronze vessels, elaborate gold jewelry, wheeled vehicles, and ornaments of coral and amber, but the plain graves do not appear to have been as affected by the increased presence of foreign substances in the rich graves as were the plain graves in Late Hallstatt Württemberg.

Manufacturing subsystem. As in Late Hallstatt Württemberg, the rich graves of the Early La Tène Saarland contain a variety of locally made luxury objects indicative of new specialized industries in working gold and bronze serving the needs of the elite. Unclear in the Early La Tène case is the location and organization of the industrial activities, since no evidence for the presence of economic centers has yet been identified. Aside from the elite luxury goods, it is unclear whether the production of bronze, iron, and pottery materials was centralized to the extent that it was at the Heuneburg (p. 83 above). Further research on large samples of objects recovered from both rich and plain graves would provide additional data on the organization of manufacturing activities in the Early La Tène context.

Settlement subsystem. None of the settlements excavated so far provides evidence of habitation sites comparable to the centers of Late Hallstatt Württemberg. Nor do large cemeteries exist which would suggest such concentrations of population. From the cemetery evidence Schindler (1965, 35) and Haffner (1976, 148–149) suggest that the settlement pattern was one of single farmsteads and hamlets. No substantial changes are apparent in the settlement organization during the Hallstatt and Early La Tène Periods.

Social subsystem. During most of the Hallstatt Period there is little differentiation in grave assemblages in the Saarland (Haffner 1966*a*, 130). At the end of the Late Hallstatt and start of the Early La Tène Period differentiation begins to become apparent. Richer graves are characterized by wheeled vehicles, wooden burial chambers, and exceptionally large tumuli. A very few such graves contain materials of the latest Hallstatt tradition (Schindler 1968, 62–65), but the majority contain Etruscan bronze vessels and local products of the Early La Tène tradition. None of the known rich Early La Tène graves is as richly outfitted as some of the Late Hallstatt burials in Württemberg and eastern France, such as Eberdingen-Hochdorf, Grafenbühl, and Vix. A difference in social organization is also suggested by the character of the gold jewelry. In the Late Hallstatt context, the gold neck rings present in so many of the graves are very similar to one another in form and decoration (Paret 1941–1942; Zürn 1970, 122–123 fig. 78). The similarity of these gold rings implies a standardized production at the centers around which they are found. Their frequent occurrence in rich graves at some distance from the centers suggests that they served as badges of status among the lesser chiefs in the Late Hallstatt social system (Zürn 1970, 122–128; Frankenstein and Rowlands 1978). The gold neck rings and other gold jewelry in the Early La Tène context are not so standardized, but each piece is different from all others. Each appears to have been commissioned individually and not manufactured as one of a series. This aspect of the gold jewelry supports the model of independent and roughly equal headmen or chiefs in the Saarland, in contrast to the structured hierarchy of big chiefs and lesser chiefs in Late Hallstatt Württemberg.

The changes which took place in the Early La Tène Saarland were thus different from those in Late Hallstatt Württemberg. In the two contexts, the appearance of a series of rich graves, containing Mediterranean luxury imports, ornate gold jewelry, ornamental weapons, and wheeled vehicles, is similar. Associated with this new elite group in each case is evidence for the development of new crafts industries in gold and bronze, and in foreign materials such as amber and coral, to serve the needs of the elite. In the Saarland there is no evidence for the emergence of centers of industrial and commercial activity nor of population. Neither does the quantity of foreign materials (amber, coral, glass, lignite, and jet) increase in the plain graves as it did in the plain graves in Late Hallstatt Württemberg. Finally, the burial evidence in the

Saarland does not suggest a ranked hierarchy of chiefs, nor is there clear evidence for distinctions between centers and hinterlands.

6.2 *Effects in central Europe*

The interactions between central Europeans and Etruscans brought about less severe dislocations in the cultural system of the Early Iron Age Saarland than did those between central Europeans and Greek traders in southern France. Among the individuals from the Saarland who went to northern Italy may have been some headmen of small hamlet communities who brought with them other members of their families and communities. If such a headman and his followers went to the commercial centers of the Po Plain to take advantage of the economic growth there, he may have enlisted the cooperation of his family and community in acquiring the sought-after prestige objects. Such cooperation may have been stimulated through the headman's giving communal feasts and redistributing a variety of material goods (Sahlins 1960*b*; 1963). Thus both common persons from the Early Iron Age Saarland and privileged individuals such as heads of families and small communities could have acquired the desired bronze vessels in northern Italy and returned home with them.

Once back in the Saarland, these individuals may have made use of their new prestige objects to gain further prestige and wealth by making strategic gifts to influential persons, by using the vessels to pay high bride-prices for wealthy brides, and perhaps by using them to trade for other goods, for services, and to build up obligations. Once in possession of such prestige goods from Italy (and perhaps others of organic substances which do not survive as well, such as the silk in the Altrier grave), the holders were in a favorable position to offer incentives and rewards (through giving feasts and other forms of redistribution) to their relatives and other members of their societies who would join in efforts of production to enhance the wealth, status, and power of the emerging headman or chief and thereby of his group (Sahlins 1960*a*, *b*; 1963). In such a way the specialized crafts industries producing gold jewelry, bronze vessels and other ornaments, and wheeled vehicles could be started and maintained by the emerging headmen in the Saarland. Active production of surplus materials by local communities, such as copper and iron, would have made possible the development of exchange systems for the importation of amber, coral, glass, gold, lignite, jet, and other materials represented in the rich graves and occasionally in the others.

There is no evidence in settlement structure and activities, distribution of objects, or burial patterns, that the emerging headmen organized production or trade on a scale approaching that apparent at the Heuneburg and other Late Hallstatt centers, probably because no customer was demanding products in the quantities sought by western

Greek traders. No centers developed; there was no great influx of foreign materials represented in the plain graves; and there is no evidence for the growth of a hierarchical structure among the elite, with big chiefs at centers and lesser chiefs coordinating production and transportation of materials at smaller sites. The absence of any standard badge of chiefly authority comparable to the gold neck rings in Late Hallstatt Württemberg underscores this absence of a centralized hierarchical structure in the cultural system.

The change in the Early La Tène context was one involving the introduction of a series of new objects into the Saarland and surrounding areas from the Mediterranean world, the emergence of a group of individuals controlling these objects and acquiring considerable material wealth in new kinds of fine crafts products, the growth of specialized crafts industries to serve their needs, and the development of a new art style based upon the forms and motifs of Etruscan bronze vessels and jewelry (Frey and Schappach 1973; von Hase 1973). In contrast to the Late Hallstatt instance, no profound reorganization of the economic and social subsystems of the society was brought about.

7
Conclusion

This book has presented a case study in the investigation of contact between societies and of changes brought about as a result of that contact. I have attempted to develop a general methodology for the archaeological study of contact and change. Through the examination of one particularly well-documented instance, I have tried to demonstrate the application of this methodology in such a way that it might be adopted by other archaeologists, with appropriate revisions and adaptations, for the study of other prehistoric contexts.

Contact has been an important factor in culture change throughout man's existence on earth. Interaction with other groups of human beings opens a society or a community to the influx of new raw materials, new finished products, and new ideas. The results of interaction with the outside world have played a major role in the development and growth of all societies. Besides introducing new elements, interaction brings about other changes in a society. In order for new elements brought in from outside to be adopted and integrated into a societal system, changes have to occur in that system to accommodate the new features. Many of the changes observed in historical and ethnographic contexts can be productively analyzed in terms of the introduction of new elements into the cultural system. Numerous studies of the experiences of European explorers and merchants in the Americas, Africa, and Asia have provided well-documented cases of interaction and of the resulting changes (see articles in Bohannan and Plog 1967; Walker 1972).

Prehistoric contact is frequently evident in the archaeological record particularly in the form of trade objects. The existence of trade necessarily implies contact, however direct or indirect it might be. In the last decade, trade studies in archaeology have demonstrated the vast quantity of evidence for exchange in prehistoric contexts, and have developed useful techniques for the investigation of trade systems. Yet few have concerned themselves with the culture changes which came about as a result of the contact and interaction between societies indicated by that trade (see Adams 1974).

Investigators in the field of cultural anthropology and related disciplines (especially social anthropology and sociology), through their concern with the study of cultural systems, their make-up and processes, have developed methodologies for the study of contact between societies and of the changes which occur as a result of interaction (Redfield *et al.* 1936; Herskovits 1938; Barnett 1953; Barnett *et al.* 1954; Rogers and Shoemaker 1971). Some of the methods so developed are directly applicable to archaeological problems. The present study is an attempt to demonstrate the value of such research strategies in studying mechanisms of interactions and processes of change in a prehistoric context.

Investigations in cultural and social anthropology provide important information on the circulation of goods in traditional societies. Mauss, Firth, Sahlins, and others have explained the principles by which goods circulate in non-Western societies. Of particular significance is the social context of exchange. The circulation of goods can be viewed as a form and expression of social interactions between members of a society and between members of different societies. This aspect of social behavior is integrated into the societal system as a whole, and does not exist as a separate economic sphere as it does today (Polanyi 1944). Of special importance for the understanding of systems of exchange is the role played by the leader of the social unit – the chief – who acts as a 'center' in the flow of goods.

Cultural anthropology also provides a rich body of data on interaction between societies and the resulting changes. Numerous case studies offer specific examples of contact and change, while theoretical works (Barnett 1953; Rogers and Shoemaker 1971) aim at describing and explaining the regularities apparent in different instances of contact and change. This literature provides a vital insight into the range of factors which affect the mechanisms of interaction and the processes of change. On the basis of such regularities we can often predict the kinds of changes likely to occur as a result of contact in any given situation. The archaeologist can make use of such regularities in the formulation of models for application to archaeological data.

Since the best evidence of contact in prehistoric contexts is often trade goods, as in the case explored in this study, it is in terms of these objects that a method has been outlined here. The types of goods traded and the contexts in which they appear can yield valuable information about the interactions. Among the most productive questions which can be asked are the following: What social stratum in the society was getting the trade goods? What kinds of objects were being traded? What was the purpose and value of the objects in their societies of origin? Were the objects mass produced goods or specially made pieces? Are the trade objects concentrated at particular sites or evenly scattered throughout the cultural landscape? Do different kinds of trade goods show different patterns of distribution? Were imported objects imitated by local craftsmen? As I have tried to demonstrate in the text, the posing of such questions can lead the investigator to important information about the interactions and the kinds of changes occurring.

The approach taken in this study depends upon the belief that patterned regularities exist in human behavior and in processes of culture change (Linton 1936; Kroeber 1948). The interpretation of the archaeological evidence presented here is based on information provided by cultural anthropologists about behavior and change in contemporary societies whose economic and social organization is probably not very different from those of the prehistoric societies under investigation. I have assumed that processes of culture change in the past operated according to the same principles as in recent times, and have attempted to account for the observed patterns of interaction and change in terms familiar to anthropologists and archaeologists working today.

Bibliography

SOURCES

Caesar. *The Gallic war*. Translation by H. J. Edwards. Loeb Classical Library, Harvard University Press. Cambridge, Mass. (1966).

Diodorus of Sicily. Translation by C. H. Oldfather. Loeb Classical Library, Harvard University Press, Cambridge, Mass. (1954).

Dionysius of Halicarnassus. *The Roman antiquities*. Translation by E. Cary. Loeb Classical Library, Harvard University Press, Cambridge, Mass. (1939).

Herodotus. Translation by A. D. Godby. Loeb Classical Library, Harvard University Press, Cambridge, Mass. (1963).

Livy. Translation by B. O. Foster. Loeb Classical Library, Harvard University Press, Cambridge, Mass. (1967).

Pliny. *Natural history*. Translation by H. Rackham. Loeb Classical Library, Harvard University Press, Cambridge, Mass. (1960).

Polybius. *The histories*. Translation by W. R. Paton. Loeb Classical Library, Harvard University Press, Cambridge, Mass. (1968).

Strabo. *Geography*. Translation by H. L. Jones. Loeb Classical Library, Harvard University Press, Cambridge, Mass. (1917).

Tacitus. *The complete works*. Translation by A. J. Church and W. J. Brodribb. Modern Library, New York (1942).

MODERN WORKS

Adams, R. McC. (1974). Anthropological perspectives on ancient trade. *Current Anthropology*, **15**, 239–249.

(1975). The emerging place of trade in civilizational studies. In Sabloff, J. A. and Lamberg-Karlovsky, C. C. (eds.), *Ancient civilization and trade*, pp. 451–465. University of New Mexico Press, Albuquerque.

(1977). World picture, anthropological frame. *American Anthropologist*, **79**, 265–279.

Alfieri, N. and Arias, P. E. (1958). *Spina: Die neuentdeckte Etruskerstadt und die griechischen Vasen ihrer Gräber*. Hirmer, Munich.

Ames, D. W. (1962). The rural Wolof of the Gambia. In Bohannan, P. and Dalton, G. (eds.), *Markets in Africa*, pp. 29–60. Northwestern University Press, Evanston, Ill.

Andrewes, A. (1967). *Greek society*. Penguin, Harmondsworth.

Angeli, W. (1970). Die Erforschung des Gräberfeldes von Hallstatt und der 'Hallstattkultur'. In *Krieger und Salzherren: Hallstattkultur im Ostalpenraum*, pp. 14–39. Römisch-Germanisches Zentralmuseum, Mainz.

Arnold, R. (1957). A port of trade: Whydah on the Guinea coast. In Polanyi,

K., Arensberg, C. M. and Pearson, H. W. (eds.), *Trade and market in the early empires: economies in history and theory*, pp. 154–176. Free Press, New York.

Aufdermauer, J. (1963). *Ein Gräberfeld der Hallstattzeit bei Mauenheim, Ldkrs. Donaueschingen.* Badische Fundberichte, Sonderheft 3, Freiburg.

Aurigemma, S. (1960). *La necropoli di Spina in Valle Trebba.* 'L'Erma' di Bretschneider, Rome.

Bailey, B. L. (1940). The exportation of Attic black-figure ware. *Journal of Hellenic Studies*, **60**, 60–70.

Barnett, H. G. (1953). *Innovation: the basis of cultural change.* McGraw-Hill, New York.

Barnett, H. G., Broom, L., Siegel, B. J., Vogt, E. Z. and Watson, J. B. (1954). Acculturation. *American Anthropologist*, **56**, 973–1000.

Beazley, J. D. (1947). *Etruscan vase-painting.* Clarendon, Oxford.

(1950). The world of the Etruscan mirror. *Journal of Hellenic Studies*, **69**, 1–17.

Beazley, J. D. and Magi, F. (1939). *La raccolta Benedetto Guglielmi nel museo Gregoriano etrusco.* Città del Vaticano, Rome.

Beck, C. W., Liu, T. and Nunan, R. (1975). Die Herkunft der Bernsteinfunde vom Hagenauer Forst. *Bericht der Staatlichen Denkmalpflege im Saarland*, **22**, 5–17.

Belshaw, C. S. (1965). Traditional exchange and modern markets. Prentice-Hall, Englewood Cliffs, New Jersey.

Benoit, F. (1955). Amphores grecques d'origine ou de provenance marseillaise. *Revue d'Etudes Ligures*, **21**, 32–43.

(1956*a*). Relations de Marseille grecque avec le monde occidental. *Revue d'Etudes Ligures*, **22**, 5–32.

(1956*b*). Epaves de la côte de Provence: typologie des amphores. *Gallia*, **14**, 23–34.

(1965). *Recherches sur l'hellénisation du Midi de la Gaule.* Annales de la Faculté des Lettres, Aix-en-Provence, No. **43**.

Bermond Montanari, G. (1969). La necropoli protostorica di S. Martino in Gattara (Ravenna). *Studi Etruschi*, **37**, 213–228.

Bersu, G. (1922). Die Heunenburg (Markung Upflamör, O. A. Riedlingen). *Fundberichte aus Schwaben*, N.S. **1**, 46–60.

Bersu, G. and Goessler, P. (1924). Der Lochenstein bei Balingen. *Fundberichte aus Schwaben*, N.S. **2**, 73–103.

Bertaux, J.-P. (1977). Das Briquetage an der Seille in Lothringen. *Archäologisches Korrespondenzblatt*, **7**, 261–272.

Bertrand, A. and Reinach, S. (1894). *Les Celtes dans les vallées du Pô et du Danube.* Ernest Leroux, Paris.

Biel, J. (1978). Das frühkeltische Fürstengrab von Eberdingen-Hochdorf, Landkreis Ludwigsburg. *Denkmalpflege in Baden-Württemberg*, **7**, 168–175.

(1979). Ein Fürstengrabhügel der späten Hallstattzeit bei Eberdingen-Hochdorf, Kreis Ludwigsburg. *Archäologische Ausgrabungen 1978*, 27–35.

Bittel, K. (1934). *Die Kelten in Württemberg.* De Gruyter, Berlin.

Bittel, K. and Rieth, A. (1951). *Die Heuneburg an der oberen Donau.* W. Kohlhammer, Stuttgart and Cologne.

Blanc, A. (1958). Le commerce de Marseille dans le bassin du Rhône d'après les trouvailles de céramique. *Revue archéologique de l'Est et du Centre-Est*, **9**, 113–121.

Bloch, M. (1953). *The historian's craft.* Translation by P. Putnam. Knopf, New York.

(1961). *Feudal society*. Translation by L. A. Manyon. University of Chicago Press, Chicago.
Bloch, R. (1968). *Les Etrusques*, 5th edition. Presses Universitaires de France, Paris.
Boardman, J. (1964). *The Greeks overseas*. Penguin, Harmondsworth.
(1973). *The Greeks overseas*, 2nd edition. Penguin, Harmondsworth.
Boethius, A. (ed.), (1962). *Etruscan culture, land and people*. Translation by N. G. Sahlin. Columbia University Press, New York.
Bohannan, P. and Dalton, G. (eds.), (1962). *Markets in Africa*. Northwestern University Press, Evanston, Ill.
Bohannan, P. and Plog, F. (eds.), (1967). *Beyond the frontier: social process and cultural change*. Natural History Press, Garden City.
Böhner, K. (1970). Die Franken. In Böhner, K., Ellmers, D. and Weidemann, K. (eds.), *Das frühe Mittelalter: Führer durch das Römisch-Germanische Zentralmuseum in Mainz*, pp. 75–125. Zabern, Mainz.
Bohnsack, D. (1976). Bernstein und Bernsteinhandel. In Hoops, J. (ed.), *Reallexikon der germanischen Altertumskunde*, 2nd edition, vol. 2, pp. 290–292. De Gruyter, Berlin.
Bökönyi, S. (1974). *History of domestic mammals in central and eastern Europe*. Akadémiai Kaidó, Budapest.
von Bothmer, D. (1965). Review of Diehl, E., *Die Hydria* (1964). *Gnomon*, **37**, 599–608.
Bouloumié, B. (1968). Les oenochoés à bec en bronze des musées d'Etruria centrale e méridionale. *Mélanges d'archéologie et d'histoire*, **80** (2), 399–460.
(1973). Les oenochoés en bronze du type *Schnabelkanne* en France et en Belgique. *Gallia*, **31**, 1–35.
Braudel, F. (1972). *The Mediterranean and the Mediterranean world in the age of Philip II*. Translation by S. Reynolds. Harper and Row, New York.
Brown, J. A. (ed.), (1971). *Approaches to the social dimensions of mortuary practices*. Memoirs of the Society for American Archaeology, 25.
Brown, W. L. (1960). *The Etruscan lion*. Clarendon, Oxford.
Burford, A. (1972). *Craftsmen in Greek and Roman society*. Thames and Hudson, London.
Cambi, L. (1957). Problemi della metallurgia etrusca. In *Tyrrhenica: soggi di studi etruschi*, pp. 97–116. Accademia di Scienze e Lettere, Milan.
Camporeale, G. (1969). *I commerci di Vetulonia in età orientalizzante*. Sansoni, Florence.
Carcopino, J. (1957). *Promenades historiques aux pays de la dame de Vix*. L'Artisan du livre, Paris.
Carr, E. H. (1961). *What is history?* Macmillan, London.
Cary, M. (1924). The Greeks and ancient trade with the Atlantic. *Journal of Hellenic Studies*, **44**, 166–179.
(1949). *The geographic background of Greek and Roman history*. Clarendon, Oxford.
Champion, S. (1976). Coral in Europe: commerce and Celtic ornament. In Duval, P.-M. and Hawkes, C. (eds.), *Celtic art in ancient Europe*, pp. 29–37. Seminar Press, London.
Chang, K. C. (1975). Ancient trade as economics or as ecology. In Sabloff, J. A. and Lamberg-Karlovsky, C. C. (eds.), *Ancient civilization and trade*, pp. 211–224. University of New Mexico Press, Albuquerque.
Charbonneaux, J. (1953). Le mobilier funéraire de la tombe de Vix. *La Revue des Arts*, **3**, 198–202.
(1959). *Les bronzes grecs*. Presses Universitaires de France, Paris.
Charles, J. A. (1975). Where is the tin? *Antiquity*, **49**, 19–24.

Chevallier, R. (1962*a*). L'Italie du nord au seuil de l'histoire: Villanoviens et Etrusques. *Latomus*, **21**, 99–123.
(1962*b*). La Celtique du Pô: positions des problèmes. *Latomus*, **21**, 356–370.
Childe, V. G. (1950). *Prehistoric migrations in Europe*. Instituttet for Sammenlignende Kulturforskning, Oosterhout.
Chorley, R. J. and Haggett, P. (eds.), (1971). *Models in geography*. Methuen, London.
Cianfarani, V. (1969). *Antiche civiltà d'Abruzzo*. De Luca, rome.
Cipolla, C. M. (1970). Chinese mandarins and the self-ringing bell. In Cipolla, C. M., *European culture and overseas expansion*, pp. 149–170. Penguin, Harmondsworth.
Clark, G. (1957). *Archaeology and society*, 3rd edition. Methuen, London.
Clarke, D. L. (1968). *Analytical archaeology*. Methuen, London.
(1972). Models and paradigms in contemporary archaeology. In Clarke, D. L. (ed.), *Models in archaeology*, pp. 1–60. Methuen, London.
(1976). The Beaker network – social and economic models. In Lanting, J. N. and van der Waals, J. D. (eds.), *Glockenbecher Symposium*, pp. 459–477. Fibula-Van Dishoeck, Bussum/Haarlem.
Clavel-Lévêque, M. (1974). Das griechische Marseille: Entwicklungsstufen und Dynamik einer Handelsmacht. In Welskopf, E. C. (ed.), *Hellenische Poleis*, vol. 2, pp. 855–969. Akademie-Verlag, Berlin.
Colonna, G. (1974). Richerche sugli Etruschi e sugli Umbri a nord degli Appennini. *Studi Etruschi*, **42**, 3–24.
Cook, R. M. (1959). Die Bedeutung der bemalten Keramik für den griechischen Handel. *Jahrbuch des Deutschen Archäologischen Instituts*, **74**, 114–123.
(1962). *The Greeks until Alexander*. Thames and Hudson, London.
(1972). *Greek painted pottery*, 2nd edition. Methuen, London.
Crivelli, A. (1946). Presentazione dal ripostiglio di un fonditore di bronzi dell'epoca del ferro scoperto ad Arbedo. *Revue des Etudes Ligures*, **12**, 59–79.
Curtin, P. D. (1975). *Economic change in precolonial Africa*. University of Wisconsin Press, Madison.
Dalton, G. (1977). Aboriginal economies in stateless societies. In Earle, T. K. and Ericson, J. E. (eds.), *Exchange systems in prehistory*, pp. 191–212. Academic Press, New York.
Dämmer, H.-W. (1978). *Die bemalte Keramik der Heuneburg*. Philipp von Zabern, Mainz.
Dayet, M. (1967). Recherches archéologiques au 'camp du Château' (Salins) (1955–1959). *Revue archéologique de l'Est et du Centre-Est*, **18**, 52–106.
Déchelette, J. (1913*a*). *Manuel d'archéologie préhistorique, celtique, et gallo-romaine*, vol. 2, pt 2: *Premier âge du fer*. Picard, Paris.
(1913*b*). Le tumulus de la Motte Saint-Valentin (Commune de Courcelles-en-Montagne, Haute-Marne). In Déchelette, J., *La collection Millon*, pp. 101–151. Geuthner, Paris.
(1914). *Manuel d'archéologie préhistorique, celtique, et gallo-romaine*, vol. 2, pt 3: *Second âge du fer*. Picard, Paris.
Dehn, W. (1940). Thomm 'Hübel'. *Trierer Zeitschrift*, **15**, 49.
(1950). Vor- und frühgeschichtliche Bodendenkmale aus dem Ries. *Jahrbuch des Historischen Vereins für Nördlingen und das Ries*, **23**, 5–52.
(1951). Einige Bemerkungen zu süddeutschem Hallstattglas. *Germania*, **29**, 25–34.
(1957). Die Heuneburg beim Talhof unweit Riedlingen (Kr. Saulgau): Periode IV nach den Ergebnissen der Grabungen 1950 bis 1955. *Fundberichte aus Schwaben*, N.S. **14**, 78–99.

(1962–1963). Frühe Drehscheibenkeramik nördlich der Alpen. *Alt-Thüringen*, **6**, 372–382.
(1965). Die Bronzeschüssel aus dem Hohmichele, Grab VI, und ihr Verwandtkreis. *Fundberichte aus Schwaben*, N.S. **17**, 126–134.
(1969). Keltische Röhrenkannen der älteren Latènezeit. *Památky Archaeologické*, **60**, 125–133.
(1971). Hohmichele Grab 6 – Hradenin Grab 28 – Vače (Watsch) Helmgrab: Ein Nachtrag zu den späthallstättischen Bronzeschüsseln. *Fundberichte aus Schwaben*, N.S. **19**, 82–88.
(1974). Einige Bemerkungen zum eisenzeitlichen Befestigungswesen in Mitteleuropa. In *Symposium zu Problemen der jüngeren Hallstattzeit in Mitteleuropa*, pp. 125–136. Slovakian Academy of Sciences, Bratislava.
Dehn, W. and Frey, O.-H. (1962). Die absolute Chronologie der Hallstatt- und Frühlatènezeit Mitteleuropas auf Grund des Südimports. In *Congresso Internazionale delle Scienze Preistoriche e Protostoriche* **6**, *Atti*, vol. 3, pp. 197–208.
Dennis, G. (1883). *The cities and cemeteries of Etruria*, 3rd edition. John Murray, London.
Diehl, E. (1964). *Die Hydria: Formgeschichte und Verwendung im Kult des Altertums.* Zabern, Mainz.
van Dorp, P. A. and van Royen, R. A. (1977). The Tarasque de Noves. *Talanta*, **8–9**, 33–51.
Drack, W. (1949–1950). Hallstatt II/I-Bronzen und -Keramik von Lenzburg, Kt. Aargau. *Jahrbuch der Schweizerischen Gesellschaft für Urgeschichte*, **40**, 232–256.
(1950). Die Früheisenzeit der Schweiz im Überblick. In *Congrès International des Sciences Préhistoriques et Protohistoriques* **3**, *Actes*, pp. 279–281.
(1957). Die Hallstattzeit im Mittelland und Jura. In *Repertorium der Ur- und Frühgeschichte der Schweiz*, vol. 3: *Die Eisenzeit der Schweiz*, pp. 7–14. Schweizerische Gesellschaft für Urgeschichte, Zurich.
(1964). *Ältere Eisenzeit der Schweiz: Die Westschweiz. Materialhefte zur Ur- und Frühgeschichte der Schweiz*, vol. 4.
(ed.) (1969). *Ur- und frühgeschichtliche Archäologie der Schweiz*, vol. 2: *Die jüngere Steinzeit.* Schweizerische Gesellschaft für Ur- und Frühgeschichte, Basel.
(ed.) (1971). *Ur- und frühgeschichtliche Archäologie der Schweiz*, vol. 3: *Die Bronzezeit.* Schweizerische Gesellschaft für Ur- und Frühgeschichte, Basel.
(1972–1973). Waffen und Messer der Hallstattzeit aus dem schweizerischen Mittelland und Jura. *Jahrbuch der Schweizerischen Gesellschaft für Urgeschichte*, **57**, 119–168.
(1974). Die späte Hallstattzeit im Mittelland und Jura. In Drack, W. (ed.), *Ur- und frühgeschichtliche Archäologie der Schweiz*, vol. 4: *Die Eisenzeit*, pp. 19–34. Schweizerische Gessellschaft für Ur- und Frühgeschichte, Basel.
Driehaus, J. (1965). 'Fürstengräber' und Eisenerze zwischen Mittelrhein, Mosel und Saar. *Germania*, **43**, 32–49.
(1966). Zur Verbreitung der eisenzeitlichen Situlen im mittelrheinischen Gebirgsland. *Bonner Jahrbücher*, **166**, 26–47.
Duby, G. (1974). *The early growth of the European economy.* Translation by H. B. Clarke. Cornell University Press, Ithaca.
Ducati, P. (1928–1929). Una tomba di Felsina. *Dedalo*, **9**, 323–353.
(1937). *Tarquinii, fasc. I: Le pitture delle Tombe delle Leonesse e dei Vasi Dipinti.* Monumenti della pittura antica scoperti in Italia. La Libreria dello Stato, Rome.

von Duhn, F. (1926). Italien. In Ebert, M. (ed.), *Reallexikon der Vorgeschichte*, vol. 6, pp. 286–296. De Gruyter, Berlin.

Dunbabin, T. J. (1948). *The western Greeks*. Clarendon, Oxford.

Dušek, S. (1977). Zur sozialökonomischen Interpretation hallstattzeitlicher Fundkomplexe der Südwest-Slowakei. In Herrmann, J. (ed.), *Archäologie als Geschichtswissenschaft*, pp. 177–185. Deutsche Akademie der Wissenschaften, East Berlin.

Earle, T. K. (1977). A reappraisal of redistribution: complex Hawaiian chiefdoms. In Earle, T. K. and Ericson, J. E. (eds.), *Exchange systems in prehistory*, pp. 213–232. Academic Press, New York.

Earle, T. K. and Ericson, J. E. (eds.), (1977). *Exchange systems in prehistory*. Academic Press, New York.

Eichler, J. (1961). Mineralogische und geologische Untersuchungen von Bohnerzen in Baden-Württemberg. *Neues Jahrbuch für Mineralogie*, **97**, 51–111.

Engels, H.-J. (1967). *Die Hallstatt- und Latènekultur in der Pfalz*. Pfälzische Gesellschaft zur Förderung der Wissenschaften, Speyer.

(1972). Der Fürstengrabhügel von Rodenbach. *Bonner Hefte zur Vorgeschichte*, **3**, 25–52.

Engels, H.-J. and Kilian, L. (1970). Das Hügelgräberfeld von Miesau, Kreis Kusel. *Mitteilungen des Historischen Vereins der Pfalz*, **68**, 158–182.

Erb, H. (1969). Ur- und frühgeschichtliche Pfade, Siedlungen und Streufunde längs der San Bernardinoroute von der Luzisteig bis in die Mesolcina. *Schriftenreihe des Rätischen Museums, Chur*, **5**, 3–17.

Filow, B. D. (1927). *Die archäische Nekropole von Trebenischte am Ochridasee*. De Gruyter, Berlin.

Finley, M. I. (1959). Was Greek civilization based on slave labour? *Historia*, **8**, 145–164.

(1962). Classical Greece. In *Deuxième conférence internationale d'histoire économique*. pp. 11–35. Mouton, Paris.

(1965). *The world of Odysseus*. Viking Press, New York.

(1973). *The ancient economy*. Chatto and Windus, London.

Firth, R. (1929). *Primitive economics of the New Zealand Maori*. Routledge, London.

(1965). *Primitive Polynesian economy*, 2nd edition. Routledge and Kegan Paul, London.

Fischer, F. (1967). Alte und neue Funde der Latène-Periode aus Württemberg. *Fundberichte aus Schwaben*, N.S. **18**, pt 1, 61–106.

(1973). KEIMHΛIA: Bemerkungen zur kulturgeschichtlichen Interpretation des sogenannten Südimports in der späten Hallstatt- und frühen Latène-Kultur des westlichen Mitteleuropa. *Germania*, **51**, 436–459.

Flannery, K. V. (1968*a*). The Olmec and the valley of Oaxaca: a model for inter-regional interaction in Formative times. In *Dumbarton Oaks Conference on the Olmec*, pp. 79–117. Dumbarton Oaks, Washington, D.C.

(1968*b*). Archaeological systems theory and early Mesoamerica. In Meggers, B. J. (ed.), *Anthropological archaeology in the Americas*. pp. 67–87. Anthropological Society of Washington, Washington, D.C.

Foster, G. M. (1962). *Traditional cultures and the impact of technological change*. Harper and Brothers, New York.

Frankenstein, S. and Rowlands, M. J. (1978). The internal structure and regional context of Early Iron Age society in southwestern Germany. *Institute of Archaeology Bulletin* **15**, 73–112.

Frei, H. (1965–1966). Der frühe Eisenerzbergbau im nördlichen Alpenvorland. *Jahresbericht der bayerischen Bodendenkmalpflege*, **6–7**, 67–137.
Frey, O.-H. (1955). Eine etruskische Bronzeschnabelkanne. *Annales littéraires de l'Université de Besançon*, ser. 2, vol. 2, fasc. 1, 4–30.
(1957). Die Zeitstellung des Fürstengrabes von Hatten im Elsass. *Germania*, **35**, 229–249.
(1963). Zu den 'rhodischen' Bronzekannen aus Hallstattgräbern. *Marburger Winckelmann-Programm*, pp. 18–26. Kunstgeschichtliches Seminar, Marburg/Lahn.
(1969). *Die Entstehung der Situlenkunst.* De Gruyter, Berlin.
(1971*a*). Fibeln vom westhallstättischen Typus aus dem Gebiet südlich der Alpen. In *Oblatio: Raccolta di studi di antichità in onore del Prof. Aristide Calderini*, pp. 355–386. Noseda, Como.
(1971*b*). Die Goldschale von Schwarzenbach. *Hamburger Beiträge zur Archäologie*, **1** (pt 2), 85–100.
(1976). The chariot tomb from Adria. In Megaw, J. V. S. (ed.), *To illustrate the monuments: essays on archaeology presented to Stuart Piggott*, pp. 171–179. Thames and Hudson, London.
Frey, O.-H. and Schwappach, F. (1973). Studies in early Celtic design. *World Archaeology*, **4**, 339–356.
Fried, M. H. (1960). On the evolution of social stratification and the state. In Diamond, S. (ed.), *Culture in history*, pp. 713–731. Columbia University Press, New York.
(1967). *The evolution of political society.* Random House, New York.
Fries, C. (1962). Forest and soil in Etruria. In Boethius, A. (ed.), *Etruscan culture, land and people.* Translated by N. G. Sahlin, pp. 231–276. Columbia University Press, New York.
Gall, P. L. and Saxe, A. A. (1977). The ecological evolution of culture: the state as predator in succession theory. In Earle, T. K. and Ericson, J. E. (eds.), *Exchange systems in prehistory*, pp. 255–268. Academic Press, New York.
Gallet de Santerre, H. (1962). A propos de la céramique grecque de Marseille. *Revue des Etudes Anciennes*, **64**, 378–403.
Gardiner, P. (1952). *The nature of historical explanation.* Clarendon Press, Oxford.
Garscha, F. and Rest, W. (1938). Eine Hallstatt- und Latène-Siedlung am Mägdeberg (Hegau). *Marburger Studien*, pp. 54–69. Wittich, Darmstadt.
Gerhard, E. (1856). Etruskischer Goldschmuck aus den Mosellanden. *Bonner Jahrbücher*, **23**, 131–134, 194–196.
Gerlach, R. (1967). *Tierknochenfunde von der Heuneburg.* Naturwissenschaftliche Untersuchungen zur Vor- und Frühgeschichte in Württemberg und Hohenzollern, vol. 7, Stuttgart.
Gersbach, E. (1969). Heuneburg-Aussensiedlung – jüngere Adelsnekropole. *Fundberichte aus Hessen*, supplement 1, 29–34.
(1971). Vorläufige Ergebnisse der Ausgrabungen im Bereich der Südostecke der Burg 1959–1969: Die Siedlungsstadien der Periode IV. In Kimmig, W. and Gersbach, E., Die Grabungen auf der Heuneburg 1966–1969. *Germania*, **49**, 61–91.
(1975). Das Modell der Heuneburg. In *Ausgrabungen in Deutschland 1950–1975*, vol. 3, pp. 317–319. Römisch-Germanisches Zentralmuseum, Mainz.
(1976). Das Osttor (Donautor) der Heuneburg bei Hundersingen (Donau). *Germania*, **54**, 17–42.

(1978). Ergebnisse der letzten Ausgrabungen auf der Heuneburg bei Hundersingen (Donau). *Archäologisches Korrespondenzblatt*, **8**, 301–310.

Geyr von Schweppenburg, M. and Goessler, P. (1910). *Hügelgräber im Illertal bei Tannheim.* Paul Neff, Esslingen.

Gibson, G. D. (1962). Bridewealth and other forms of exchange among the Herero. In Bohannan, P. and Dalton, G. (eds.), *Markets in Africa*, pp. 617–639. Northwestern University Press, Evanston, Ill.

Goessler, P. and Veeck, W. (1927). *Verzeichnis der vor- und frühgeschichtlichen Altertümer.* Museum der Stadt, Ulm.

Grierson, P. (1959). Commerce in the Dark Ages. *Transactions of the Royal Historical Society*, ser. 5, **9**, 123–140.

Griffo, P. and von Matt, L. (1968). *Gela: the ancient Greeks in Sicily.* New York Graphic Society, Greenwich, Conn.

Gsell, S. (1891). *Fouilles dans la nécrople de Vulci.* Ernest Thorin, Paris.

Günther, A. (1934). Gallische Wagengräber im Gebiet des Neuwieder Beckens. *Germania*, **18**, 8–14.

Haevernick, T. E. (1960). *Die Glasarmringe und Ringperlen der Mittel- und Spätlatènezeit auf dem europäischen Festland.* Habelt, Bonn.

(1975). Hallstatt-Glasringe und Haguenauer Perlen. *Trierer Zeitschrift* **38**, 63–73.

(1978). Urnenfelderzeitliche Glasperlen. *Zeitschrift für Schweizerische Archäologie und Kunstgeschichte*, **35**, 145–157.

Haffner, A. (1964). Das frühlatène Gräberfeld von Theley. *Bericht der Staatlichen Denkmalpflege im Saarland*, **11**, 121–147.

(1965). Späthallstattzeitliche Funde aus dem Saarland. *Bericht der Staatlichen Denkmalpflege im Saarland*, **12**, 7–34.

(1966*a*). Die Hallstatt- und Latènezeit im Saarland. In *Führer zu vor- und frühgeschichtlichen Denkmälern*, vol. 5: *Saarland*, pp. 28–45. Zabern, Mainz.

(1966*b*). Das Fürstinnengrab von Besseringen, Kreis Merzig-Wadern. In *Saarland* (see *idem* 1966*a*), pp. 170–172.

(1966*c*). Die Fürstengräber von Weiskirchen, Kr. Merzig-Wadern. In *Saarland* (see *idem* 1966*a*), pp. 212–216.

(1966*d*). Das Fürstengrab von Theley, Kr. St. Wendel. In *Saarland* (see *idem* 1966*a*), pp. 205–207.

(1969). Ein Grabhügel der Späthallstattzeit von Riegelsberg, Ldkr. Saarbrücken. *Bericht der Staatlichen Denkmalpflege im Saarland*, **16**, 49–60.

(1971). Ein hallstattzeitlicher Eisenschmelzofen von Hillesheim, Kr. Daun. *Trierer Zeitschrift*, **34**, 21–29.

(1976). *Die westliche Hunsrück-Eifel-Kultur.* De Gruyter, Berlin.

Hagen, E. E. (1962). *On the theory of social change.* Dorsey Press, Homewood, Ill.

Haggett, P. (1965). *Locational analysis in human geography.* Edward Arnold, London.

Hanks, L. M. (1957). Five generalizations on the structure of foreign contact: a comparison of two periods in Thai history. In *Proceedings, 1957 Spring Meeting, American Ethnological Society*, pp. 72–75.

Hartmann, A. (1970). *Prähistorische Goldfunde aus Europa: Spektralanalytische Untersuchungen und deren Auswertung.* Gebr. Mann, Berlin.

(1978). Ergebnisse spektralanalytischer Untersuchung späthallstatt- und latènezeitlicher Goldfunde vom Dürrnberg, aus Südwestdeutschland, Frankreich und der Schweiz. In Pauli, L. (ed.), *Der Dürrnberg bei Hallein III*, pp. 601–617. Beck, Munich.

von Hase, F.-W. (1973). Unbekannte frühetruskische Edelmetallfunde mit

Maskenköpfen: mögliche Vorbilder keltischer Maskendarstellungen. *Hamburger Beiträge zur Archäologie*, **3**, pt 1, 51–64.

Hasebroek, J. (1933). *Trade and politics in ancient Greece.* Translation by L. M. Fraser and D. C. Macgregor. Bell, London.

Hatt, J. (1958). Encore le problème des relations entre Grecs et Celtiques (à propos de J. Carcopino, *Promenades historiques aux pays de la dame de Vix*). *Revue archéologique de l'Est et du Centre-Est*, **9**, 152–155.

(1959). *Histoire de la Gaule romaine.* Payot, Paris.

(1960). Les invasions celtiques en Italie du nord: leur chronologie. *Bulletin de la Société Préhistorique Française*, **57**, 362–372.

Hawkes, C. and S. (eds.), (1973). *Greeks, Celts and Romans: Studies in venture and resistance.* Dent, London.

Hawkes, C. F. C. and Smith, M. A. (1957). On some buckets and cauldrons of the Bronze and Early Iron Ages. *Antiquaries Journal*, **37**, 131–198.

Hencken, H. (1958). Syracuse, Etruria, and the north. *American Journal of Archaeology*, **62**, 259–272.

(1974). Bracelets of lead–tin alloy from Magdalenska gora. *Situla*, **14–15**, 119–127.

Hensel, W. (1970). Remarques sur les origines des villes en Europe centrale. In *Atti del convegno di studi sulla città etrusca e italica preromana*, **1**, 323–328.

Herlihy, D. (1971). The economy of traditional Europe. *Journal of Economic History*, **31**, 153–164.

Héron de Villefosse, A. (1887). Anse d'amphore en bronze appartenant au Musée du Louvre. *Gazette archéologique*, 263–266.

Herrmann, H.-V. (1966). *Die Kessel der orientalisierenden Zeit*, pt 1: *Kesselattaschen und Reliefuntersätze.* De Gruyter, Berlin.

(1970). Die südländischen Importstücke des Fürstengrabes von Asperg. In Zürn, H., *Hallstattforschungen in Nordwürttemberg*, pp. 24–34. Staatliches Amt für Denkmalpflege, Stuttgart.

Herskovits, M. J. (1938). *Acculturation: the study of culture contact.* J. J. Augustin, New York.

(1940). *The economic life of primitive peoples.* Knopf, New York.

(1952). *Economic anthropology.* Knopf, New York.

Heurgon, J. (1964). *Daily life of the Etruscans.* Translation by J. Kirkup. Weidenfeld and Nicholson, London.

Hill, J. N. (1977). Systems theory and the explanation of change. In Hill, J. N. (ed.), *Explanation of prehistoric change*, pp. 59–103. University of New Mexico Press, Albuquerque.

Hill, J. N. (ed.), (1977). *Explanation of prehistoric change.* University of New Mexico Press, Albuquerque.

Hocart, A. M. (1936). *Kings and councillors: an essay in the comparative anatomy of human society.* Faculty of Arts, Egyptian University, Cairo.

Hodson, F. R. (1968). *The La Tène cemetery at Münsingen-Rain.* Stämpfli, Bern.

Hollstein, E. (1973). Jahrringkurven der Hallstattzeit. *Trierer Zeitschrift*, **36**, 37–55.

(1976). Die Holzfunde aus dem Magdalenenberg bei Villingen und ihre zeitliche Einordnung (Dendrochronologie). In Spindler, K., *Der Magdalenenberg bei Villingen*, Führer zu vor- und frühgeschichtlichen Denkmälern in Baden-Württemberg, vol. 5, pp. 97–112. Theiss, Stuttgart.

Homann-Wedeking, E. (1958). Von spartanischer Art und Kunst. *Antike und Abendland*, **7**, 63–72.

Homans, G. C. (1958). Social behavior as exchange. *American Journal of Sociology*, **63**, 597–606.

Howard, S. and Johnson, F. P. (1954). The Saint-Valentin Vases. *American Journal of Archaeology*, **58**, 191–207.
Hoving, T. (1975). (ed.) *From the lands of the Scythians: ancient treasures from the museums of the U.S.S.R., 3000 B.C.–100 B.C.* Metropolitan Museum of Art, New York.
Humphreys, S. C. (1967). Archaeology and the economic and social history of classical Greece. *La Parola del Passato*, **116**, 374–400.
(1969). History, economics and anthropology: the work of Karl Polanyi. *History and Theory*, **8**, 165–212.
Hundt, H.-J. (1969). Über vorgeschichtliche Seidenfunde. *Jahrbuch des Römisch-Germanischen Zentralmuseums*, **16**, 59–71.
(1970) Gewebefunde aus Hallstatt: Webkunst und Tracht in der Hallstattzeit. In *Krieger und Salzherren: Hallstattkultur im Ostalpenraum*, pp. 53–71. Römisch-Germanisches Zentralmuseum, Mainz.
Hus, A. (1971). *Vulci étrusque et étrusco-romaine.* Klincksieck, Paris.
Izikowitz, K. G. (1951). *Lamet: hill peasants in French Indochina.* Etnologiska Museet, Göteborg.
Jacobsthal, P. (1929). Rhodische Bronzekannen. *Jahrbuch des Deutschen Archäologischen Instituts*, **44**, 198–223.
(1934). Bodenfunde griechischer Vasen nördlich der Alpen. *Germania*, **18**, 14–19.
(1944). *Early Celtic art.* Clarendon, Oxford.
Jacobsthal, P. and Langsdorff, A. (1929). *Die Bronzeschnabelkannen.* Heinrich Keller, Berlin-Wilmersdorf.
Jahn, A. (1852). Die Ausgrabungen zu Grächwyl, Amts Aarberg, Kanton Bern. *Bonner Jahrbücher*, **18**, 81–93.
Jankuhn, H. (1969). *Vor- und Frühgeschichte vom Neolithikum bis zur Völkerwanderungszeit*, Deutsche Agrargeschichte, vol. 1. Eugen Ulmer, Stuttgart.
Jannoray, J. (1955). *Ensérune.* De Boccard, Paris.
Jantzen, U. (1955). *Griechische Greifenkessel.* Gebr. Mann, Berlin.
Jehl, M. and Bonnet, C. (1968). La pyxide d'Appenwihr (Haut-Rhin). *Gallia*, **26**, 295–300.
Joachim, H.-E. (1968). *Die Hunsrück-Eifel-Kultur am Mittelrhein.* Böhlau, Cologne.
Joachim, W. and Biel, J. (1977). Untersuchung einer späthallstatt-frühlatènezeitlicher Siedlung in Kornwestheim, Kreis Ludwigsburg. *Fundberichte aus Baden-Württemberg*, **3**, 173–203.
Joffroy, R. (1954). *Le trésor de Vix (Côte-d'Or).* Presses Universitaires de France, Paris.
(1960*a*). *L'Oppidum de Vix et la civilisation hallstattienne finale dans l'Est de la France.* Bernigaud, Dijon.
(1960*b*). Le bassin et le trépied de Saint-Colombe (Côte-d'Or). *Fondation Eugène Piot: Monuments et Mémoirs*, **51**, 1–23.
(1962). *Le trésor de Vix.* Fayard, Paris.
(1976). Les civilisations de l'Age du Fer en Bourgogne. In *La préhistoire française*, vol. 2: Guilaine, J. (ed.), *Les civilisations néolithiques et protohistoriques de la France*, pp. 816–825. CNRS, Paris.
Johansen, F. (1971). *Reliefs en bronze d'Etrurie.* Translation by G. Merad. Glyptothèque Ny Carlsberg, Copenhagen.
Jucker, H. (1966). Bronzehenkel und Bronzehydria in Pesaro. *Studia Oliveriana*, **13–14**, 1–128.
(1973). Altes und Neues zur Grächwiler Hydria. In *Zur griechischen Kunst: Festschrift Hansjörg Bloesch*, pp. 42–62. Francke Verlag, Bern.

Jucker, H. and I. (1955). *Kunst und Leben der Etrusker.* Kunsthaus, Zurich.
Jullian, C. (1908). *Histoire de la Gaule*, vols. 1 and 2. Hachette, Paris.
Keesing, F. M. (1939). *The Menomini Indians of Wisconsin: a study of three centuries of cultural contact and change.* American Philosophical Society, Memoir 10.
Keller, J. (1965). *Das keltische Fürstengrab von Reinheim.* Römisch-Germanisches Zentralmuseum, Mainz.
(1970). Zur Datierung des keltischen Fürstengrabes von Reinheim. In *Actes du VIIe Congrès International des Sciences Préhistoriques et Protohistoriques*, pp. 796–798. Prague.
Kilian-Dirlmeier, I. (1970). Bemerkungen zur jüngeren Hallstattzeit im Elsass. *Jahrbuch des Römisch-Germanischen Zentralmuseums*, **17**, 84–93.
Kimmig, W. (1940). *Die Urnenfelderkultur in Baden.* De Gruyter, Berlin.
(1950). Ein Wagengrab der frühen Latènezeit von Laumersheim (Rheinpfalz). *Germania*, **28**, 38–50.
(1958). Kulturbeziehungen zwischen der nordwestalpinen Hallstattkultur und der mediterranen Welt. In *Actes du colloque sur les influences helléniques en Gaule*, pp. 75–87. Bernigaud, Dijon.
(1964). Ein attisch schwarzfiguriges Fragment mit szenischer Darstellung von der Heuneburg a. d. Donau. *Archäologischer Anzeiger*, 467–475.
(1968). *Die Heuneburg an der oberen Donau.* Gesellschaft für Vor- und Frühgeschichte in Württemberg und Hohenzollern, Stuttgart.
(1969). Zum Problem späthallstättischer Adelssitze. In *Siedlung, Burg and Stadt*, pp. 96–113. Deutsche Akademie der Wissenschaften, East Berlin.
(1971). Grabungsverlauf und Funde. In Kimmig, W. and Gersbach, E., Die Grabungen auf der Heuneburg 1966–1969, *Germania*, **49**, 21–60.
(1974). Zum Fragment eines Este-Gefässes von der Heuneburg an der oberen Donau. *Hamburger Beiträge zur Archäologie*, **4**, 33–102.
(1975*a*). Die Heuneburg an der oberen Donau. In *Ausgrabungen in Deutschland 1950–1975*, pp. 192–211. Römisch-Germanisches Zentralmuseum, Mainz.
(1975*b*). Early Celts on the upper Danube: excavations at the Heuneburg. In Bruce-Mitford, R. (ed.), *Recent archaeological excavations in Europe*, pp. 32–64. Routledge and Kegan Paul, London.
Kimmig, W. and Hell, H. (1958). *Vorzeit an Rhein und Donau.* Jan Thorbecke, Lindau.
Kimmig, W. and Rest, W. (1954). Ein Fürstengrab der späten Hallstattzeit von Kappel am Rhein. *Jahrbuch des Römisch-Germanischen Zentralmuseums*, **1**, 179–216.
Kimmig, W. and von Vacano, O.-W. (1973). Zu einem Gussform-Fragment einer etruskischen Bronzekanne von der Heuneburg a. d. oberen Donau. *Germania*, **51**, 72–85.
Knorringa, H. (1926). *Emporos: data on trade and traders in Greek literature from Homer to Aristotle.* H. J. Paris, Amsterdam.
Koenen, C. (1906). Gallisches Kriegergrab bei Urmitz. *Bonner Jahrbücher*, **114–115**, 330–339.
Kossack, G. (1959). *Südbayern während der Hallstattzeit.* De Gruyter, Berlin.
(1964). Trinkgeschirr als Kultgerät der Hallstattzeit. In Grimm, P. (ed.), *Varia Archaeologica*, pp. 96–105. Deutsche Akademie der Wissenschaften, East Berlin.
(1970). *Gräberfelder der Hallstattzeit an Main und Fränkischer Saale.* Lassleben, Kallmünz.
(1972). Hallstattzeit. In Kunkel, O. (ed.), *Vor- und frühgeschichtliche Archäologie in Bayern*, pp. 85–100. Bayerischer Schulbuch-Verlag, Munich.

(1974). Prunkgräber. In Kossack, G. and Ulbert, G. (eds.), *Studien zur vor- und frühgeschichtlichen Archäologie*, pp. 3–33. Beck, Munich.
Kroeber, A. L. (1948). *Anthropology*. Harcourt, Brace, New York.
Kromer, K. (1959). *Das Gräberfeld von Hallstatt*. Sansoni, Florence.
(1963). *Hallstatt: die Salzhandelsmetropole des ersten Jahrtausends vor Christus in den Alpen*. Naturhistorisches Museum, Vienna.
(1964). *Von frühem Eisen und reichen Salzherren: Die Hallstattkultur in Österreich*. Im Wollzeilen, Vienna.
Lagrand, C. and Thalmann, J.-P. (1973). *Les habitats protohistoriques de Pègue (Drôme)*. Centre de documentation de la préhistoire alpine, Grenoble.
Lang, A. (1974). *Die geriefte Drehscheibenkeramik der Heuneburg*. De Gruyter, Berlin.
(1976). Neue geriefte Drehscheibenkeramik von der Heuneburg. *Germania*, **54**, 43–62.
Langlotz, E. (1966). *Die kulturelle und künstlerische Hellenisierung der Küsten des Mittelmeers durch die Stadt Phokaia*, Arbeitsgemeinschaft für Forschung des Landes Nordrhein-Westfalen, Geisteswissenschaften, vol. 130. Westdeutscher Verlag, Cologne.
Laslett, P. (1973). *The world we have lost: England before the Industrial Age*, 2nd edition. Charles Scribner's Sons, New York.
Laviosa Zambotti, P. (1953). Stirpi e civiltà preistoriche e protostoriche in Val Padana; L'invasione gallica in Val Padana. In *Storia di Milano*, vol. 1, pp. 17–110. Treccani, Milan.
Lepore, E. (1970). Strutture della colonizzazione focea in Occidente. *La Parola del Passato*, **130–133**, 19–54.
Lerat, L. (1958). L'Amphore de bronze de Conliège (Jura). In *Actes du colloque sur les influences helléniques en Gaule*, pp. 89–98. Bernigaud, Dijon.
Lewis, O. (1942). *The effects of White contact upon Blackfoot culture, with special reference to the role of the fur trade*. J. J. Augustin, New York.
Liebschwager, C. (1972). Zur Frühlatènekultur in Baden-Württemberg. *Archäologisches Korrespondenzblatt*, **2**, 143–148.
Liepmann, U. (1968). Fragmente eines Dreifusses aus Zypern in New York und Berlin. *Jahrbuch des Deutschen Archäologischen Instituts*, **83**, 39–57.
Lindenschmit, L. (1870). *Die Altertümer unserer heidnischen Vorzeit*, vol. 2. Mainz.
(1881). *Die Altertümer unserer heidnischen Vorzeit*, vol. 3. Mainz.
(1904). Museographie: Mainz, Sammlung des Vereins zur Erforschung der rhein. Geschichte und Altertümer. *Westdeutsche Zeitschrift für Geschichte und Kunst*, **23**, 351–373.
Linton, R. (1936). *The study of man*. Appleton-Century, New York.
(1940). *Acculturation in seven American Indian tribes*. Appleton-Century, New York.
Lopez, R. S. (1945). Silk industry in the Byzantine Empire. *Speculum*, **20**, 1–42.
Lurie, N. C. (1959). Indian cultural adjustment to European civilization. In Smith, J. M. (ed.), *Seventeenth century America*, pp. 33–60. University of North Carolina Press, Chapel Hill.
Maier, F. (1958). Zur Herstellungstechnik und Zierweise der späthallstattzeitlichen Gürtelbleche Südwestdeutschlands. *Berichte der Römisch-Germanischen Kommission*, **39**, 131–249.
(1974). Gedanken zur Entstehung der industriellen Grosssiedlung der Hallstatt- und Latènezeit auf dem Dürrnberg bei Hallein. *Germania*, **52**, 326–347.
Maisant, H. (1972). Die Öffnung von drei Grabhügeln der späten

Hallstattzeit auf der 'Steinrausch' in Saarlouis-Fraulautern 1970/71. *Bericht der Staatlichen Denkmalpflege im Saarland*, **19**, 43–64.
(1973). Grabhügel der Hallstattzeit in Saarlouis-Fraulautern. *Bericht der Staatlichen Denkmalpflege im Saarland*, **20**, 61–106.
Malinowski, B. (1922). *Argonauts of the western Pacific*. Routledge, London.
Malinowski, T. (1971). Über den Bernsteinhandel zwischen den südlichen baltischen Ufergebieten und dem Süden Europas in der frühen Eisenzeit. *Praehistorische Zeitschrift*, **46**, 102–110.
Mansfeld, G. (1973). *Die Fibeln der Heuneburg*. De Gruyter, Berlin.
Mansuelli, G. A. (1960). La cité étrusque de Marzabotto et les problèmes de l'Etrurie padane. *Comptes rendus de l'Académie des Inscriptions*, 65–84.
Mansuelli, G. A. and Scarani, R. (1961). *L'Emilia prima dei Romani*. Il Saggiatore, Milan.
Mariën, M. (1962). Eigenbilzen et Hallein. In *Collection Latomus, Hommages à Albert Grenier*, **58**, 1113–1116.
Mauss, M. (1967). *The gift: forms and functions of exchange in archaic societies*. Translation by I. Cunnison. Norton, New York.
Maxwell-Hyslop, K. R. (1956). Urartian bronzes in Etruscan tombs. *Iraq*, **18**, 150–167.
Megaw, J. V. S. (1966). The Vix burial. *Antiquity*, **40**, 38–44.
(1970). *Art of the European Iron Age*. Harper and Row, New York.
(1975). The Orientalizing theme in early Celtic art: east or west? *Alba Regia, Annales Musei Stephani Regis*, **14**, 15–33.
von Merhart, G. (1952). Studien über einige Gattungen von Bronzegefässen. In *Festschrift des Römisch-Germanischen Zentralmuseums*, vol. 2, pp. 1–71. Mainz.
Mildenberger, G. (1963). Griechische Scherben vom Marienberg in Würzburg. *Germania*, **41**, 103–104.
Millotte, J. P. (1963). *Le Jura et les Plaines de Saône aux âges des métaux*. Les Belles Lettres, Paris.
(1976*a*). Les civilisations de l'Age du Fer dans le Jura. In *La préhistoire française*, vol. 2: Guilaine, J. (ed.), *Les civilisations néolithiques et protohistoriques de la France*, pp. 724–733. CNRS, Paris.
(1976*b*). Les civilisations de l'Age du Fer dans l'Est de la France. In *La préhistoire française*, vol. 2: Guilaine, J. (ed.), *Les civilisations néolithiques et protohistoriques de la France*, pp. 835–846.
Minns, E. H. (1913). *Scythians and Greeks: a survey of ancient history and archaeology of the north coast of the Euxine from the Danube to the Caucasus*. Cambridge University Press, London.
Minto, A. (1955). L'Antica industria mineraria in Etruria ed il porto di Populonia. *Studi Etruschi*, **23**, 291–319.
Moberg, C.-A. (1977). La Tène and types of society in Scandinavia. In Markotic, V. (ed.), *Ancient Europe and the Mediterranean: studies presented in honour of Hugh Hencken*, pp. 115–120. Aris and Phillips, Warminster.
Momigliano, A. (1975). The Celts and the Greeks. In Momigliano, A., *Alien wisdom: the limits of hellenization*, pp. 50–73. Cambridge University Press, London.
Monumenti antichi (1890–). Reale Accademia dei Lincei, Milan.
Muhly, J. D. (1973). *Copper and tin*. Connecticut Academy of Arts and Sciences, Transaction 43, New Haven.
Müller-Karpe, H. (1959). *Beiträge zur Chronologie der Urnenfelderzeit nördlich und südlich der Alpen*. De Gruyter, Berlin.
Murdock, G. P. (1949). *Social structure*. Macmillan, New York.
Nenquin, J. (1961). *Salt: a study in economic prehistory*. De Tempel, Brugge.

Neuffer, E. M. (1974). *Hallstatt: frühe Kelten in Baden-Württemberg*. Exhibition catalogue, Landesdenkmalamt, Freiburg.
Neugebauer, K. A. (1923–1924). Die Bronzeindustrie von Vulci. *Archäologischer Anzeiger*, **38–39**, 302–326.
(1943). Archäische vulcenter Bronzen. *Jahrbuch des Deutschen Archäologischen Instituts*, **58**, 206–278.
Neuninger, H. and Pittioni, R. (1959). Woher stammen die blauen Glasperlen der Urnenfelderkultur? *Archaeologia Austriaca*, **26**, 52–66.
Neuninger, H., Pittioni, R. and Preuschen, E. (1969). *Salzburgs Kupfererzlagerstätten und Bronzefunde aus dem Lande Salzburg*. *Archaeologia Austriaca*, supplement 9.
Neustupný, J. (1970). Essai d'explication de la fonction des stations préhistoriques fortifées en Europe centrale. *Atti del convegno di studi sulla città etrusca e italica preromana*, **1**, 339–343.
Noble, J. V. (1965). *The techniques of painted Attic pottery*. Watson-Guptill, New York.
Notizie degli scavi di antichità. Hoepli, Milan.
Odner, K. (1972). Ethno-historic and ecological settings for economic and social models for an Iron Age society: Valldalen, Norway. In Clarke, D. L. (ed.), *Models in archaeology*, pp. 623–651. Methuen, London.
Osterhaus, U. (1969). Zu verzierten Frühlatènewaffen. *Fundberichte aus Hessen*, supplement 1, pp. 134–144.
Otto, K.-H. (1955). *Die sozialökonomischen Verhältnisse bei den Stämmen der Leubinger Kultur in Mitteldeutschland*. Ethnographisch-Archäologische Forschungen, vol. 3, pt 1, East Berlin.
Paret, O. (1921). *Urgeschichte Württembergs*. Strecker and Schröder, Stuttgart.
(1933–1935). Ein Fund aus dem Fürstengrabhügel Rauher Lehen bei Ertingen. *Fundberichte aus Schwaben*, N.S. **8**, 73–75.
(1935). Das Fürstengrab der Hallstattzeit von Bad Cannstatt. *Fundberichte aus Schwaben*, N.S. 8, supplement 1.
(1935–1938). Ein zweites Fürstengrab der Hallstattzeit von Stuttgart-Bad Cannstatt. *Fundberichte aus Schwaben*, N.S. **9**, 55–60.
(1938). Das Hallstattgrab von Sirnau bei Esslingen. *Fundberichte aus Schwaben*, N.S. **9**, 60–66.
(1941–1942). Der Goldreichtum im hallstättischen Südwestdeutschland. *IPEK*, **15–16**, 76–85.
(1951). Das reiche späthallstattzeitliche Grab von Schöckingen (Kr. Leonberg). *Fundberichte aus Schwaben*, N.S. **12**, 37–40.
Pareti, L. (1947). *La Tomba Regolini-Galassi*. Tipografica Poliglotta Vaticana, Vatican City.
Pauli, L. (1971). *Die Golasecca-Kultur und Mitteleuropa: ein Beitrag zur Geschichte des Handels über die Alpen*. Hamburger Beiträge zur Archäologie, vol. 1, no. 1.
(1972). *Untersuchungen zur Späthallstattkultur in Nordwürttemberg*. Hamburger Beiträge zur Archäologie, vol. 2, pt 1.
(1974). Review of Lang, A., *Die Drehscheibenkeramik der Heuneburg*. *Bonner Jahrbücher*, **174**, 682–687.
(1978). *Der Dürrnberg bei Hallein III*. Beck, Munich.
Pellegrini, G. (1896). Di alcune tombe della necropoli vulcente. *Notizie degli scavi*, N.S **23**, 286–290.
Penninger, E. (1960). Vorläufiger Bericht über die neugefundenen latènezeitlichen Gräber vom Dürrnberg bei Hallein. *Germania*, **38**, 353–363.

Perron, E. (1882). Tumulus de la vallée de la Saône supérieure. *Revue archéologique*, **65–73**, 129–140.
Peschel, K. (1971). Zur Frage der Sklaverei bei den Kelten während der vorrömischen Eisenzeit. *Ethnographisch-Archäologische Zeitschrift*, **12**, 527–539.
Peyre, C. (1963). L'Armement défensif des Gaulois en Emilie et en Romagne. *Studi Romagnoli*, **14**, 255–277.
(1969). Problèmes actuels de la recherche sur la civilisation celtique dans la Cispadane. *Revue archéologique*, 165–177.
Philippaki, B. (1967). *The Attic stamnos.* Clarendon, Oxford.
Piggott, S. (1965). *Ancient Europe.* Aldine, Chicago.
(1977). A glance at Cornish tin. In Markotic, V. (ed.), *Ancient Europe and the Mediterranean: studies presented in honour of Hugh Hencken*, pp. 141–145. Aris and Phillips, Warminster.
Piroutet, M. (1928). Essai de classification du Hallstattien franc-comtois. *Revue archéologique*, **28**, 220–281.
(1930*a*). A propos de la limite entre le Hallstattien et le La Tène I. *Bulletin de la Société Préhistoire Française*, **27**, 76–80.
(1930*b*). Tableau des subdivisions chronologiques du Hallstattien franc-comtois. *Bulletin de la Société Préhistorique Française*, **27**, 387–391.
Pittioni, R. (1966). Grächwil und Vix handelsgeschichtlich gesehen. In *Helvetia Antiqua: Festschrift Emil Vogt*, pp. 123–128. Conzett and Huber, Zurich.
(1976*a*). Beiträge zur Kenntnis der urzeitlichen Kupferbergwesens um Jochberg und Kitzbühel, Tirol. *Archaeologia Austriaca*, **59–60**, 243–264.
(1976*b*). Bergbau – Kupfererz. In Hoops, J. (ed.), *Reallexikon der germanischen Altertumskunde*, 2nd edition, vol. 2, pp. 251–256. De Gruyter, Berlin.
Pleiner, R. (1962). *Staré evropské kovářství (Alteuropäisches Schmiedehandwerk).* Československá Akademie Ved, Prague.
(1976). Bergbau – Eisenerz. In Hoops, J. (ed.), *Reallexikon der germanischen Altertumskunde*, 2nd edition, vol. 2, pp. 258–261.
Polanyi, K. (1944). *The great transformation.* Rinehart, New York.
(1957). The economy as instituted process. In Polanyi, K., Arensberg, C. M. and Pearson, H. W. (eds.), *Trade and markets in the early empires: economies in history and theory*, pp. 243–270. Free Press, New York.
(1959). Anthropology and economic theory. In Fried, M. (ed.), *Readings in cultural anthropology*, pp. 161–184. Crowell, New York.
Polenz, H. (1971). Zur Schnabelkanne von Oberwallmenach, Loreleykreis. *Nassauische Annalen*, **82**, 1–30.
(1973). Zu den Grabfunden der Späthallstattzeit im Rhein-Main-Gebiet. *Bericht der Römisch-Germanischen Kommission*, **54**, 107–202.
Powell, T. G. E. (1958). *The Celts.* Thames and Hudson, London.
Primas, M. (1972). Zum eisenzeitlichen Depotfund von Arbedo (Kt. Tessin). *Germania*, **50**, 76–93.
(1974). Die Hallstattzeit im alpinen Raum. In Drack, W. (ed.), *Ur- und frühgeschichtliche Archäologie der Schweiz: Die Eisenzeit*, pp. 35–46. Schweizerische Gesellschaft für Ur- und Frühgeschichte, Basel.
(1977). Die Bronzefunde vom Montlingerberg (Kanton St. Gallen): Ein Beitrag zur Frage des prähistorischen Verkehrs. In Frey, O.-H. (ed.), *Festschrift zum 50jährigen Bestehen des Vorgeschichtlichen Seminars Marburg*, pp. 107–127. Kempkes, Gladenbach.
Py, M. (1968). Les fouilles de Vaunage et les influences grecques en Gaule méridionale (commerces et urbanisation). *Revue des Etudes Ligures*, **34**, 57–106.

Randsborg, K. (1973). Wealth and social structure as reflected in Bronze Age burials. In Renfrew, C. (ed.), *The explanation of culture change*, pp. 565–570. University of Pittsburgh Press, Pittsburgh.

(1974). Social stratification in Early Bronze Age Denmark. *Praehistorische Zeitschrift*, **49**, 38–61.

Rathje, W. L. (1970). Socio-political implications of lowland Maya burials. *World Archaeology*, **1**, 359–374.

(1971). The origins and development of Lowland Classic Maya civilization. *American Antiquity*, **36**, 275–287.

(1972). Praise the gods and pass the metates: a hypothesis of the development of Lowland rainforest civilizations in Mesoamerica. In Leone, M. P. (ed.), *Contemporary archaeology*, pp. 365–392. Southern Illinois University, Carbondale.

Redfield, R. (1947). The folk society. *American Journal of Sociology*, **52**, 293–308.

(1953). *The primitive world and its transformations*. Cornell University Press, Ithaca.

Redfield, R., Linton, R. and Herskovits, M. J. (1936). Memorandum for the study of acculturation. *American Anthropologist*, **38**, 149–152.

Reim, H. (1968). Zur Henkelplatte eines attischen Kolonettenkraters vom Uetliberg (Zürich). *Germania*, **46**, 274–285.

Reinach, S. (1899). Le corail dans l'industrie celtique. *Revue celtique*, **20**, 13–29, 117–131.

Reinecke, P. (1902). Zur Kenntnis der La Tène-Denkmäler der Zone nordwärts der Alpen. *Festschrift des Römisch-Germanischen Zentralmuseums*, pp. 53–109. Mainz.

(1911*a*). Kleinfunde aus Brandgräbern der frühen Hallstattzeit Südwestdeutschlands (pp. 231–234); Tongefässe aus Brandgräbern der frühen Hallstattzeit Südwestdeutschlands (pp. 235–247); Grabfunde der zweiten Hallstattstufe aus Süddeutschland (pp. 315–323); Grabfunde der dritten Hallstattstufe aus Süddeutschland (pp. 399–408); Funde der Späthallstattstufe aus Süddeutschland (pp. 144–150). In *Altertümer unserer heidnischen Vorzeit*, vol. 5.

(1911*b*). Grabfunde der ersten La Tènestufe aus Nordostbayern (pp. 281–287); Grabfunde der zweiten La Tènestufe aus der Zone nordwärts der Alpen (pp. 330–337); Grabfunde der dritten La Tènestufe aus dem bayerischen Donautal (pp. 288–294); Funde vom Ende der La Tènezeit aus Wohnstätten bei Karlstein unweit Reichenhall, Oberbayern (pp. 364–369). In *Altertümer unserer heidnischen Vorzeit*, vol. 5.

Renfrew, C. (1969). Trade and culture process in European prehistory. *Current Anthropology*, **10**, 151–169.

(1972). *The emergence of civilization: the Cyclades and the Aegean in the third millennium B.C.* Methuen, London.

(1973). (ed.). *The explanation of culture change: models in prehistory*. University of Pittsburgh Press, Pittsburgh.

(1974). Beyond a subsistence economy: the evolution of social organization in prehistoric Europe. In Moore, C. B. (ed.), *Reconstructing complex societies*, pp. 69–95. Bulletin of the American Schools of Oriental Research, vol. 20, supplement.

(1975). Trade as action at a distance: questions of integration and communication. In Sabloff, J. A. and Lamberg-Karlovsky, C. C. (eds.), *Ancient civilization and trade*, pp. 3–59. University of New Mexico Press, Albuquerque.

Richter, G. M. A. (1923). *The craft of Athenian pottery.* Yale University Press, New Haven.
Riek, G. (1962). *Der Hohmichele.* De Gruyter, Berlin.
Rieth, A. (1938). *Vorgeschichte der schwäbischen Alb.* Kabitzsch, Leipzig.
(1942). *Die Eisentechnik der Hallstattzeit.* Kabitzsch, Leipzig.
(1950). Werkstattkreise und Herstellungstechnik der hallstattzeitlichen Tonnenarmbänder. *Zeitschrift für Schweizerische Archäologie und Kunstgeschichte,* **11**, 1–16.
Riis, P. J. (1939). Rod-tripods. *Acta Archaeologica* (Copenhagen), **10**, 1–30.
(1941). *Tyrrhenika: an archaeological study of the Etruscan sculpture in the Archaic and Classical Periods.* Munksgaard, Copenhagen.
(1959). The Danish bronze vessels of Greek, early Campanian and Etruscan manufacture. *Acta Archaeologica* (Copenhagen), **30**, 1–50.
Rochna, O. (1962). Hallstattzeitliches Lignit- und Gagat-Schmuck: zur Verbreitung, Zeitstellung und Herkunft. *Fundberichte aus Schwaben,* N.S. **16**, 44–83.
Rochna, O. and Mädler, K. (1974). Die Sapropelit- und Gagatfunde vom Dürrnberg. In Moosleitner, F., Pauli, L. and Penninger, E. (eds.), *Der Dürrnberg bei Hallein II,* pp. 153–167. Beck, Munich.
Roebuck, C. (1950). The grain trade between Greece and Egypt. *Classical Philology,* **45**, 236–247.
(1959). *Ionian trade and colonization.* Archaeological Institute of America, New York.
Rogers, E. S. (1964). The fur trade, the government and the central Canadian Indian. *Arctic Anthropology,* **2**, 37–40.
Rogers, E. A. and F. Shoemaker (1971). *The communication of innovations.* Free Press, New York.
Rolland, H. (1949). L'expansion du monnayage de Marseille dans le pays celto-ligure. *Revue des Etudes Ligures,* **15**, 139–148.
(1951). *Fouilles de Saint-Blaise (Bouches-du-Rhône).* CNRS, Paris.
Rolley, C. (1962). Trouvailles méditerranéennes en Basse-Bourgogne. *Bulletin de correspondance hellénique,* **86**, 476–493.
(1964). Le trépied d'Auxerre. *Bulletin de Correspondance hellénique,* **88**, 442–443.
Rowlands, M. J. (1973). Modes of exchange and the incentives for trade, with reference to later European prehistory. In Renfrew, C. (ed.), *The explanation of culture change,* pp. 589–600. University of Pittsburgh Press, Pittsburgh.
Sabloff, J. A. and Lamberg-Karlovsky, C. C. (1975), (eds.). *Ancient civilization and trade.* University of New Mexico Press, Albuquerque.
Sahlins, M. (1960*a*). Political power and the economy in primitive society. In Dole, G. E. and Carneiro, R. L. (eds.), *Essays in the science of culture in honor of Leslie A. White,* pp. 390–415. Crowell, New York.
(1960*b*). Production, distribution, and power in a primitive society. In Wallace, A. F. C. (ed.), *Men and cultures: selected papers of the Fifth International Congress of Anthropological and Ethnological Sciences,* pp. 495–500. University of Pennsylvania Press, Philadelphia.
(1963). Poor man, rich man, big man, chief: political types in Melanesia and Polynesia. *Comparative Studies in Society and History,* **5**, 285–303.
(1965). On the sociology of primitive exchange. In Banton, M. (ed.), *The relevance of models for social anthropology,* pp. 139–236. Tavistock, London.
(1972). The domestic mode of production: intensification of production. In Sahlins, M., *Stone Age economics,* pp. 101–148. Tavistock, London.

Sangmeister, E. (1969). Die Hallstattgräber im Hagenauer Forst und die relative Chronologie der jüngeren Hallstattkultur im Westen. *Fundberichte aus Hessen*, supplement 1, pp. 154–187.

Savignoni, L. (1897). Di un bronzetto arcaico dell'acropoli di Atene e di una classe di tripodi di tipo greco-orientale. *Monumenti antichi*, 277–376.

Schaaff, U. (1969). Versuch einer regionalen Gliederung frühlatènezeitlicher Fürstengräber. *Fundberichte aus Hessen*, supplement 1, pp. 187–202.

(1971). Ein keltisches Fürstengrab von Worms-Herrnsheim. *Jahrbuch des Römisch-Germanischen Zentralmuseums*, **18**, 51–113.

Schaeffer, C. F. A. (1930). *Les tertres funéraires préhistoriques dans la Fôret de Hagenau: les tumulus de l'Age du Fer.* Imprimerie de la Ville, Haguenau.

Schefold, K. (1950). Die Stilgeschichte der frühen keltischen Kunst. *Praehistorische Zeitschrift*, 34–35, pt 2, 11–17.

Schiek, S. (1954). Das Hallstattgrab von Vilsingen. In *Festschrift für Peter Goessler: Tübinger Beiträge zur Vor- und Frühgeschichte*, pp. 150–167. Kohlhammer, Stuttgart.

(1956). Fürstengräber der jüngeren Hallstatt-Kultur in Südwestdeutschland. Doctoral dissertation, University of Tübingen.

(1959). Vorbericht über die Ausgrabung des vierten Fürstengrabhügels bei der Heuneburg. *Germania*, **37**, 117–131.

Schindler, R. (1961). Latènegräber in Marpingen, Kr. St. Wendel. *Germania*, **39**, 468–472.

(1965). *Führer durch das Landesmuseum für Vor- und Frühgeschichte.* Saarbrücken.

(1966). Die Fürstengräber von Schwarzenbach. In *Saarland*, Führer zu vor- und frühgeschichtlichen Denkmälern, vol. 5, pp. 216–218. Zabern, Mainz.

(1968). *Studien zum vorgeschichtlichen Siedlungs- und Befestigungswesen des Saarlandes.* Paulinus, Trier.

(1974). Frühlatènegräber beim Bau der Ferngasleitung im Kreis Birkenfeld. *Trierer Zeitschrift*, **37**, 33–47.

(1976). Fragen zur römischen Eisenverhüttung im Moselland. *Trierer Zeitschrift*, **39**, 45–59.

Schröder, M. (1963). Die Südwestdeutsche Hallstattkultur. In Roeren, R. and Schröder, M., *Kleine Vor- und Frühgeschichte Württembergs im Gang durch das Württembergische Landesmuseum*, pp. 22–28. Kohlhammer, Stuttgart.

Schröter, P. (1975). Zur Besiedlung des Goldberges im Nördlinger Ries. In *Ausgrabungen in Deutschland 1950–1975*, vol. 1, pp. 98–114. Römisch-Germanisches Zentralmuseum, Mainz.

Schüle, W. (1965). Nordalpines Hallstatt-Gold und Südwesteuropa. *Fundberichte aus Schwaben*, N.S. **17**, 173–180.

Schultze-Naumburg, F. (1969). Eine griechische Scherbe vom Ipf bei Bopfingen/Württemberg. *Fundberichte aus Hessen*, supplement 1, pp. 210–212.

Schwab, H. (1975). Châtillon-sur-Glâne: ein Fürstensitz der Hallstattzeit bei Freiburg im Üechtland. *Germania*, **53**, 79–84.

(1976). Un oppidum de l'époque de Hallstatt près de Fribourg en Suisse. *Mitteilungsblatt der Schweizerischen Gesellschaft für Ur- and Frühgeschichte*, **7**, 2–11.

Schweitzer, R. (1971). Découverte de tessons attiques à figures noires au Britzgyberg près d'Illfurth. *Bulletin du Musée Historique de Mulhouse*, **79**, 39–44.

(1973). Le Britzgyberg – station du Hallstatt. *Bulletin du Musée Historique de Mulhouse*, **81**, 43–64.

Scullard, H. H. (1967). *The Etruscan cities and Rome*. Cornell University Press, Ithaca.
Seibold, E. (1959). Die Bodenschätze. In Wagner, G. (ed.), *Die schwäbische Alb*, pp. 41–45. Burkhard, Essen.
Seltman, C. T. (1957). *Wine in the ancient world*. Routledge, London.
Semple, E. C. (1931). *The geography of the Mediterranean region: its relation to ancient history*. Holt, New York.
Service, E. R. (1962). *Primitive social organization*. Random House, New York.
Shefton, B. B. (1979). *Die 'rhodischen' Bronzekannen*. Philipp von Zabern, Mainz.
Shennan, S. (1975). The social organization at Branč. *Antiquity*, **49**, 279–288.
Sherratt, A. G. (1972). Socio-economic and demographic models for the Neolithic and Bronze Ages of Europe. In Clarke, D. L. (ed.), *Models in archaeology*, pp. 477–542. Methuen, London.
Sieveking, J. (1908). Bronzener Volutenkrater in München. *Münchener Jahrbuch für bildende Kunst*, **2**.
Sperber, L. (1979). Nachuntersuchung der hallstattzeitlichen Fürstengrabhügel auf dem Giessübel bei Hundersingen, Gemeinde Herbertingen, Kreis Sigmaringen. *Archäologische Ausgrabungen 1978* (Bodendenkmalpflege in den Reg.-Bez. Stuttgart und Tübingen), pp. 35–39.
Spicer, E. H. (1952). *Human problems in technological change*. Russell Sage Foundation, New York.
(1961). Types of contact and processes of change. In Spicer, E. H. (ed.), *Perspectives in American Indian culture change*, pp. 517–544. University of Chicago Press, Chicago.
Spindler, K. (1971). *Magdalenenberg I*. Neckar-Verlag, Villingen.
(1972). *Magdalenenberg II*. Neckar-Verlag, Villingen.
(1973). *Magdalenenberg III*. Neckar-Verlag, Villingen.
(1975*a*). Zum Beginn der hallstattzeitlichen Besiedlung auf der Heuneburg. *Archäologisches Korrespondenzblatt*, **5**, 41–45.
(1975*b*). Grabfunde der Hallstattzeit vom Magdalenenberg bei Villingen im Schwarzwald. In *Ausgrabungen in Deutschland 1950–1975*, vol. 1, pp. 221–242. Römisch-Germanisches Zentralmuseum, Mainz.
(1976). *Magdalenenberg IV*. Neckar-Verlag, Villingen.
(1977). *Magdalenenberg V*. Neckar-Verlag, Villingen.
Sprater, F. (1928). *Die Urgeschichte der Pfalz*. Pfälzische Gesellschaft zur Förderung der Wissenschaften, Speyer.
Stahl-Weber, M. and Schweitzer, r. (1972). *10 ans de recherches archéologiques: région de Mulhouse*. Musée Historique, Mulhouse.
Steiner, P. (1929). Das erste Wagenbegräbnis der frühen Eisenzeit in der Eifel. *Trierer Zeitschrift*, **4**, 145–147.
(1930). Eine vorgeschichtliche Plateaufeste im Trevererland. In *Schumacher-Festschrift*, pp. 166–177. Wilckens, Mainz.
Ströbel, R. (1961). Ausgrabung am Dreifältigkeitsberg. *Tuttlinger Heimatblätter*, N.S. **19–21**, 75–81.
Strong, D. E. (1966*a*). *Greek and Roman gold and silver plate*. Methuen, London.
(1966*b*). *Catalogue of the carved amber in the Department of Greek and Roman Antiquities*. British Museum, London.
Struever, S. and Houart, G. L. (1972). An analysis of the Hopewell Interaction Sphere. In Wilmsen, E. N. (ed.), *Social exchange and interaction*, pp. 47–79. Museum of Anthropology, University of Michigan.
Szilágyi, J. G. (1951–1952). Zur Frage des etruskischen Handels nach dem Norden. *Acta Antiqua* (Budapest), **1**, 419–454.

Thill, G. (1972). Frühlatènezeitlicher Fürstengrabhügel bei Altrier. *Hémecht*, **4**, 487–501.

Tischler, O. (1885). Über Gliederung der La-Tène-Periode und über die Dekorierung der Eisenwaffen in dieser Zeit. *Correspondenz-Blatt der Deutschen Gesellschaft für Anthropologie, Ethnologie, un Urgeschichte*, **16**, 157–161.

Torbrügge, W. (1968). *Prehistoric European art*. Abrams, New York.

Tourtellot, G. and Sabloff, J. A. (1972). Exchange systems among the ancient Maya. *American Antiquity*, **37**, 126–135.

Trigger, B. (1974). The archaeology of government. *World Archaeology*, **6**, 95–106.

Ucko, P. (1969). Ethnography and archaeological interpretation of funerary remains. *World Archaeology*, **1**, 262–280.

Uenze, H. P. (1964). Zur Frühlatènezeit in der Oberpfalz. *Bayerische Vorgeschichtsblätter*, **29**, 77–118.

Vallet, G. (1950). Athènes et l'Adriatique. *Mélanges d'archéologie et d'histoire*, **62**, 33–52.

(1958). *Rhégion et Zanclé*. De Boccard, Paris.

Vallet, G. and Villard, F. (1955). Un atelier de bronziers: sur l'école du cratère de Vix. *Bulletin de correspondence hellénique*, **79**, 50–74.

Villard, F. (1956). Vases de bronze grecs dans une tombe étrusque du VIIe siècle. *Fondation Eugène Piot: Monuments et Mémoires*, **48**, fasc. 2, 25–53.

(1960). *La céramique grecque de marseille (VIe–IVe siècle)*. De Boccard, Paris.

Viollier, D. (1916). *Les sépultures du second âge du fer sur le plateau suisse*. Georg and Co., Geneva.

Von Föhr, J. (1892). *Hügelgräber auf der schwäbischen Alb*. Kohlhammer, Stuttgart.

Vulić, N. (1934). La nécropole archaique de Trebenischte. *Revue archéologique*, 26–38.

Wackernagel, H. G. (1930). Massalia. In *Paulys Real-Encyclopädie der classischen Altertumswissenschaft*, vol. 28, pp. 2130–2152. Metzler, Stuttgart.

Wahle, E. (1940–1941). Zur ethnischen Deutung frühgeschichtlicher Kulturprovinzen. *Sitzungsberichte der Heidelberger Akademie der Wissenschaften*, 2nd paper, Phil.-Hist. Klasse.

Walker, D. E. (ed.), (1972). *The emergent native Americans: a reader in culture contact*. Little, Brown, Boston.

Walters, H. B. (1899). *Catalogue of the bronzes, Greek, Roman, and Etruscan, in the Department of Greek and Roman Antiquities*. British Museum, London.

Wasowicz, A. (1966). A l'époque grecque: le peuplement des côtes de la mer Noire et de la Gaule méridionale. *Annales economies, sociétés, civilisations*, pp. 553–572.

(1975). *Olbia pontique et son territoire*. Annales Littéraires de l'Université de Besançon, Paris.

Webster, T. B. L. (1972). *Potter and patron in classical Athens*. Methuen, London.

Wells, C. M. (1974). The ethnography of the Celts and of the Algonkian-Iroquoian tribes. In Evans, J. A. S. (ed.), *Polis and imperium: studies in honour of Edward Togo Salmon*, pp. 265–278. Hakkert, Toronto.

Wells, P. S. (1978). The excavations at Stična in Slovenia by the Duchess of Mecklenburg, 1905–1914. *Journal of Field Archaeology*, **5**, 215–226.

Wells, P. S. and Bonfante, L. (1979). West-central Europe and the Mediterranean: the decline in trade in the fifth century B.C. *Expedition*, **21**, 18–24.

White, J. R. (1975). Historic contact sites as laboratories for the study of culture change. In South, S. (ed.), *The Conference on Historic Site Archaeology, Papers*, **9**, 153–163.

Wiedmer-Stern, J. (1908). *Das gallische Gräberfeld bei Münsingen (Kanton Bern)*. Bern.

Wild, J. P. (1970). *Textile manufacture in the northern Roman provinces*. Cambridge University Press, London.

Will, E. (1954). Trois quarts de siècle de recherches sur l'économie grecque antique. *Annales economies, sociétés, civilisations*, **9**, 7–22.

(1958). Archéologie et histoire économique. *Etudes d'archéologie classique*, **1**, 149–166.

(1962). La Grece archaïque. In *Deuxième conférence internationale d'histoire économique*, pp. 41–106. Mouton, Paris.

Willey, G. R., Di Peso, C. C., Ritchie, W. A., Rouse, I., Rowe, J. H. and Lathrap, D. W. (1955). An archaeological classification of culture contact situations. *Memoirs of the Society for American Archaeology*, **11**, 1–30.

Wilmsen, E. N. (ed.), (1972). *Social exchange and interaction*. Museum of Anthropology, University of Michigan.

Wyss, R. (1974). Technik, Wirtschaft, Handel und Kriegswesen der Eisenzeit. In *Ur- und frühgeschichtliche Archäologie der Schweiz*, vol. 4: Drack, W. (ed.), *Die Eisenzeit*, pp. 105–138. Schweizerische Gesellschaft für Ur- und Frühgeschichte, Basel.

(1975). *Der Schatzfund von Erstfeld*. Gesellschaft für das Schweizerischer Landesmuseum, Zurich.

Zannoni, A. (1876–1884). *Gli scavi della Certosa di Bologna*. Regia Tipografia, Bologna.

Zuffa, M. (1975). I commerci ateniese nell'Adriatico e i metalli d'Etruria. *Emilia Preromana*, **7**, 151–179.

Zürn, H. (1942). Zur Chronologie der späten Hallstattzeit. *Germania*, **26**, 116–124.

(1952). Zum Übergang von Späthallstatt zu Latène im südwestdeutschen Raum. *Germania*, **30**, 38–45.

(1957*a*). *Katalog Zainingen*. Staatliches Amt für Denkmalpflege, Stuttgart.

(1975*b*). Zur Chronologie der Alb-Salem Keramik. *Germania*, **35**, 224–229.

(1969). Hohenasperg (Kreis Ludwigsburg), a princely stronghold of the Late Hallstatt Period, and its graves. In *Field guide to prehistoric sites in Württemberg and Bavaria*, pp. 5–6. Römisch-Germanische Kommission, Frankfurt.

(1970). *Hallstattforschungen in Nordwürttemberg*. Staatliches Amt für Denkmalpflege, Stuttgart.

INDEX